MODERN SACRED ART
AND THE CHURCH OF ASSY

PIERRE BONNARD, *Saint Francis of Sales*
OIL ON CANVAS, ALTAR DECORATION

WILLIAM S. RUBIN

MODERN SACRED ART

AND THE CHURCH OF ASSY

COLUMBIA UNIVERSITY PRESS, New York and London, 1961

ACKNOWLEDGMENTS

For aid in preparing this book I am indebted to the participating artists who gave their time to discussions of their own works. Jean Lurçat, Germaine Richier, Jacques Lipchitz, and Marc Chagall were particularly generous in this regard. In the case of those artists who were already deceased at the time of my researches, documentation was naturally difficult to obtain, and for that reason I am especially indebted to Mme Fernand Léger for allowing me to study and photograph the unpublished watercolor and gouache studies for her husband's mosaic at Assy. Georges Rouault permitted me to study a rarely seen painting in his private collection, used as a model for a window at Assy, and his daughter, Isabelle, was most generous in providing information relating to her father's activities in the Sacred Art Movement.

Canon Jean Devémy, founder of Notre-Dame-de-Toute-Grâce, gave me invaluable first-hand material on its history and made available to me the architect's plans and other important documents. Father Pie-Raymond Régamey discussed most frankly the problems raised by the church and made available to me his file of clippings on the dispute it aroused, as well as relevant texts, some of them unpublished, from the papers of the late Father Marie-Alain Couturier. All direct quotations for which no source is given are verbatim transcriptions edited from electrically recorded interviews.

This book is based on a study written between 1956 and 1958 and presented the following year as a doctoral dissertation in the Department of Fine Arts and Archaeology of Columbia University. Throughout the preparation of the study my sponsor, Professor Meyer Schapiro, gave constant encouragement and creative criticism. My previous work with him as a graduate student,

ACKNOWLEDGMENTS

more than anything else, inspired me with the desire to explore this area of scholarship. Professors Everard Upjohn and George Collins read the text before its presentation and made many valuable suggestions. To Professor Rudolf Wittkower, Chairman of the Department of Fine Arts and Archaeology, I owe not only valuable advice, but also the enthusiastic support which led eventually to the publication of this book.

Miss Marian Kuhn gave me extensive secretarial and editorial assistance in the preparation of the original manuscript for which I am profoundly grateful. The work of turning an academic dissertation into a book was in the hands of Vergene F. Leverenz, an editor of the Columbia University Press. Her surgery has filled me with admiration. For the design of the book I am indebted to Eugenia Porter.

WILLIAM S. RUBIN

New York, N.Y.
July, 1961

CONTENTS

CONTENTS

ILLUSTRATIONS

ix

ILLUSTRATIONS

MODERN SACRED ART

AND THE CHURCH OF ASSY

INTRODUCTION

January, 1950, marked the beginning of the semicentennial Jubilee Year of the Catholic Church. From his balcony in the façade of St. Peter's, Pope Pius XII greeted the advance guard of a great army of faithful, whose numbers soon exceeded even the optimistic forecasts of Vatican officials. These pilgrims constituted a living index to the popular religious revival under way in the Western world since the end of the Second World War. But if the clerics and pious believers embraced by the Bernini colonnades had always been a part of the religious landscape, testimony of a more novel sort was being taken in New York, where the editors of the *Partisan Review* were preparing a symposium of articles entitled "Religion and the Intellectuals." "One of the most significant tendencies of our time, especially in this decade," their editorial statement began,

has been the new turn toward religion among the intellectuals. . . . There is no doubt that the number of intellectuals professing religious sympathies, beliefs, or doctrines is greater now than it was ten or twenty years ago, and that this number is continually increasing or becoming more articulate.[1]

Nowhere did this religious rebirth seem to be proceeding more productively on all levels of society than in France, where the efforts of the friars of the Dominican Order of Preachers and the Catholic lay intelligentsia had once again made the Church a viable force and a social and spiritual challenge even to the community of artists and intellectuals. While Léon Bloy, Jacques Maritain, and other heroic forerunners of this movement had constituted an

---

[1] "Religion and the Intellectuals: A Symposium," *Partisan Review*, XVII, No. 2 (February, 1950), 103.

1

embattled few with little support among the clergy, the New Gallicanism was spearheaded by the Dominicans and had a firm hold among the younger seminarians of all orders.

If churchmen seemed to be reentering the intellectual life of France after long hibernation, they were participating with no less vigor in the world of the plastic arts, from which they had been absent even longer. In August, 1950, the Dominican-inspired church of Notre-Dame-de-Toute-Grâce at Assy was consecrated amid great jubilation and even greater hope that it represented the commencement of a "Renaissance" of sacred art. The appearance there of religious works which, in power and purity, recalled those of the great ages of faith, certainly seemed symptomatic of a genuine religious revival. For the first time in centuries, great artists had directed their efforts towards church art. Bonnard, Chagall, Leger, Lipchitz, Lurçat, Matisse, and Rouault had all contributed significantly. Side by side with works of the pious Catholic Rouault one saw those of Jews, atheists, and even Communists—a revolutionary situation that struck the keynote of a new evangelical spirit.

Esthetically less perfect a whole than the subsequent Matisse chapel at Vence or the Corbusier church at Ronchamp, the church of Assy was nevertheless the first and by far the most ambitious of those sponsored by the Dominican-led Sacred Art Movement. Even before its dedication in 1950, the church had become the center of an increasingly bitter dispute which was to cause a marked rupture between the liberal and conservative wings of the clergy and laity during the following years. The violent polemics on both sides involved not only the French Church, but also the Vatican, usually through the voice of the Congregation of the Holy Office. As its destiny was linked to the fortunes of the entire liberal religious movement in France, the church of Assy and its decorations were vehemently attacked and defended by an army of critics, most of whom had seen only a few photographs of the works in question.

Clearly, an evaluation of the church of Assy can be made only in the context of a discussion of the New Gallicanism in general and the Sacred Art Movement in particular. An understanding of the latter, in turn, must pivot upon a study of the decadence of religious art which the Dominicans were endeavoring to overcome and of the efforts of Marie-Alain Couturier, o.p., and Pie-Raymond Régamey, o.p., to reanimate sacred art both by their activities and their writings in the pages of *L'Art sacré.*

Despite the almost endless torrent of polemical literature that has emerged from the "querelle de l'art sacré," no serious examination of the works themselves or of the history of the entire experiment has yet been undertaken. To fill this documentary vacuum I began the present study, convinced that an analysis of the works and the historical factors involved would throw light upon the revival of religious art, and perhaps upon the renascence of French Catholicism in general. Though deeply sympathetic with the aims of the Dominicans and interested in the possible revival of sacred art, I had no a priori convictions about the church of Assy. My conclusions developed *en passage,* as it were, out of investigation of the facts and examination of the works.

Part I. THE REVIVAL OF SACRED ART

I. DECADENCE AND THE DOMINICANS

An accelerating decadence has characterized sacred art since the beginning of the eighteenth century, but only during the last forty years has enlightened Catholicism recognized the problem. Toward the end of the First World War, the Catholic poet Paul Claudel courageously pronounced contemporary churches "heavily laden confessions." Their ugliness, he insisted, was the "demonstration to all the world of sins and shortcomings, weakness, poverty, timidity of faith and feeling, disgust with the supernatural, domination by conventions and formulae . . . worldly luxury, avarice, boasting, sulkiness, Pharisaism and bombast." [1] Today, though high Church authorities do not seriously treat this cancer, they do not deny its existence.

THE DECADENCE OF SACRED ART

The beginning of the decrepitude of sacred art was signaled by the Church's endorsement of the academic ideal that emerged in the sixteenth and seventeenth centuries. Academicism is really a mode of feeling and seeing, or, perhaps better, of not feeling and not seeing. Its growth reflects the development of rigorous structurings within society, and its institutionalized and hence conservative character made it a defensive mode par excellence for Catholic art after the Reformation, particularly in France. From the end of the sixteenth century onward, the clergy—much like secular officialdom— clung increasingly to academicism.

[1] Paul Claudel, "Lettre à Alexandre Cingria," *Positions et propositions* (Paris: Gallimard, 1934), p. 226. My translation is adapted from that of Jacques Maritain, *Art and Scholasticism with Other Essays,* trans. by J. F. Scanlan (New York, Scribner, 1930), p. 161.

DECADENCE AND THE DOMINICANS

The orthodox reaction determined by the Council of Trent was translated on the practical daily level into a conformism in all things. Caravaggio was rejected . . . Rembrandt scorned. But people fainted before faded efforts of Guido Reni, Carlo Dolci and Mignard. Theological conformism—pious, social, intellectual—led to artistic conformism.[2]

"Acceptable" stereotypes of religious art ensued, built on convention, allegory, and genre painting. These modes have since been preferred above others by the Vatican Commissions on Sacred Art and, indeed, the neo-Raphaelesque form has represented the taste of the recent popes.[3]

The sterility of the academic style became more marked after the enfranchisement of the middle class through the French Revolution and the subsequent crystallization of bourgeois values and religious taste. Motivated by a desire for legitimacy and a sense of continuity with the aristocracy it had replaced, the upper middle class not only embraced academicism but put it in the service of a sentimentality and pietism that brought about the absolute nadir of sacred art. In the entire nineteenth century only one important church decoration was realized—and that by the atheist Delacroix. But, when his Chapel of the Holy Angels in the Church of Saint-Sulpice in Paris was finished in 1861, it was roundly condemned. Had there not been a revolution in 1848, Delacroix would never have received a religious commission of such importance and one which so discontented the increasingly defensive clergy. It was, in effect, a "pure and unique accident" [4] in the history of religious art.

[2] Pie-Raymond Régamey, "Les Étapes de l'académisme," *L'Art sacré,* New Series, October, 1947, No. 10, pp. 245–87.

[3] The *Madonna and Child* by Barabino (Figure 1), a prize-winning entry in the Holy Year exhibition (1950) of religious art in Rome, typifies this neoclassical ideal.

Modern art and medieval art are sometimes paired by the Popes in opposition to the antique and Renaissance heritage recalled by Barabino's picture. Pius XI, for example, in the dedication of the Vatican Pinacoteca, spoke of modern art as "often scandalously ugly, reflecting only incapacity or impatience in general cultural preparation, and in drawing (this above all) . . . which lead to deformations . . . too much like certain figurations found in manuscripts of the darkest Middle Ages when the good antique traditions had been lost in barbaric upheavals and the new light of the Renaissance had not yet dawned." Quoted by Celso and Giovanni Costantini, *Fede ed arte,* II (1946), 213.

[4] Yves Florenne, "Prière pour un agonisant: fin de l'art sacré?" *Mercure de France,* CCCXVII, No. 1073 (January–April, 1953), 54–62.

8

Ingres, meanwhile, became the model for liturgical art; not so much in his own subtly individualized painting as in the vapid repetitions of his conventions in the work of his followers. Partially blinded by the theoretical arguments of the day, Ingres himself was unable to make satisfactory judgments on the art of others, and when the curé of Saint-Sulpice asked his opinion of the Delacroix frescoes, he angrily replied: "Rest assured, my dear Curé, there *is* a hell." Yet before the canvases of Hippolyte Flandrin, the *NB* most characteristic religious artist of his day, Ingres was transported with joy and cried out: "I have not been useless. Oh Phidias! Oh Raphael! Painting is not dead." [5]

By this time the increasingly sentimental and bourgeois character of religious practice had produced some characteristic saints, the extreme case of this phenomenon being St. Thérèse de l'Enfant Jésus. "Her own personal bad taste," writes Father Régamey (further amplified in our time by the art of her basilica at Lisieux), "does not seem to be a casual accident." [6]

A further symptom of the post-Renaissance decline of sacred art was the spread of cheap and gaudy religious ornament known in German as *Kitsch* (for good reasons the word has passed into other languages). Though *Kitsch* is a phenomenon that can be traced back at least to late antiquity, some of its modern forms spring directly from the fussy and flamboyant decoration that weighed down many Baroque churches. This decor was often created in plaster, glass, and wood, in keeping with Baroque love for the mélange of materials. Manipulated by a master like Bernini, such materials are magnificently transformed, but in lesser hands they degenerate into superfluous trash. During the Rococo, the taste for *Kitsch* was compounded until such claptrap virtually camouflaged the interiors of some churches.

Such decorative malpractice obtained not only in many new churches, but also was carried out in the "renovation" of older ones, including some of the

[5] Régamey, "Les Étapes de l'académisme," *L'Art sacré*, New Series, October, 1947, No. 10, pp. 245–87. The taste for Flandrin is still strong in Catholic circles. Father Guy-Jean Auvert, a leading exponent of the Vatican position in France, groups him with Angelico and Ribera as "outstanding artistic manifestations of divine grace." *Défense et illustration de l'art sacré* (Paris: Nouvelles Editions Latines, 1956), p. 122.

[6] Régamey, "Les Conditions de l'art sacré dans le monde moderne," *La Vie intellectuelle*, 16th year, No. 12, December, 1948, pp. 8–34.

great medieval cathedrals, now considered "gothic and barbaric." "It was in 1753," wrote Etienne Houvet in his study of the Cathedral of Chartres, "that the Canons began their devastation of the choir . . . covering the columns with a vulgar stucco . . . and adding the eight bas reliefs which are the despair of lovers of the Middle Ages." [7]

The so-called "art of Saint-Sulpice" is a special brand of *Kitsch*—that which is produced commercially in series. Though it is to be found everywhere (we have our equivalent in the United States), this "art" is widely sold in religious stores in the neighborhood of Saint-Sulpice in Paris—hence its common appellation. Though the larger part is purchased for private devotion, much of it finds its way into the sanctuary. There is little difference, in most cases, between these serially manufactured images and more expensive hand-made *Kitsch*. The Dominican editors of *L'Art sacré* made this clear in a series of juxtaposed illustrations. One paired an original oil of *St. Thérèse of Lisieux* by a certain Sister Céline and a "Happy Anniversary" card in the style of the serial devotional art of Saint-Sulpice.[8] They were indistinguishable in character.

But the acceptability of sulpician products even in *milieux* supposedly seriously interested in the amelioration of sacred art is reflected in the criticism to which the Dominicans' confrontation was subjected by the Italian review *Arte cristiana*. After disparaging the Dominican critique of the Céline work as a kind of sacrilege, the editors went on to argue the justice of the fact that an effigy of a saint should resemble a greeting-card image of "Happy Anniversary." [9]

The position of the Vatican and conservative Church circles with respect to the art of Saint-Sulpice is complicated by contradictions in theory and practice. Vatican authorities object to this art not primarily in terms of its

[7] Etienne Houvet, *Cathedrale de Chartres* (Paris, 1926), VII, 8. Sometimes such renovation was limited to the elimination of older works as at Notre-Dame-de-Paris and the cathedral of Reims, where the canons replaced all the twelfth-, thirteenth-, and fourteenth-century windows with white glass. Cf. G. G. Coulton, *Art and the Reformation* (Cambridge: The University Press, 1953), p. 451.

[8] Chanoine Ledeur, "Conseils fraternels," *L'Art sacré*, January–February, 1951, No. 5–6, pp. 15–17.

[9] Eva Tea, "Le Immagine sacré," *Arte cristiana*, XXXIX, No. 2 (February, 1952), 32–35.

style or character, but because it is manufactured. Canon law No. 1399 forbids the decoration of churches with images of holy figures reproduced in series, thus arguing implicitly that the spark of genius can be present only in unique artistic creations. High prelates in Italy and France have, consequently, often attacked this "industrial shoddy." But the hand-made *Kitsch* prototypes which receive church blessing are, paradoxically, indistinguishable from their serial duplications.

Much has been written about this problem, particularly since 1950, as a result of the debate aroused by the church of Assy and subsequent modern churches. But a good part of clerical criticism of the art of Saint-Sulpice has arisen not so much from a sincere objection to it as from a need to provide leverage for an attack upon genuine modern art. The clergy, wrote André Rousseau,

tend simultaneously to oppose confectionary statuary and the "outrages" of modern art, while searching for a *juste milieu* on the road to health for Christian art. This would be fine. But the actual situation is nevertheless quite different, and here is what it appears to be: With respect to modern art, the cries of scandal are so loud that the Bishop orders removal of the scandalous object, the Crucifix of Assy [see below, pp. 51–52]; on the other side—Oh, well, on the other side nothing happens. I have never heard that scandalized opinion . . . has ever demanded the removal of a caramel St. Thérèse or a whipped cream Virgin of Lourdes. Let us say more: if there had not been an incident like that of the Crucifix of Assy, I wonder if there would have been so much thought about denying the sulpician images we see honored everywhere.[10]

There is, indeed, no question but that the art of Saint-Sulpice has much support among high ecclesiastical and lay authorities. Monsignor Labourt, Vicar-General of Paris and President of the Diocesan Commission for Sacred Art and Liturgy, notes approvingly that "if this art has few defenders, it retains many partisans. It is inexpensive and essentially readable."[11] For Gaston Bardet, Belgian architect and city planner and an important figure in Vatican art circles, the art of Saint-Sulpice "is not suspect except of frivolousness, it is not [like modern art] a heresy. It remains within the

[10] André Rousseau, "Encore l'art sacré," *Le Figaro,* August 4, 1951, p. 8.
[11] Le Chanoine Labourt, "Réponse à une enquête sur l'art sacré: presentée par Maurice Brillant," *La Croix,* May 10, 1952, pp. 2–3.

11

Church. . . ." [12] Monsignor Touzé, director of the vast church building program known as the Chantiers du Cardinal, has long been an important and eloquent defender of the art of Saint-Sulpice as that of the "Chrétien moyen." [13]

A united front of manufacturers and ecclesiastics, Father Régamey observed, helps insure the persistence of the art of Saint-Sulpice.

The merchants are prospering more than ever; the large majority of the clergy calls on them, rather than on true creators, for what it wants. . . . In order to better attack Assy everyone declares himself now an enemy of the production of Saint-Sulpice, but no one really combats it. I could show how the counselors of the clergy encourage it.[14]

The apparent advantage of *Kitsch* and sulpician art, as far as the Church is concerned, would appear to be its innocuousness, its lack of the power to move or to challenge. It is an art that can be looked at without being seen. And it can never arouse sentiments which the Church might find questionable.

The average churchgoer does not appear to desire emotional engagement by religious art, and thus the imagery of Saint-Sulpice fully satisfies his taste —or lack of it. Since he prefers sentimentality to suffering and sacrifice, he rejects the art of Rouault in favor of *Kitsch*-like "Coca-Cola" Christs (Figure 2) which derive from stereotypes of advertising and motion pictures. The perpetuity of *Kitsch* thus marks the adaptation by the Church of today's "popular" art. It reflects submission to the taste of the "Chrétien moyen" and so constitutes an unconscious secularization. Church authorities of the Middle Ages and the Renaissance did not choose their art to suit the taste of the man on the street, and it is improbable that such a practice, especially in

[12] Gaston Bardet, "Una Polemica si allarga," *Arte cristiana*, XXXVIII, No. 11–12 (November–December, 1951), 129–130.

[13] His acquaintance with the art of our era can be gauged from his assertion that Cubism and Impressionism (he takes Impressionism to be the later movement) "lasted no longer than a flower. What trace have they left in the history of art?" Msgr. Paul Louis Touzé, "L'Art sacré," *Le Christ dans la banlieue*, 18th year, No. 8, 1951, p. 3.

[14] Régamey, "La Querelle de l'art sacré," *La Vie intellectuelle*, 19th year, No. 11, November, 1951, pp. 3–48.

12

our times, could produce a genuine sacred art—or, for that matter, any art at all.

The rise of the art of Saint-Sulpice is intimately connected with the disappearance of folk imagery and the decline of rural craftsmanship. The artisans of Saint-Sulpice have in effect replaced the carvers of the wayside calvaries. Contemporary Catholic artists like Henri Charlier [15] blame the disappearance of popular religious art on the French Revolution, which abolished the "corporations" and made it more difficult to hand down a tradition of artisanship.[16] But this was a minor factor compared with the rise of industrialism and its attendant social changes.[17] By 1850 technological advances had caused a crisis in rural artisanship, and the clergy had already turned wholeheartedly towards the manufacturers. Even the Abbé Hurel, a friend of Manet and the only later nineteenth-century prelate who showed any interest in the living art of the period, was a typical representative of prevailing clerical sentiment when he wrote that he was happy to see "poorly formed" rustic altars replaced by new ones, manufactured in series, which had "a quality of style, design, and form exempt from the grotesque fantasies . . . that traverse the mind of the village mason or sculptor." [18]

In keeping with the mood of the new industrialized society and its prin-

[15] Henri Charlier, "À propos du Christ de l'église d'Assy," *Écrits de Paris,* September, 1951, pp. 50–55.

[16] It is interesting that as a result of a nostalgic respect for "folk" craftsmanship and a misguided, antihistorical hope for its revival, Canon Devémy accepted the request of a local auto-didact, Constant Demaison, to sculpt the roof beams of the church of Assy. The result was a heavy-handed archaism wholly out of harmony with the other decorations of the church.

[17] André Malraux rightly observes that there cannot be a true popular art today "because there is no more people." "De l'art et des masses," *Liberté de l'esprit,* 3d year, No. 22, June, 1951, pp. 177–80.

[18] Abbé J. A. Hurel, *L'Art religieux contemporain* (Paris: Didier, 1868), p. 336. Compare this view of an advanced cleric with the attitude of a secular critic like Champfleury, who prized folk and native art highly.

By the nineteenth century such folk art as persisted was no longer religious, but republican and anticlerical. Even in the eighteenth century and before, while popular art reflected deep belief in Christ and the saints, it showed nothing but ridicule for the clerics. Cf. Meyer Schapiro, "Courbet and Popular Imagery," *Journal of the Warburg and Courtauld Institutes,* IV, No. 3–4 (1940–41), 164–91.

13

ciple of division of labor, there soon developed a hitherto rare phenomenon: artists who were "specialists" in religious art.[19] This came about in part through an increased need for church decorations just at a time when most artists were separating themselves from religious life and thereby (in clerical opinion) rendering themselves no longer useful in this connection. As the themes and the liturgical necessities of sacred art became unfamiliar, schools were established to teach artists what they had previously assimilated from tradition and from their cultural environment. Artists studying in these liturgical schools (e.g., the Scuola Beato Angelico) soon lost contact almost completely with the active and creative developments outside seminary walls.[20]

The clergy, of course, came into contact only with this group of specialized religious artists. And, whereas productive relationships between artists and the clergy had existed in all the great eras of Christian art, there was not, in the period from the French Revolution to the time of the church of Assy, a single significant liaison between cleric and artist. "For two centuries at least, even the most advanced representatives of the clergy never sought a dialogue with the artists of their time, but rather with those who represented neither their time—nor even art." [21]

A further correlate of industrialism which was to affect sacred more than profane art was the development of photography. This did much to spread the taste for the most literal and sentimental realism. "Finish," by which was meant the bringing of the image to a plane of realistic imitation in which brushwork, drawing, and other elements of the *facture* were buried, became a central standard of judgment in religious art and is even today insisted upon

[19] Cf. Bernard Dorival, "Le Divorce de l'art et du public," *L'Art sacré,* January–February, 1951, No. 5–6, pp. 4–8.

[20] So strongly has the school idea imbued modern Catholicism that even Jacques Maritain, though he rejects the idea of such specialized schools as a final solution, concedes that in the face of the present decadent situation they may well be necessary, given the "peculiar conditions" surrounding ecclesiastical or sacred art. Jacques Maritain, *Art and Scholasticism with Other Essays,* trans. by J. F. Scanlan (New York: Scribner, 1930), p. 159, note.

[21] Florenne, "Prière pour un agonisant: fin de l'art sacré?" *Mercure de France,* CCCXVII, No. 1073 (January–April, 1953), 54–62.

by Vatican authorities.[22] Since the creative artists of the last hundred years (beginning with Manet) have explored and exploited painterly values as positive elements in themselves, the gap between bourgeois church art and modern painting has become immense. "An abyss," Rouault called it.

Look at Bouguereau side by side with Cezanne. . . . One admits there is a gift, but a detestable gift. There is a derisive merit in his work, but a merit, nevertheless, because not everybody could do it. And it is that which they have confused with the masterpieces of the past, because it is *finished*.[23]

In addition to academicism, the "aristocratic" branch of the decadence, and the art of Saint-Sulpice, its "popular" counterpart, two other styles remain to be described to complete the survey of sacred art as it stood on the eve of the activities of the Dominicans. These may be described as the "historical" and the "modernistic" modes.

Consisting largely of neo-Romanesque, neo-Byzantine, and neo-Gothic formulations, the historical styles had their origins in the revivals of the late eighteenth and nineteenth centuries. Supported by the Vatican "when liberally reworked with intelligence and modern sensibility," [24] they have persisted in

[22] Cf. Michele Guerrisi, "L'Arte religiosa e la crisi del gusto contemporaneo," *Fede ed arte,* 1st year, No. 3, March, 1953, pp. 77–84.

The demand for that academic finish which Cezanne called "le fini des imbéciles" receives support from a law of Tridentine origin incorporated in the modern canon as No. 1279, para. 3. This law states that every sacred image must reflect "due decency and respectability." Decency is regularly interpreted as referring to the esthetic and material formulation of the work, and respectability to the morality of the image *qua* image. Thus, among other things, we are told that decency means that the work of art be "finished, not sketched" (*abbozzata*). Cf. Goffredo Mariani, *La Legislazione ecclesiastica in materia d'arte sacra* (Rome: Ferrari, 1945), p. 106.

Starting with St. Thomas, who had postulated completeness as an essential aspect of beauty, Jacques Maritain has also to insist that the religious work of art must be "finished." But Maritain denies that this means "academic finish" and interprets it "according to the peculiar style of the work and the means taken to achieve it." "Some Reflections on Religious Art," in *Art and Scholasticism with Other Essays,* p. 111.

[23] Georges Rouault, "Réponse à une enquête sur l'art sacré: présentée par Maurice Brillant," *La Croix,* May 11, 1952, p. 2.

[24] Giovanni Costantini, "Norme pratiche per l'ordinazione e esecuzione delle opere d'arte sacra," *Fede ed arte,* 1st year, No. 5, May, 1953, pp. 149–51.

church decoration, largely through the support of Catholics of "Integrist" persuasion, long after disappearing from the secular scene.

Integrism, a view common in the extreme right wing of the clergy and laity, is based upon the concept of retaining absolute "integrity" of the structure of the faith through detachment of the Church from the modern world. Convinced that Catholicism is a total, fixed, and absolute ideal, Integrism is inflexible and brooks no criticism; nor does it allow any compromise whatever in the face of a changing world situation. The Integrist looks forward (or backward) to a world that will be completely Catholic. He strives to achieve a dogmatic unanimity and consistency which he mistakenly believes to have existed in the Middle Ages.

Logically, most of the Integrists favor art forms drawn not from the Renaissance, but from the Middle Ages, the most important of these being the neo-Byzantine style, which most nearly corresponds to the Integrists' rigidly hieratic views. This preference, of course, extends to reactionary social and political policies that derive from such a view of history as that epitomized by Paul Scortesco, one-time Rumanian Ambassador to the Vatican and a leading figure in Integrist circles. For him culture has sustained a continuous decline since the Middle Ages, the five major retrogressive steps being the Renaissance, the Reformation, the philosophy of the Enlightenment, the French Revolution with its attendant democracy, and Marxism.[25]

The Integrists have sometimes been criticized even by high clergy, as, for instance, the late Joseph Cardinal Suhard, Archbishop of Paris, who warned against "making yesterday's forms today's ideal" or confusing "the integrity of doctrine with the maintenance of its passing exterior character," [26] but they remain, nevertheless, a powerful group with many important representatives in the hierarchy. Their view has been particularly favored by the members of the Holy Office, whose leaders, Giuseppe Cardinal Pizzardo and Alfredo Cardinal Ottaviani, are referred to even by other clergy as "men of the

[25] Paul Scortesco, *Satan voici ta victoire* (Paris: Nouvelles Éditions Latines, 1953), p. 10 and *passim*.

[26] Joseph Cardinal Suhard, *Essor ou déclin de l'église* (pastoral letter; Paris: Lahure, 1947), pp. 36–39.

Middle Ages." [27] As a group, the Integrists have formed the major opposition ✓ to the Dominican-inspired Sacred Art Movement.

The results of such archaizing taste may be seen in any number of churches, in Italy in particular, as, for example, the apse mosaic of San Giorgio alla Vittoria in Reggio Calabria, created in 1954 by Angelo Marelli of the Scuola Beato Angelico (Figure 3). It is fascinating to observe the degree to which this anemic work dissipates the power of its Byzantine prototypes through a complete misunderstanding of the esthetic unity of the older works.[28] Marelli has employed a series of offensively sugary tonalities entirely out of keeping with the content and structure of his image. The deeper, saturated colors of true Byzantine mosaics suggest not only mystery, but also celestial royalty and wealth. The mint green and orange of the San Giorgio apse belong not to the vocabulary of spiritual and hieratic art, but to modern sentimental decor. They would be more at home in a *Kitsch* painting of the Riviera than they are here. The gesture of the Christ Pantocrator is wholly without decision; he seems to be tiredly posing in a manner akin to the spiritless celebrations of the liturgy described by Father Régamey.[29] His almost caricatural

[27] At the opposite extreme are lay and clerical figures who have tried to infuse certain principles of Marxism into their Catholic mystique. Known as "Progressivists," they were condemned by Pius XII. But the term has come to be used as a kind of slander against the Dominicans and other noncommunist religious liberals. See, for example, Scortesco, *Saint Picasso peignez pour nous* (Paris: Nouvelles Éditions Latines, 1953), p. 62, and Auvert, *Défense et illustration de l'art sacré*, p. 157.

[28] More immediate prototypes for this style may be found in the work of the brethren of the Benedictine abbey of Beuron (Germany). These artists adhered to no single style, though most of their work had a hieratic byzantinizing character. The school was founded by Professor Peter (later Father Desiderius) Lenz. In trying to create an art that would adjust well to architecture Lenz generally rejected modeling and minimized his use of perspective. Egyptian and Greek archaic art especially appealed to the Beuron monks, and these styles rank with Byzantine and trecento Italian painting as their main sources. Activities reached their peak at Beuron around 1890, when the style exerted considerable influence on sacred art in France and Italy as well as in Germany. Cf. Joseph Kreitmaier, "Die Beuroner Kunstschule," *Stimmen aus Maria Laach*, LXXXVI (1913), 48–66.

[29] "The modern era," Régamey insists, "is precisely the epoch of the most profound liturgical decadence, and one of the reasons for it is an abuse of obeisance. In effect, the majority of clerics no longer conceive of the liturgical celebration as the ensemble of means of par-

face lacks the transcendent insistence and intensity of true Byzantine examples. We can hardly expect more in a world where the hieratic order of the society that generated Byzantine imagery has largely disintegrated, and though this hieratic structure persists within the Church, it constitutes an increasingly lonely island.

While opposed to historical styles in general, the Dominicans prefer the spirit of the Romanesque to that of the Byzantine, considering it more in keeping with the nature of modern experience, particularly in France. "It is clear," wrote Father Couturier,

that Assy, Vence, and Audincourt . . . are antipodal to the Byzantine and its spirit. At a time when the Church lives practically in diaspora and when immense sections of cultural and social life have eluded it—when at least its institutions and its people are in constant inferiority—conceptions, doctrines, and attitudes of a Byzantine type cannot but be fallacious.[30]

The most recent form of religious painting favored by some diocesan commissions consists of "modernistic" imagery based on softened formulas derived from the art of 1905–30. Though it would seem to be the most laudable of religious styles, as it is moving in the right direction, it is actually the most

---

ticipating in the mysteries of Christ, but rather as the dismissal of a debt." Régamey, "Les Conditions de l'art sacré dans le monde moderne," op. cit. The "abuse of obeisance" of which Father Régamey speaks is a subtle reference to the Rome-inspired resistance on the part of many clerics to the innovations and reanimation of the service sponsored by an energetic and highly spirited Liturgical Movement, supported widely by French Dominicans. This resistance is strengthened by frequent pronouncements from Rome, particularly by papal statements such as Mediator Dei. In this regard the Pope warned: ". . . we observe with considerable anxiety and some misgiving that elsewhere certain enthusiasts, over eager in their search for novelty, are straying beyond the path of sound doctrine and prudence. Not seldom, in fact, they interlard their plans and hopes for a revival of the sacred liturgy with principles which compromise the holiest of causes in theory or practice, and sometimes even taint it with errors touching Catholic faith and ascetical doctrine." Pius XII, Mediator Dei, Encyclical Letter on the Sacred Liturgy, November 20, 1947 (rev. ed.; New York: America Press, 1954), p. 16. "It has pained us grievously to note, venerable brethren, that such innovations are being actually introduced, not merely in minor details but in matters of major importance as well. We instance, in point of fact, those who make use of the vernacular in the celebration of the august eucharistic sacrifice. . . ." Ibid., p. 35.

[30] Couturier, "Byzance et nos efforts," L'Art sacré, May–June, 1953, No. 9–10, pp. 26–27.

insidious, for it allows its supporters to believe that they are indeed incorporating modern art into the church. This type of painting has constantly exemplified for various critics in the debate on sacred art a solution in the *juste milieu:* a "healthy modernity equidistant from banality and outrage." [31] Such derivative modernism has been practiced by Catholic converts like *converts* Albert Gleizes and Gino Severini, and by a host of lesser artists.[32]

The election of the *juste milieu* must lead to polite decadence, for it functions under the misguided idea that truth is necessarily found somewhere between two extremes. Artistic truth is absolute—it "bloweth where it listeth" —and in the end the Church must face the fact that creation is never a compromise. The liberal Catholic critic Yves Florenne signaled the only possible solution when he argued that "the Church has been created to live in the extreme." In art the insistence on moderation, he observed, "leads to the acceptance, out of concern for being up-to-date . . . of marginal moderate works by Picasso (neoclassic) while holding the art . . . of Rouault for a sin." [33]

THE DOMINICANS ENGAGÉS

It was in the face of the decadence we have been describing that the group of energetic Dominicans who constitute the nucleus of the Sacred Art Movement began their revolutionary activities. But their progress in the years just after the Second World War depended on a balance of forces and a coalition of interests peculiar to the modern Gallican Church.

The French have steadily disputed the subject of religion since the Revolution, when the Church lost substantial masses of the lower middle and working classes. The landed gentry and the peasantry remained within the Church and have since constituted the core of the French Right—a combination of

[31] Régamey, *Art sacré au XXe siècle?* (Paris: *Éditions du Cerf,* 1952), p. 411.

[32] Among the most sincere but pathetic practitioners of this art "entre Assy et Saint-Sulpice" are the group of artist-monks busily living out a medieval myth in isolation at the monastery of La-Pierre-qui-vire (Yonne). Examples of their work may be seen in the periodical *Zodiaque.*

[33] Florenne, "Prière pour un agonisant: fin de l'art sacré?" *Mercure de France,* CCCXVII, No. 1073 (January–April, 1953), 54–62.

19

conservatives, clericals, legitimists, and others who have been in constant struggle against the anti-clericals, liberals, and working-class parties.

Since the Revolution, power has alternated between these two groups. The Rightist position was at its zenith under Napoleon III; the Left reached its maximal power during the Third Republic. The force of these oppositions was somewhat mitigated by the situation obtaining during the First World War. Conservative clerics, though they disliked the Republic, were also intensely nationalist. Consequently, an entente developed between the two groups against the common enemy from without. This understanding persisted in the Second World War, with the exception of the monarchist clericals of the *Action française,* whose opposition to the Republic was so fanatic that they supported Germany against it. The *Action française,* however, lost much of its prestige after its condemnation by Rome. On the eve of the Second World War, Catholic youth was looking elsewhere than toward fascism or exaggerated nationalism.

Though the spirit of traditional Gallicanism is still to be found among older clerics, many of the younger abbés now graduating from the seminaries have new ideals. This change goes back to radical Catholic writing around the turn of the century. Léon Bloy attacked the complacency of French bourgeois life with the fury of an Old Testament prophet; Charles Péguy, a Republican, tried to reconcile the struggle for social liberty with the French medieval heritage. Paul Claudel, François Mauriac, Georges Bernanos, and Jacques Maritain all broadened what had become a lay Catholic revival.

After a youth devoted to radical ideals, Maritain came under the influence of Léon Bloy and converted dramatically to Catholicism. In time he became a leader of the neo-Thomist movement which had been set under way and given great impetus by Pope Leo XIII.[34] However questionable Maritain's scholastic theory of art, it was to be of more direct value to the

[34] It is important to keep in mind that Maritain belongs to the philosophical rather than the theological branch of the movement. His free interpretation of Thomas Aquinas, like that of Gilson and Simon, is far removed from that of conservative, literalistic exegists like Father Garrigou-Lagrange, French theologian at the Angelicum, the Dominican university in Rome. The fame of Maritain among American intellectuals may obscure the fact that in clerical circles in Rome he is considered a rather marginal figure.

Sacred Art Movement than the work of any other Catholic intellectual.

Another vital and more recent source of ideas for the New Catholicism was Emmanuel Mounier's review, *Esprit*. Mounier, who had been deeply influenced by Maritain, believed in the efficacy of the sacraments but was otherwise intensely anticlerical. He lived ascetically, starting cells of his existentialist-inspired "personalist" movement all over France. Like Maritain, Bernanos, and many of the French clergy, Mounier participated in the Resistance, and it was partly due to the prestige thus gained that *Esprit* enjoyed a tremendous following among young people. These in turn gave the Dominicans vigorous support in their post-war struggles against the Vatican. *Esprit* stood for a liberalized, antidoctrinaire Catholicism similar to that which Father Couturier preached and practiced in his relations with artists.

It is natural that the French clergy should have felt the impact of this movement. Young priests read Maritain, Mauriac, Bernanos, and *Esprit*. A few French Jesuits were active in it, but the Dominicans constituted the major force of the new clerical avant-garde. They attempted to lead from within a revolution in which the old idea that the Church is a "priests party" would be abolished, and in which personal contact with the real social and intellectual problems of the French masses would lead to a rehabilitation of the vital spirit of the Church.

It seems surprising, at first, that the French Dominicans, whose brethren in Italy, Ireland, and elsewhere preserve their traditional association with inquiry into heresy and condemnation of books, should be the leaders of the New Gallicanism. But the possibility of this radical identity follows naturally from the unique structure of the Dominican constitution. The organization of the order is loosely constructed along egalitarian lines that provide for elections from the bottom upward,[35] and, consequently, it has developed in a

[35] The friars of each convent elect a Prior who then with two delegates from the body of friars participates in the election of a Provincial Prior. These, with two delegates from each province, elect the Master-General of the order, who resides in Rome. The government of the order is carried on by Chapters which meet every four years and which are alternately constituted of Provincials, Priors, and delegates. Any specific piece of legislation must be approved by three Chapters and hence takes twelve years to pass, making authoritarian control of the order impossible.

21

manner quite opposite to that of the Vatican, where during the last few hundred years authority has been more and more vested in the hands of the Pope,[36] insuring a hierarchy more absolute than ever obtained in medieval or Renaissance times. The elasticity of the Dominican organization allows for considerable variation of opinion; the rules of its constitution are not binding under sin and can be waived if they interfere with preaching or teaching.

The social aspect of this Gallican revolution centered around the Dominican-inspired movement of the *prêtres-ouvriers,* or Worker-Priests. The desire for a religion that would be *engagé* necessitated the abolition of the old and widespread clerical view that the world was a dangerous place lying beyond seminary walls. Priests, it was argued, should not live in a ghetto, seeing only other priests in a closed society of protection and mutual esteem. They should join with the citizenry, particularly with the working classes, to establish a new, spiritually inspired system of social justice.

The Worker-Priest movement began in the days of the German Occupation, when young priests, fleeing from the Gestapo, became involved in the Resistance or found themselves in forced labor battalions. In 1943 Cardinal Suhard assigned two priests of the Young Christian Workers Movement to draw up a report on the relationship of the Church and the working classes. Their observations led to an official experiment in which France was to be treated as a "missionary country" (i.e., one in which large sections of the community are not Christian). Young priests began working full time in factories and workshops, wearing the same clothing as the workers and sharing their lot. They were distinguished from the workers only by being unmarried and by saying Mass. To many people it seemed as though the Church had at last found an answer to the challenge of modern times in a revival of the spirit of piety and love that animated early Christianity.

The Worker-Priest movement was encouraged by various Dominican publications, most of them issuing from Les Editions du Cerf, which was soon to reactivate the review *L'Art sacré,* publication of which had been suspended during the war. Fathers Couturier and Régamey endeavored to

---

[36] The Cardinals who elect the Pope are appointees of the previous Pope and completely dependent upon the new one after election.

22

bring to bear the same spirit of missionary *engagement* and openness to new ideas in an attempt to reanimate sacred art. They understood clearly that in the face of centuries of decadence only a radical program could succeed in recreating a nexus between the current of living art and that of the church.

The question of a revival of sacred art was not, however, a wholly new one. Tentative efforts had been made in this direction in France even in the nineteenth century. But, putting aside Delacroix's Chapel of the Holy Angels in the church of Saint-Sulpice as an historical accident, the only essays of any importance occurred in the last decade of the century in connection with the work of the Symbolists.

Though at the time his work went totally unnoticed in religious circles, some present-day Catholic critics retroactively cite Paul Gauguin as an important precursor of the revival of sacred art.[37] But although Gauguin made a number of pictures with manifestly religious subject matter, they were conceived from the point of view of the nonbeliever. In the *Yellow Christ,* for example, religious experience, though viewed with sympathy and even longing, is considered outside the realm of the artist's private sensibility. In the Tahitian scenes with Christian subject matter (e.g., *Nativity*) the Western religious element is incongruously superimposed in a literal manner on the Tahitian situation. The conflict in these pictures between the pseudo-religious overlay and Gauguin's more sincere interest in the pattern and color of tropical landscape, life, and dress is manifest in *Ia Orana Maria,* where the angel crying "Hail, Mary" is almost invisible owing to his dissolution in the intricate patterns of foliage and fabric. In any case, despite the curious popularity of Gauguin today even in some of the most conservative Catholic quarters,[38] his work was really isolated from the development of a modern tradition in religious art except indirectly, through his influence on the symbolist esthetic of the Nabis, of which group Maurice Denis was a member.

It was with the work of Denis, who in 1890 showed his first religious paint-

---

[37] Pichard, *L'Art sacré moderne,* p. 24.

[38] The integrist Paul Scortesco rationalizes his love for Gauguin by insisting that "This great artist . . . was not of his time." *Saint Picasso peignez pour nous,* p. 67. He later remarks that Gauguin's work "renders possible once again a Christian art." *Ibid.,* p. 79.

23

ing, *Le Mystère Catholique,* that a modest but continuous tradition of modern sacred imagery was initiated. This incipient revival of sacred art was implemented by a school which Denis founded in his atelier with the help of Georges Desvallieres. Through his teaching Denis exercised a widespread influence on Christian painting until his death in 1943.[39] But if his own pale and overrefined *fin de siècle* palette and excessive stylization of gesture and costume palled in time, it became unbearable in the saccharine works of his followers, who to this day specialize in a self-consciously naïve style aimed at recapturing the quality of older popular imagery.[40] A better theorist than painter, Denis's greatest importance lies in having argued the primacy of plastic over literary values, thus paving the way for a reconsideration of the whole problem of religious art from the esthetic point of view.[41]

In 1917 the Catholic painter Alexandre Cingria published *La Décadence de l'art sacré,*[42] which, in spite of its brevity, omissions, and oversimplifications, constituted the first serious confrontation of the problem of modern religious art. Essentially an accusatory critique, it elicited considerable interest throughout Catholic intellectual and artistic circles, one upshot being the now famous letter of Paul Claudel cited at the beginning of this chapter. Cingria soon implemented his criticism with a practical program. A painter, glazier, and mosaicist with an inexhaustible fund of energy, he gathered optimistic, if not deeply talented, young artists around him, and his "Group of St. Luke" decorated dozens of churches, mostly in French Switzerland.

Cingria was also instrumental in obtaining the collaboration of one-time Futurist Gino Severini, who around 1920 had reverted to the Catholic faith

[39] The "Atelier de l'Art Sacré" was directed by Denis under the patronage of the Catholic Institute of Paris. Its members, who were dedicated to a communal life of piety, called each other "companion" and generally emulated the Nazarenes.

[40] Cf. Régamey, "Cinq tendances dominates," *Cahiers de l'art sacré,* 1946, No. 3, pp. 17–29.

[41] His famous definition, describing a picture as a "two dimensional surface covered with colors arranged in a particular order," is more important for the history of religious art than for modern art in general, its countless citations in books on modern painting notwithstanding. For the former it was an implicit program, for the latter simply a verbal summation of an already established painterly attitude.

[42] Alexandre Cingria, *La Décadence de l'art sacré* (Lausanne: Cahiers Vaudois, 1917).

24

of his youth. This spiritual transformation paralleled a change in his art from decorative (or "synthetic") Cubism to a neoclassicism based on an elaborate set of mathematical principles.[43] But even as he gave up Cubism Severini recognized that movement as "the basis of the new classicism which is forming," [44] and, in contradistinction to the opinion still voiced in Vatican quarters,[45] he argued that there is no inherent contradiction between Cubism and Catholicism. In fact, he observed, the mathematical and philosophical meditations begun in his Cubist period favored his return to the Catholic religion.

Severini demanded absolute artistic liberty, refusing to accept stylistic dictation from without, but at the same time he agreed that sacred art must conform to its destination and function. This delicate balance, which under certain practical conditions would seem untenable except through compromise, became the kernel of the position taken by Jacques Maritain, who subsequently worked to give it theological legitimacy.

In the meantime, interest in a modern religious art was growing, and many new groups of artists were formed. L'Arche, founded in 1918, united, among others, the Benedictine architect Dom Bellot, Ferdinand Py, and Henri Charlier. Jean Hébert-Stevens and his wife, Pauline Peugniez, established an atelier that was to advance interest in modern stained glass, an area in which Marguerite Huré and young Father Couturier, both of whom later created windows for Assy, were active.[46] By 1920 the Salon d'Automne recognized the importance of this movement and the growing public it attracted to the

---

[43] Cf. Gino Severini, *Du Cubisme au classicisme* (Paris: Povolozsky, 1921). In addition to extended mathematical speculations, Severini here reproduces a group of pictures from 1919–20 which span his change in style.

[44] *Ibid.*, p. 21.

[45] Vatican critic Michele Guerrisi ("L'Estetica del cubismo," *Fede ed arte,* 1st year, No. 7, July, 1953, pp. 194–97) considers Cubism "an erring theoretical principle . . . a useless and fastidious polemic." Picasso's production is "an artistic joke." Some measure of the author's understanding of this art may be gauged by his reference in these works to "the representation of the cube."

[46] The windows of the crypt and the nave at Assy represent that segment of the decoration which belongs to this tastefully "modernistic" phase of the Sacred Art Movement, which continued even as the Dominicans were engaging the masters of modern painting for the decoration of other parts of the church.

extent of reserving a special section for its artists. Before 1920 it was doubted that religious art could be modern. Now the question was whether modern religious art could be good.

During this period Severini numbered Jacques Maritain among his friends, and the latter came in time to believe that Cubism, "despite its tremendous deficiencies," might represent the "childhood of an art once more pure." [47] Through his deep friendship with Rouault and now with Severini, Maritain understood "that the first duty of the artist . . . is to be unshakably faithful to his own truth,[48] to the individual and incommunicable truth about himself and about things which is obscurely revealed to him and which must take shape in his work." [49]

The situation Maritain faced was one in which most truly creative artists, responding to the loss of integrity of social and spiritual institutions, had made painting itself a principle of order, a way of life, and, finally, almost a religion. Some new theological formulation was necessary if the genuine artist was to be able to function freely within a Church which cannot doctrinally admit to any primacy outside itself. Since neither the artists nor the Church could be reformed, the resolution had to be a semantic one.

Maritain accomplished this with a cleverly contrived neo-Thomist thesis that appeared at once to nullify the conflict of prerogatives between artist and Church and give the legitimacy of philosophical and theological tradition to his position. His reading of Thomas Aquinas turned the saint into a virtual exponent of pure painting. "Art . . . ," went Maritain's interpretation,

remains outside the line of human conduct, with an end, rules, and values which are not those of the man, but of the work to be produced. That work is everything for art—one law only governs it—the exigencies and good of the work. . . . I will try to translate into English this vigorous Aristotelian and scholastic definition . . . as the "undeviating determination of the work to be done." [50]

[47] Maritain, *Art and Scholasticism with Other Essays,* p. 42.

[48] Rouault has always insisted that the artist "ne doit obéir qu'à son ordre intérieur," and Maritain's *Art and Scholasticism with Other Essays* was admittedly written with him in mind. Raïssa Maritain, *Adventures in Grace* (New York: Longmans, Green, 1945), p. 159.

[49] Maritain, "On Artistic Judgment," *Liturgical Arts,* XI, No. 2 (February, 1943), 46–47.

[50] Maritain, *Art and Scholasticism with Other Essays,* pp. 6–7.

But this isolation of the work from theological obligation is balanced by the fact that for the artist *qua* man, i.e., the man working, "the work to be done of itself comes into the line of morality, and so is merely a means. If the artist were to take for the final end of his activity, that is to say for beatitude, the end of his art or the beauty of his work, he would be, purely and simply, an idolator." [51] The artist thus remains subject to the order of religion even if the work he creates is excused. Since, Maritain continued, the "manner of action follows the disposition of the agent and, as a man is, so are his works," it follows that Christian art [52] will be produced in any instance of a Christian artist at work (regardless of the manifest subject matter). But only in those instances; that is, Christian art cannot be produced (as Severini agreed) by nonreligious artists. *NB* Though the last part of this formulation was not to suit their purposes, the Dominicans found its central propositions a useful theological starting point and a source of legitimacy for their more radical program.

Maritain's synthesis had been constructed in part from a passage in which Thomas defined the beautiful as that which gives pleasure to the eye and which resides in the due proportion, completeness, finish, and color of the object. But though this definition appears to resemble views propounded in modern esthetics, the relationship is illusory. The success of Maritain's formula depended on a certain shift in the meaning of Thomas's observations. As Meyer Schapiro observes,

the formula of Thomas concerns natural beauty, the physical charm of men, women, animals, and plants. When he speaks of art he has nothing to say about the beautiful; art is for him skilled work of any kind, whether of the carpenter, logician or surgeon, and its perfection lies in the achievement of a practical end. The modern concept of fine art . . . is apparently unknown to him. The beautiful is not artistic, but natural, and the work of art is not beautiful, but useful.[53]

[51] *Ibid.,* p. 58.

[52] Maritain defines sacred art (which "is in a state of absolute dependence upon theological wisdom") as a subdivision of Christian or religious art distinguished by its liturgical function and ecclesiastical location. *Ibid.,* p. 111 and *passim.*

[53] Meyer Schapiro, "On the Aesthetic Attitude in Romanesque Art," in *Art and Thought, Essays in honor of Dr. Ananda K. Coomaraswamy* (London: Luzac and Co., 1947), p. 148. The

DECADENCE AND THE DOMINICANS

But, however it may have been a distortion of Aquinas, Maritain's thesis was a response to a real need for a *modus vivendi* between Catholic modern artists and the Church. His apologia has seen continuous service since its publication.

In the meantime, church decoration had become a more and more important

medievalist G. G. Coulton (*Art and the Reformation,* Appendix XXII, pp. 560–62) also criticizes Maritain along the same general lines, observing that the Scholastics did not "devote themselves to the consideration of 'fine art' in the more specialized sense. . . . To them, all 'mechanical arts' are in the same category; the ploughman is an artist in the same sense as the sculptor or painter. This is perfectly natural; at the time when Aquinas was writing in Paris, the painters were enrolled in the saddlers' gild, for the reason that saddles were commonly painted . . . . we shall therefore conclude that philosophers who did not distinguish between a painter and a saddler, writing for a public to whom this distinction was equally irrelevant, were philosophers who had not devoted much thought to theories of 'fine art.' . . . [moreover] Maritain boldly substitutes his own contradictory ideas for the words of Saint Thomas, on the plea that, if Saint Thomas had devoted more direct thought to the matter, and written more explicitly, this is what he would have said. . . . [In one passage, Saint Thomas] agrees with Aristotle that it is the business of the state authorities to control the artist, by compulsion if necessary, in the exercise of his art. In order to escape from a conclusion so unacceptable to modern readers, Maritain pleads that Saint Thomas, here, would doubtless allow to the 'fine arts' that indulgence and freedom which he and Aristotle explicitly allow to the speculative sciences. But is not this plea a plain example of what Bossuet stigmatized as 'the worst of intellectual vices—the belief that things are so because we should like them to be so'? When Saint Thomas, in enumerating the 'mechanical arts' so carefully includes 'fine art' and distinguishes all alike from the speculative sciences, do we not do him a very poor compliment by supposing that he would have meant just the opposite if he had possessed M. Maritain's . . . clearness of thought? The whole passage shows how the author, while persuading himself that he follows Saint Thomas, is really voicing the catchwords of a modern clique. The Scholastics, all through this book are scarcely more than a convenient excuse for temperamental divagations."

In his *Creative Intuition in Art and Poetry* (New York: Meridian, 1955), Maritain has described both "useful arts" and "fine arts" as virtues of the Practical Intellect, but he distinguished between them (p. 47) by assigning "fine arts" a place among the liberal arts, explaining that the ancients did not recognize this "because any manual labor bore in their eyes the stamp of the servile condition." Though here and elsewhere in this recent book Maritain has restated the thesis of *Art and Scholasticism,* he was careful not to ascribe the placement of the "fine arts" in the liberal arts to the Scholastics directly, though the reader is left with the impression that his whole view follows directly from Saint Thomas. Nowhere has Maritain taken up or attempted to refute the criticisms of Coulton, and the whole "legitimizing" structure of the earlier thesis has thus fallen to the ground.

concern in France. In 1931 Cardinal Verdier, assisted by Monsignor Touzé, opened the ambitious series of church constructions known as the Chantiers du Cardinal. By 1938 ninety-two churches were finished, and, sustained by charity, the work continues to this day. In 1935 Joseph Pichard founded the review *L'Art sacré,* which during the following years fought a valiant war for minimal taste and quality in church decoration, a war in which, with respect to the Chantiers du Cardinal, most of the battles were lost.

By 1937 some of the best artists in the modernist group had gathered enough support among the clergy and lay community to make a frontal attack on the traditionalists, an action which was, in effect, a prelude to the great debate on sacred art that developed after the war around the church of Assy. This initial move took the form of a project for filling in a number of the blank windows of Notre-Dame-de-Paris with modern stained glass. Father Couturier and Paul Bony (both later active at Assy) were among the participants. Cardinal Verdier considered the windows a success, and they were publicly praised by such artists as Denis, Frièsz, Dufy, and Bonnard.[54] Nevertheless, their installation caused great alarm and consternation among the more conservative elements in the clergy and the lay community. Objections focused not on the rather mediocre quality of the particular works,[55] but on the whole principle of the use of modern art in the church, particularly in a Gothic cathedral. After long discussions, the incriminated windows were quietly removed, and, the war having broken out, this little drama was soon forgotten.

Good intentions notwithstanding, the Catholic modernist movement, as it stood on the eve of the Second World War, had produced no outstanding works, for the participating artists were either men of small talent or, like Severini and Gleizes, past their artistic prime. By this time it was clear to Father Couturier and other interested Dominicans that lesser talents would never suffice to bring about the desired resurrection of sacred art. Little by

[54] Régamey, "La Querelle des vitraux," *L'Art sacré,* 5th year, No. 38, February, 1939, pp. 49–53.

[55] François Mathey ("Situation du vitrail en France," *Quadrum,* December, 1957, No. 4, pp. 84–98) rightly considers the Notre-Dame windows "a timid step" by artists whose "good intentions could not rise to the demands of the program."

29

little a more daring position began to be explored. It was expressed primarily through the review, *L'Art sacré,* which Fathers Couturier and Régamey had rescued from impending bankruptcy with the help of lay financial support. This shift from the editorial regime of Joseph Pichard, whose goals were limited by an innocuous "modernistic" taste, marked the counterpart, on the level of critical activity, of the practical events which were just getting under way at Assy.

In March, 1939, on his return from Rome where he was working in the church of Santa Sabina, Father Couturier stopped at Assy. There his old friend Canon Devémy and the architect Maurice Novarina asked him to collaborate in planning and executing the decoration of Notre-Dame-de-Toute-Grâce, then under construction. A trip to Paris with the Canon led to the first Rouault window, and in June and August Father Couturier returned to Assy to further elaborate his plans. On December 30 he embarked for New York, charged with preaching Lent to the French colony of the city. The outbreak of war arrested plans for Assy [56] and lengthened Father Couturier's stay in America to five years.

It was in America that this brilliant and always independent Dominican was to develop fully his new position. His friendship here with such exiles from France as Maritain, Maurois, Focillon, Léger, Chagall, Dalí, and Stravinsky led him to an exhaustive reconsideration of the problem of sacred art viewed apart from the conditions and traditions actually existing in France. The patriotic and romantic spirit of wartime, the great disasters and realignments of values that took place, all favored the radicality of the conclusions that he was to draw and, with the coming of peace, put into practice with the aid of Father Régamey. In America both Léger and Chagall spoke with him of the possibility of a collaboration. It crystallized in the Church of Assy.

[56] With the exception of the contact made during the war with Bonnard, who was approached independently by the Canon Devémy.

2. GENESIS OF THE CHURCH OF ASSY

When Father Couturier made his fateful call at Assy in 1939, he found a thriving community at a site where a little over a decade before there had been only rock cliffs and rich virgin forests. There, high above the Arve River, at an altitude of 1,000 meters, the plateau of Assy forms the second step of the gigantic ladder that terminates in the Désert de Plate. In 1928 Doctors Tobé and Terrasse chose the area facing Saint-Gervais and the chain of Mont Blanc as the location for the sanatorium of Sancellemoz. Other sanatoria followed in rapid succession—the Mont Blanc (1929), Roc des Fiz (1932), the Martel de Janville (1937)—and with them a number of pensions, small hotels, and private villas. Stores and services of all kinds took root on the plateau to meet the needs of tubercular patients, convalescents, and their families, and though the war interrupted this development somewhat, the village has flourished increasingly in the last decade.

By 1937 the large number of Catholic patients in the area necessitated the creation of an independent parish, and the bishop of Annecy confided to Father Jean Devémy the task of planning and administering the building of a new church to be placed subsequently in the hands of the Dominicans. Father Devémy had himself been a patient and later a chaplain at Sancellemoz, and was much in sympathy with the taste and sentiments of Assy's transient population, "open to the influences of the outside world and yet predisposed to inward contemplation." [1]

The absence of an indigenous population with deep-rooted local traditions and provincial biases is an important factor in the development of the modern

[1] F. Stahly, "The Church of Assy," *Graphis*, V, No. 26 (1949), 128–33, 203–5.

taste that came to characterize the church of Assy. But in those first days nothing could have been further from the mind of Father Devémy than the program which later led some of the greatest artists of the century to contribute their efforts. The Canon has insisted that his first notion of a church for this community was of "something completely traditional and in good taste." His main concern was that the church should be of high quality. "I come from the very solid country of the north; we like only the best and cannot tolerate *'camelote'* —third class merchandise." Even as the project took on its revolutionary character Canon Devémy denied any intention of shattering tradition, arguing that the innovations were simply the result of a search for the finest art. The church of Assy, he insisted, "is not a manifest of art; Assy has not pretended to give a lesson; Assy has not wished to create a prototype." [2] Not all these sentiments were shared by the Dominican fathers who gradually assumed the dominant role in the disposition of the church.

Until it entered its post-war phase, the iconographic plan for the Church of Notre-Dame-de-Toute-Grâce developed in a rather haphazard manner. At Easter time in 1938, when the crypt was under way, Canon Devémy called in Marguerite Huré, a religious glazier in the "modernistic" tradition, to do its windows. By fall she had executed a pedestrian series of eucharistic scenes and symbols (see Figure 8), and with the crypt thus completed, services began. At that time the architect, Maurice Novarina, pressed Canon Devémy to establish a complete plan of decorations, including subjects, locations, and materials. But the latter, feeling that he could not envisage the church adequately from plans and wishing to secure a sense of its space and atmosphere before making such decisions, left the question open. Nevertheless, the Canon did agree to commission a façade project from the Lyonais painter Zelman. This came to naught, however, as Zelman died before he could execute it.

Meanwhile, a local Savoyard artisan, Constant Demaison, had been granted permission to carve the eight great oak beams designed to support the wooden roof being made at the École Professionelle of the Abbé Lamache at Lyon. Moses (Figure 9) representing the law and Isaiah representing the prophecy of the coming of Christ were selected as appropriate for the beams nearest the

[2] "L'Eglise d'Assy et l'art sacré," *Courier de l'ouest,* January 6, 1951, p. 1.

32

GEORGES ROUAULT, *Christ aux outrages*
STAINED GLASS WINDOW, WEST FAÇADE
EXECUTED BY PAUL BONY

portal. They were followed by the four evangelists, and the group was completed by Saint Irenaeus and Saint Bernard of Citeaux, representing the beginning and the end of the great era of doctors of the Church.[3] These figures, drawn from Scripture and tradition, were to "support" the church in fact as well as metaphor. Demaison had finished four beams when the Second World War broke out; he was to finish the rest *in situ* with the coming of peace.

In 1939, as the walls of the church proper were rising, a fortunate encounter took place, which became the key to later developments. In Paris for a short sojourn, Canon Devémy was taken to an exhibition of religious art at the Petit Palais by his old friend Father Couturier. There he saw three stained glass windows based on cartoons by Rouault and executed under his supervision in the atelier of Jean Hébert-Stevens. These so pleased the Canon that he decided to request one for his church. "I had no grandiose plan for a modern church, but felt that a single window by Rouault would be enough. It would be an addition, if only by a speck, to the total of living art in the church."

Rouault graciously accepted Devémy's request and offered him his choice of three windows from which the Canon selected a seated *Christ aux outrages* (see plate). The painter was highly pleased that for the first time, as he neared the age of seventy, one of his works was to be placed in a Catholic church. By a fortuitous accident, which Canon Devémy calls "the miracle of Assy," the width of the Rouault window was exactly that of the openings reserved for windows in the wall of the west façade, which had already risen to the tribune level. Had it been too large, there might never have been a Rouault window in the church, as the Canon did not feel at the time that he could ask Rouault to make anything to fit Assy's specifications.

Work on Notre-Dame-de-Toute-Grâce was halted on the outbreak of the war, but was resumed in 1940 after the armistice with Germany. Though Canon Devémy and Father Couturier had spoken vaguely of an over-all iconographic plan, nothing had been settled, and, with the latter stranded in America by the fall of France, Devémy was forced to continue on his own.

---

[3] Meyer Schapiro has observed that the choice of St. Irenaeus was also probably influenced by the fact that this Bishop of Lyon was the only great early (second century) Gallic Church Father.

Elated by the presence of the Rouault window, he decided to make the rest of the decoration match this standard. Proceeding courageously, if naïvely, he selected artists largely on the basis of reputation, his choices being necessarily limited by wartime difficulties in communication.

Couturier and Devémy had previously chosen Saint Dominic (the church was confided to his order) and Saint Francis of Sales (once Bishop of Geneva and patron saint of the region of Assy) as subjects for the two lateral altars. To paint Saint Francis the Canon now selected Raoul Dufy, a surprising choice but understandable, as Dufy, unlike most well-known painters, was a religious Catholic and had been a friend of Devémy when both were students at the ecclesiastical college of Le Havre. But it proved impossible to make contact with Dufy, and Devémy turned to Bonnard, whose work he knew moderately well. In 1943 he traveled to Cannes, where Bonnard, after overcoming some initial skepticism, agreed to do the work (see frontispiece).

For Saint Dominic, Devémy chose André Derain, with whose post-Fauve religious pictures he was familiar. But, after first agreeing, Derain withdrew, whereupon the Canon embarked on a pilgrimage to Picasso's studio in Paris, though his familiarity with Picasso's work was limited primarily to the Blue and the Rose periods. It was his feeling that the Iberian painter would be an appropriate choice for the Spanish-born saint. Picasso was surprised but most cordial, and showed Devémy some canvases of male figures he had just completed, suggesting, probably with a touch of facetiousness, that they might serve as representations of the saint. These pictures, executed in the extremely expressionistic style of Picasso's wartime work, shocked the Canon, as they were to shock considerably less naïve sensibilities in the Salon d'Automne immediately after the cessation of hostilities in 1945. Concluding that Picasso was unsuited for the task, Devémy thanked the artist for his time and took his leave. There the matter of the Saint Dominic altar rested until 1948, when Father Couturier arranged to have Matisse make a variant (see plate) of the large ceramic mural he was preparing for the Dominican chapel at Vence.

With the coming of peace Father Couturier returned to France, and only then was an orderly iconographic program for the decorations drawn up. This program was largely the product of Couturier, who now more or less took over

34

direction of work at Assy, using the project as a practical laboratory in which to experiment with the new theories of ecclesiastical art being explored by the Dominicans in *L'Art sacré*.

Beginning with the eight windows of the nave, Father Couturier chose as subjects the Archangel Raphael, Saint Vincent of Paul, Saint Francis of Assisi, Saint Thérèse of Lisieux (north aisle), and Saint Peter, Saint Louis, Saint Joan of Arc, and Our Lady of the Seven Sorrows (south aisle). Though these saints appear at first a rather disparate group, they are linked by their involvement with sickness or cure. The Archangel Raphael (according to the guide published under Father Couturier's direction [4]) was included because he cured Tobit; Vincent of Paul, because he spent his life caring for the sick and wounded; Francis of Assisi, for his kindness to the leper; Thérèse of Lisieux, because she died of tuberculosis; [5] Peter, for curing by his shadow (Acts 5.15); Louis, because he built hospitals, personally treated the sick, and later died of the plague; and Joan of Arc for her tenderness toward the French and English wounded.

Commissions to design these windows were given to Maurice Brianchon, Paul Berçot, Paul Bony (who actually executed all but the tribune and crypt windows of the church), and Adeline Hébert-Stevens (Mme Bony). Father Couturier designed two himself. The selection of these artists reflected a conscious attempt by Couturier to keep the decoration of the aisles in the family, as it were. All are religious Catholics, and all were active in modernist circles of Church decoration before the war. Seen in the context of the other decorations, only the two windows by Berçot hold their own. Fully conscious of the disparity in quality, Father Couturier spoke, shortly before his death, of removing his own windows and replacing them with others that would rank artistically with contributions of the master artists.

Both Father Couturier and Paul Bony had participated in the ill-fated

[4] Guide (to the church of Assy), *L'Art sacré*, September–October, 1950, No. 1–2, pp. 11–15. In Hebrew the name Raphael means "healing Angel."

[5] The apropos nature of her suffering (the patients in Assy sanatoria are tuberculars) explains the inclusion of a saint who is otherwise a symbol of just that religious sentimentalism and *Kitsch* that the Dominicans oppose.

Notre-Dame-de-Paris project just before the war, and the work of Brianchon and Hébert-Stevens accords with the modernist taste evinced at that time. It therefore appears somewhat surprising that Father Couturier should have turned to these same artists seven years later, picking up the threads where they had been broken off in France, as though his wartime American adventure and its resultant spiritual and critical transformations had never taken place. The explanation, I think, lies in his desire to reward the Catholic modernists for their efforts, particularly in view of the rebuffs they had received in 1937–39. Moreover, the distribution of these commissions to artists within the Church mitigated somewhat the criticism to which the Dominicans were to be subjected for their employment of Jews, atheists, and Communists.

The radical aspect of the decorative plan for Assy began late in 1945 with the engagement of Fernand Léger to execute a mosaic façade decoration (see plate). But it seemed that shortly before the end of the war the architect, Novarina, with Canon Devémy's concurrence, had entrusted the task to two young painters named Lenormand and Idoux, who had already begun a large mural of the Sermon on the Mount. Delicate negotiations were required therefore to open the way for Léger, and his appointment was announced in 1946. Since the edifice was dedicated to the Virgin, her litanies were selected as appropriate to both the iconography of the church and the limited possibilities of the artist, an avowed Communist.

About this time Jean Lurçat was commissioned to do the tapestry for the sanctuary (see plate). Before the end of the war Canon Devémy had written him, requesting a Virgin in Majesty for this focal point in the decorative scheme. But Father Couturier understood the Marxist Lurçat's inability to work with such a subject, and in 1946 the scene of cosmic struggle from the twelfth chapter of the Apocalypse was finally agreed upon.

There were to be three windows in the tribune, which was the site of the organ. For these a simple iconography dealing with music was established. King David (Old Testament prototype of the musician), Saint Cecilia (patroness of music), and Gregory the Great (codifier of the chant) were confided in 1946 to Jean Bazaine, who was at that time still working in a semifigurative cubist style, and who, except for Rouault, is the only practicing Catholic *NB* among the famous modern artists represented at Assy.

Rouault now agreed to allow four stained glass windows to be translated from his paintings, and during the years 1946–50 they were realized under his guidance in the atelier of Paul Bony. A second seated Christ of the Passion (Figure 11) and two floral still lifes were combined with the Christ of 1939 to make a group of four windows for the west façade. The still lifes were iconographically linked to the Christs through the symbolism of Isaiah, who referred to the Messiah in metaphors of flowers, grapes, and plants. To make the connection clear, Rouault added fragments of text from Isaiah 53.7 to the still-life windows.[6] A fifth window, realized from Rouault's oil of Saint Veronica, was placed in the mortuary chapel (Figure 15). This legendary saint is appropriately associated with Calvary, supposedly having received the impress of the features of Christ on her handkerchief when she offered it to him as he was carrying the Cross. Actually, her legend is a somewhat late creation of confused origin, her name itself having been derived apparently from the term "true image," or *vera icon*.

In 1947 Jacques Lipchitz undertook to create a baptismal font with a figure of the Virgin, and Marc Chagall later consented to decorate the baptistry with a ceramic mural of the Red Sea Passage (Figure 37), a familiar Old Testament prefiguration of the sacrament of baptism. It was simple liturgical logic for the two Jewish artists participating at Assy to be originally assigned the baptistry, for this section of the church is associated with the transition from the state of Law to that of Grace.[7] Catechumens, for example, who are not allowed into the

---

[6] These texts were not in the paintings that served as models; they were added to clarify the iconographic meaning at Assy. Since the seated Christs appear to be waiting judgment in prison, they are further linked to the still lifes through the opening line of Isaiah 53.8: "He was taken from prison and judgment."

[7] Owing to difficulties in fitting both the Lipchitz and Chagall works into the small baptistry, it was subsequently decided to move the Lipchitz sculpture—now no longer attached to a font—elsewhere in the church. The shift destroyed a certain logic in the original choices, but the placement in the church proper of this work by a religious Jew has never been specifically questioned.

37

church proper, may hear the service from the baptistry. The Jewish artists were thus considered partial "outsiders," whose religion constitutes an antecedent of Catholicism, but whose confession is considered incomplete. All the modern artists working elsewhere in the church of Assy, whatever the atheism they professed, were born and baptized Catholics.[8] No Protestant artist was engaged.

In 1948, Georges Braque offered a small relief for the door of the tabernacle, and the decorative program was completed the following year when Germaine Richier was commissioned to do a bronze crucifix (Figure 53).

Though the individual works are discussed in detail in Part II, some observations regarding the iconographic scheme as a whole are in order here.

There is a striking difference between the plan of decorations at Assy and the programs of contemporary "modernist" as well as older churches. The iconography of older churches is generally based on the Church calendar, drawing primarily upon the Bible and the lives of the saints.[9] The subjects are related to dogmatic principles and are usually organized in hierarchical relationships, focused climactically on the region of the altar.[10] The same is true

[8] The only partial exception would be Rouault, who, though of Catholic extraction, spent his childhood outside the Church and was educated in Protestant schools.

[9] The foregoing is true, of course, primarily for larger churches and cathedrals, parish churches usually having had little decoration in medieval times. Though Assy is a parish church, the number, size, and disposition of its decorations constitute a system normally associated with a church of at least collegiate rank. This is equally true in the disposition of altars, the one dedicated to the tabernacle being the north lateral. Ordinarily, in parish churches, the tabernacle is placed on the central altar; in fact, Canon No. 1268, para. 3, specifically prohibits its being placed elsewhere except in churches of collegiate or cathedral size. See Mariani, *La Legislazione ecclesiastica in materia d'arte sacra,* p. 94. The program at Assy should thus properly be compared with those of larger churches of the past.

[10] This is somewhat less true of post-Reformation churches. But, in spite of many new iconographic motifs introduced following the Council of Trent, the essentials of the older programs were maintained. See Émile Mâle, *L'Art réligieux après le concile de Trente* (Paris: Colin, 1932). The rigorous attitude toward iconography of the Counter-Reform years relaxed somewhat in the Baroque period, but it is only in the eighteenth and nineteenth centuries that a marked *détente* took place. The Academicism of those years reemphasized some pre-Reformation iconographic motifs, developed a few new ones, but did not create a characteristic and systematic iconography like that of the Counter-Reform. Of the various

for modern churches as they are customarily decorated by Catholic artists, though here the programs are not so inclusive. "The repertoire of our Christian painters," notes Pichard,

is not that of the Middle Ages or the Renaissance. The opening into the subject is less large. Of the whole of Christian iconography, only certain images have been retained. . . . One may group them around the two great liturgical cycles which summarize Christian life: the Christmas cycle and the Easter cycle.[11]

At Assy, however, not even these fundamental cycles are present. Though each choice of subject has an appropriate rationale, the decoration as a whole does not constitute a sequence, much less an inclusive affirmation of the essentials of the religion. Of the sacraments, which often determine the choice of themes in older churches, only baptism is alluded to. The calendar is largely overlooked, and the structure of the hierarchy omitted. Such figures of the hierarchy as are present are juxtaposed in an anti-hieratic manner in terms of position and size. Thus Veronica is smaller and more obscurely placed than Thérèse of Lisieux, while the Archangel Raphael and Peter are smaller and further from the altar than Francis of Sales.

Surveying the decoration from within the church, one is struck by a feeling of isolation of parts, resulting to some extent from the absence of a continuous iconographic scheme. This sense of disjunction is reinforced by the marked difference in style from one work to the next. Thus, just as the musical saints of the tribune seem to have no connection with the iconography below, the style of Bazaine is at variance with that of Rouault. Yet this iconographic and stylistic discontinuity is not out of harmony with the more individualistic, less group-oriented religious experience of the convalescents at Assy.

Since there is no continuity in the iconographic program, there can be no hieratic crescendo in the sanctuary, such as leads to the Pantocrator in some

---

attempts at reviving Christian iconography in the nineteenth century Louis Brehier observes: ". . . these experiments were interesting, but too isolated, too fragmentary to permit the rediscovery of a lost tradition and the creation of a new Christian art. The history of this [religious] art in the 19th century consists of hesitations and fruitless experiments." *L'Art chrétien* (2d ed.; Paris: Laurens, 1928), p. 431.

[11] Pichard, *L'Art sacré moderne*, p. 125.

older churches. Though the fields of decoration increase in size as they near the altar, forming a visual climax, the iconography does not cooperate with this staging; indeed, it seems often to work against it. The arcade-level windows of the west façade, for example, are very small, but contain the only images of Christ (except for the Crucifix) at Assy. Proceeding eastward to the larger aisle windows, we find the lower-ranking saints, Peter and Raphael (see plan of decorations). The aisle altar fields are even larger, but are devoted to still less important saints, Francis of Sales and Dominic. Lurçat's culminating apse tapestry is immense but contains no explicit figure of the hierarchy at all. Instead, there is an apocalyptic scene of a type found generally in small format in older Christian art. Thus, where we might expect a climactic Christ Pantocrator, we find a fantasy of cosmic struggle between the Satanic beast and a woman [12] "clothed with the sun."

The tapestry of Lurçat dominates the church by its size, the brightness of its colors, and the boldness of its style, but its iconography is divided and anticlimactic. The choice of the apocalyptic theme resulted in a two-part composi-

---

[12] This figure, of course, was not meant to be the Madonna in the original text of Revelations, but she has been so identified by tradition. The cosmic symbols which surround her and the theme of the peril of childbirth relate her to the imagery of an important modern dogma, the Immaculate Conception. Mâle cites numerous examples in which such attributes as the sun, the nimbus of stars, and the moon at the feet are present in Immaculate Conceptions by seventeenth- and eighteenth-century painters. See Émile Mâle, *L'Art religieux apres le concile de Trente,* pp. 38–48. This is one of the most important post-Reformation icons and is the keystone of the dogmatic structure which the Church has built up around Mary in response to her downgrading by Protestantism. The identification of the woman of Revelations with the Virgin emphasizes her role as the "second Eve" in constant combat with the Serpent. Some versions of the Immaculate Conception actually contain the figure of Saint John, who points to his vision as a lesson for the others present, a lesson which Pius IX promulgated as dogma in 1854.

If one could accept Mâle's definition of the Immaculate Conception ("She [the Virgin] was conceived by God before the world . . ." [p. 42]), the identification with the woman of Revelations would be even more apropos as it would argue the Virgin's existence in the primordial cosmic time of John's vision. Mâle appears to be wrong here, however; his concept is at variance not only with the dogma as it was promulgated in 1854, but also with the views of the Fathers during the centuries of dispute which preceded general acceptance of the belief.

JEAN LURÇAT, *The Apocalypse*
VIEW OF SANCTUARY SHOWING TAPESTRY *in situ*

tion, with an open space in the center, where we normally expect to find the dogma ringingly summarized. Such a situation stems in part from the fact that no outstanding modern artist seems able to participate deeply enough in the spirit of a Pantocrator-type of dogmatic image to be able to render it. The Dominicans have been the first to realize this. "One would certainly prefer a Pantocrator as the dominating work in the sanctuary," writes Father Régamey, "but who today could treat such a theme better than one recites a memorized lesson?" [13] "What a frightening avowal of impotence," replied the conservative Catholic critic Madaleine Ochsé, "when the Dominican Fathers ask who will make a Pantocrator." [14]

The relatively minor role of Christ in the iconographic drama of Assy is not wholly unexpected. This has been increasingly the tendency in Catholic churches since the Reformation. Christ appears only three times at Assy, always in small format. Moreover, his role in Rouault's two Passion windows, as in the Richier Crucifix, is limited to the experience of suffering. We see no narrative scenes from his life, no scenes of transcendence or glory, and above all, no scenes of his miracles or cures.[15] The latter have been familiar since the beginning of Christian iconography and usually play an especially important role in churches which, like Assy, are dedicated to the sick. (One need only look to the imagery of Lourdes or Lisieux for a comparison.)

[13] Régamey, *Art sacré au XXᵉ siècle?* p. 334.

[14] Ochsé, *La Nouvelle Querelle des images,* p. 106.

[15] It would seem particularly significant, in this connection, that Rouault, the only great Catholic artist of our era, should imagine Christ almost exclusively as a suffering figure, and that even lesser Catholic artists (excluding academicians and archaists) should rarely attempt to picture him in glory, in resurrection, or in transfiguration. Of the moderns, only the non-representational painters, like Manessier, have attempted such themes.

Christ is a rather familiar figure in post-World War II modern figurative painting in France. Yet such different painters as Bernard Buffet and André Marchand show him always as an agonized figure. For the latter Christ is "a man from the ovens of Dachau . . . a man of the twentieth century, beaten, insulted, attacked, humiliated, reduced to the order of animals and finally burned alive in the crematories." *Cahiers de l'art sacré,* 1946, No. 7, p. 35. Buffet, with his clowns and Christs, has taken over the ascetic imagery of Rouault. But the pathos of Rouault has become bathos, and the whole of the iconography smacks of insincerity.

GENESIS OF THE CHURCH OF ASSY

In typical twentieth-century Catholic churches the gap produced by minimizing the role of Christ is filled by imagery devoted to the Virgin. Mary has come to play an extraordinarily important part in Catholic iconography, greater even than at the height of her cult during the Gothic period. This is a counterpart of the Marian orientation of the Vatican and the resultant elaboration and glorification of Mary's role in dogma and liturgy as reflected in the recent proclamation of the dogma of her bodily Assumption. At Assy, Mary is more important than Christ. She is represented in Léger's large façade mosaic, in Lipchitz's sculpture, in one of the aisle windows, and, by popular association at least, in Lurçat's tapestry.

And yet, compared with other contemporary churches, the Virgin's role, too, has been modified. Her lesser position at Assy may reflect the uneasiness of the Dominicans and of Catholic liberals in general over the Vatican tendency to enhance her role. Their opposition cannot be expressed too openly, lest they be associated with the Protestant critics who have long been laboring this point. The cult of Mary has become, in fact, the rallying point of the conservative majority within the Church.

Taken as a whole, the group of saints represented in the iconography of Assy is unusual and revealing. The stress is on the heroes of the Church, especially national ones, rather than on the sacraments, dogmas, or mysteries. In addition to the Virgin and the Archangel Raphael there are eleven saints: Peter (d. *ca.*55), Veronica (legendary), Cecilia (d. 176), Gregory (d. 604), Dominic (d. 1221), Francis of Assisi (d. 1226), Louis (d. 1270), Joan of Arc (d. 1431), Francis of Sales (d. 1622), Vincent of Paul (d. 1660), Thérèse of Lisieux (d. 1897). Whereas even in contemporary Catholic churches saints from the New Testament and from early Christianity predominate, owing to their importance in the liturgy and the crystallization of dogma, at Assy they are a feeble minority. Of the eleven only four are pre-Gothic, and two of these (Cecilia and Gregory) are included simply because they are patrons of music. Of the biblical saints only Peter is present. Three of the remaining seven (Dominic, Francis of Assisi, and Louis) are Gothic and the others post-medieval.

An unexpected majority of five of these seven (all but Francis of Assisi and Dominic) are French, the Gallican and nationalist nature of the choices being

42

especially evident in such figures as Joan of Arc,[16] St. Louis Roi, and Francis of Sales. The last-mentioned was bishop of the region of Haute-Savoie, and has tended to replace his Italian namesake in this area.[17] He was also an important figure at the court of Henry IV. Dominic, though born in Spain and represented by a large altar decoration primarily as founder of the order to which the church was confided, was also important in French religious history, having spent a good part of his life preaching to the Albigensians in the Languedoc.

The nave window of Francis of Assisi and the larger altar painting of Dominic provide representation of two of the three great orders of the Church, in proportions commensurate with their importance for the Dominicans who invented the program. The absence of the Jesuits is not accidental. In the struggle between liberals and conservatives within the Church, the Franciscans are sometimes allies of the leftist Dominicans, but the Jesuits form their major opposition.

Another unusual aspect of the iconographic program is the almost total absence of narrative imagery. None of the themes popular among even modernist Catholic artists (like the Stations of the Cross) are present. Although the saints are included on account of their acts, they are never shown in action; rather are they portrayed as simple standing figures, resembling more the

[16] Long a partisan hero in France, Joan's local festival (May 8) was declared a French public holiday by Napoleon. The Third Republic made the date a *Fête nationale* in 1920, at the time of her tardy canonization.

[17] Dr. A. van Gennep, "Essai sur le culte populaire des saints franciscains en Savoie," *Revue d'histoire franciscaine,* IV, No. 2 (April–June, 1927), 113–210 (cited in Coulton, *Art and the Reformation,* p. 289), observes that certain saints in the Savoy region "have not been suppressed in the strict sense of the word, but replaced, often through a similarity of names. The fact is specially remarkable in the case of St. Francis of Sales, who, in popular devotion, has replaced St. Francis of Assisi. . . . He has driven him out of his oldest and most venerable sanctuary in Savoy, at Chambery"; after the fifteen years' break at the Revolution, the people had forgotten the original dedication of the cathedral, and there were no protests when, at its rededication, St. Francis of Sales was imposed as the patron saint. As Francis of Assisi is often paired with Dominic, the placement of Francis of Sales at the lateral altar, opposite the one devoted to the Spanish saint, is a logical extension of the replacement process. Moreover, though the character and activities of Francis of Sales had few affinities with those of Francis of Assisi, he is now popularly adored for his simplicity, kindliness, and love of children, just those affectionate attitudes which had previously been demonstrated *vis-à-vis* the Italian saint. It is as such a figure that Bonnard represented him.

medieval "icon" than the narrative image familiar since the time of Giotto. Peter, for example, is included in the program because he healed by his shadow. But Peter is not shown doing this (as in the Brancacci Chapel fresco by Masaccio); instead, he is presented to the spectator in simple frontal position.

This absolute insistence upon the "icon" presentation is peculiar to the church of Assy among twentieth-century churches, and it may be that it results in part from the particular expressive needs of the participating modern artists. In general, narrative imagery has been foreign to modern painters. The relative isolation of a subject matter from context, which began with the *morceau* paintings of Manet and reached a climax in Cubism, leads to a symbolic image of an order wholly opposite to that of the Renaissance and Baroque.[18] At Assy, only the apocalyptic combat in the Lurçat tapestry derives from a narrative situation. But, even there, the protagonists are treated as isolated symbols rather than as engaged narrative figures.[19]

Father Couturier often remarked that he and Canon Devémy called upon the non-Catholic modern masters to work at the church of Assy in "exactly that sector which appeared spiritually open to them." [20] This statement gives the impression that the iconographic program was elaborated first, and that suitable painters were then chosen for the task. It will be clear, however, as the facts unfold in the following pages, that the subject was almost as often picked for the man as the man for the subject. The resultant iconography should thus be viewed as a compromise between the aims and desires of the Dominican Fathers and the limited liturgical possibilities of modern painters unwilling to sacrifice their integrity in commitment to an imagery they could not sincerely render.

[18] Some German Expressionist painters, Emil Nolde and Max Beckmann among them, have essayed narrative religious scenes with success. But their work is marginal to the general development of modern painting.

[19] Picasso, when confronted with a historical narrative situation in the bombing of Guernica, characteristically chose to represent the scene in hallucinatory and symbolic terms.

[20] Régamey, *L'Art sacré au XXe siècle?* p. 275.

3. THE DEBATE ON SACRED ART

The year 1950 marked the commencement of open hostilities among various factions of the Church with regard to sacred art. In the five years following the end of the Second World War the Dominicans had elaborated their theoretical position and had begun a series of practical efforts, of which the first and historically the most important, the church of Assy, was now ready for dedication. Conservative elements within the Church had looked askance upon this development, and, prodded by such Integrist reactionaries as Gaston Bardet and Charles du Mont (whose sympathies were shared by many members of the Holy Office), they fought back. Clerical and financial pressure was quietly brought to bear on the Dominicans and particularly on their review, *L'Art sacré*. In the period from 1945 to 1950 several criticisms of modern art were noted in papal addresses, and many in articles published by official reviews like *Fede ed arte*.

Reconciliation of the Dominican and conservative views had become impossible, and both sides decided to turn openly to the faithful—indeed, to the world at large—for support. The Jubilee Year of 1950 seemed admirably suited to this purpose, as world attention was more than usually focused on the Church, and as the central liturgical event, the proclamation of the dogma of the bodily Assumption of the Virgin was itself a matter of conflict between the liberal and conservative ecclesiastics. In France and elsewhere the dedication of the church of Assy attracted public attention on a vast scale (reflected in large illustrated articles in such magazines as *France Illustration* and *Life*). This was followed in the fall by a major exhibition of modern sacred art at the

Museum of Modern Art in Paris. In Rome the First International Congress of Catholic Artists took place in the beginning of September, accompanied by a large exhibition of sacred art, arranged by Vatican authorities, of a character markedly in contrast with the one taking place in Paris.

The affirmative public response to the church at Assy annoyed the Integrists exceedingly, and as the Dominicans boycotted the French delegation to the International Congress, the remaining conservative members joined those of the Italian and Belgian delegations under the leadership of Gaston Bardet to aim a concentrated attack on the "internal heresy" of modern sacred art. In the midst of confusing sessions, marked by the absence of a register of delegates and of adequate translations of the talks, Bardet presented a motion that Church authorities be urged to formulate rules to guide artists. This proposal anticipated his demand for an "Index of Sacred Art" made the following year, and its spirit may be measured by Bardet's reply to a question from the floor: "Then you would have the Church place manacles on the artists?" he was asked. "Exactly," retorted Bardet.[1] It is to the credit of the United States delegation and its chairman, Maurice Lavanoux, that with the support of delegations from Holland, Austria, Peru, and Switzerland they were able to defeat the Integrist motion. The liberal point of view was summarized in a document, elaborated by Lavanoux, stating:

1. We deny the necessity for a set of rules concerning sacred art. The difficulty in this case would be to state rules that would be applicable in a universal sense, and we feel that any such rules would be merely the expression of one particular school of thought. The directives of the Holy Father, as expressed in the encyclical *Mediator Dei,* are all that is necessary for the present time.

2. The attack on the use of reinforced concrete [2] and on modern techniques and construction is like Don Quixote tilting at windmills. The world is too large and the various needs of people in the world will be met in a normal and intelligent manner, based on liturgical requirements and a sense of tradition and that is all.

---

[1] Maurice Lavanoux, "Preliminary Report; First International Congress of Catholic Artists," *Liturgical Arts,* XIX, No. 1 (November, 1950), 4–6.

[2] Bardet's motion had also condemned this as "improper building material for churches."

3. Fanaticism in matters of sacred art is an attitude that can lead to a decadence more sterile than the one we are now endeavoring to overcome. . . .[3]

On the final day of the Congress, Pope Pius XII gave his Apostolic Benediction and delivered a short address limited, for the most part, to general statements on the cultural and spiritual value of art. True, a word of caution was given with respect to art which "needs to be explained in verbal terms" (abstract art), and the profanity of "art for art's sake" was emphasized, but the Pontiff remained characteristically aloof from the smouldering partisan contention that had animated the meetings.[4]

Press reaction to the address was nevertheless curiously strong. In many quarters the words of the Pope were interpreted as a condemnation of all abstract art, and journalists cabled from Rome to newspapers all over the world to this effect. But while there seems to be no question as to the kind of art the Pontiff was criticizing, his words were sufficiently vague to lend themselves to conflicting interpretations. Father Régamey,[5] for example, defended the abstract painting of Manessier and Bazaine as examples of precisely the kind of art that did *not* need to be explained "in verbal terms," and completely reversed the apparent intent of the Pope by viewing his statement as a condemnation of art containing involved, extrapictorial elements (i.e., "literary art"). Such an interpretation demonstrates how deeply into sophistry circumstances pushed the Dominicans, who strove to remain within the letter of the law while being outside its spirit.

By the end of the year Vatican reaction to the church of Assy and particularly to the Crucifix of Germaine Richier became more marked. This was reflected in the papal exhortation, *Menti nostre,* to the clergy of the Catholic world, which attacked

works which astonishingly deform art and yet pretend to be Christian . . . from which naturally derives the fact that there is no lack in our times of priests in-

---

[3] Lavanoux, "The Authentic Tradition and Art," *Liturgical Arts,* XXII, No. 4 (August, 1954), 122–25.

[4] Pius XII, "Address to the First International Congress of Catholic Artists," *Liturgical Arts,* XIX, No. 1 (November, 1950), 3–4.

[5] Régamey, "Rome 1950," *L'Art sacré,* January–February, 1951, No. 5–6, pp. 22–26.

fected in some way with a similar contagion . . . who have allowed themselves
to be carried away by the mania of novelty.[6]

The allusion to the church of Assy was inescapable and was more sharply
focused by an attack on "priests" who could be none other than Fathers
Couturier and Régamey.

Nor was this the only warning for the Dominicans. In 1947, Pius XII had
pointedly observed that "private individuals, even though they be clerics, may
not be left to decide for themselves in these holy and venerable matters
[liturgy and art], involving as they do the religious life of Christian society." [7]
Following the lead of the Holy Father, Gabriel Marcel, a leading Catholic
existentialist, now particularized matters by naming Fathers Couturier and
Régamey, adding that "one must not think that they are . . . the authorized
representatives of the Church." [8] Professor Marcel de Corte found it "most
astonishing if not most outrageous to see clerics placed by vocation in the
eternal . . . submit to this false prestige [modern art] and introduce the virus
into sacred art itself," [9] but such a situation hardly surprised the Catholic
sculptor Henri Charlier in view of "the drunken state of society." "Their [the
Dominicans'] opinion," added Charlier, "does not count, for they would be
nothing without their robes." [10]

To interpret the papal attack upon "deformations" of art in *Menti nostre* as
referring to anything but abstract and expressionistic painting required all the
resourcefulness of the Dominicans. Father Régamey noted legalistically that
the Pope complained of "deformations of art, and not that which one calls a
'deformation' when the artist, as he has always done, takes liberties with the
forms offered to his eyes by nature." Thus, Régamey argued, deformations *of*

[6] Cited in Mezzana, "Rome 1950," *Arte cristiana,* XXXVIII, No. 7–10 (July–October,
1951), 110–12.

[7] Pius XII, *Mediator Dei,* p. 34.

[8] Gabriel Marcel, "Lettre à *La Table ronde* sur le Christ de l'église d'Assy," *La Table
ronde,* July, 1951, No. 43, pp. 181–82.

[9] Marcel de Corte, "La Querelle de l'art sacré," *La Libre belgique,* February 5, 1952 (file
of Father Régamey).

[10] Charlier, "A propos du Christ de l'église d'Assy," *Ecrits de Paris,* September, 1951, pp.
50–55.

art, as opposed to deformations *in* art, can be interpreted simply to mean bad art, and the decision as to whether given works constitute such bad art could be left to competent people "as the Canonists, in their prudence, have always recommended." For Father Régamey, these would be the major figures of the art—not the liturgical—world, such as the directors of major museums.[11]

The overt Integrist attack upon the church of Assy began January 4, 1951. The occasion was a lecture by Canon Devémy, entitled "Does the Church of Assy Contribute to the Renewal of Christian Art?" and delivered before the Society of the Friends of Art at Angers. The lecture was widely publicized in advance, and the majority of the overflow audience was in sympathy with the Canon. This, in spite of scurrilous attacks upon Assy by a minority of the Angevin press, which called the participating artists "dangerous moral idiots" and dismissed modern art as a

vast fakery [*fumisterie*] put in motion by the art dealers who fill their pockets by means of human stupidity . . . a plot which has its end, the destruction of the old order founded on the trinity of family, country, and religion.[12]

In spite of the fact that Canon Devémy's remarks were almost all purely descriptive, and that he presented the church of Assy simply as testimony to the spirit of the patients at Assy sanatoria and not as a manifesto of modern sacred art,[13] a vociferous band of Integrists used the occasion for a partisan attack upon the whole Dominican movement. At the moment that the slide of the Richier Crucifix flashed on the screen they began a small riot, shouting "Insult!" "Sacrilege!"—and demanded to know whether Canon Devémy had been authorized by the Bishop to speak there. "The scandals accompanying the first days of modern art," reported the newspaper *Arts,* "were nothing to this." [14]

[11] Régamey, "Rome, 1950," *L'Art sacré,* January–February, 1951, No. 5–6, pp. 22–26. "The Canonists" would be quite surprised to find themselves so interpreted.

[12] Pierre Froger, "L'Art bafoué," *Courrier de l'ouest,* January 2, 1951 (file of Father Régamey).

[13] Albert Machard, "L'Église d'Assy et l'art chrétien," *Ouest-France,* January 5, 1951, p. 1.

[14] Sidoine, "Assy fait scandale à Angers," *Arts,* New Series, January 26, 1951, No. 295, pp. 1, 3.

At the door, the Integrists distributed a tract attacking the church of Assy as "an infamous profanation" and juxtaposing a photograph of the Richier Crucifix (supposedly unfavorably) with that of a Christ from a church at Limpéas, in Spain, all under the heading, "Let God not be Mocked." [15] This document, now universally referred to as "The Tract of Angers," was widely disseminated by the review *Paternité,* and was reproduced in many newspapers and magazines.

The verso of the Tract of Angers contains a text that summarizes a number of *leitmotifs* of the Integrist argument. It starts out with a verbal onslaught against

certain modern pictures which pretend to represent religious subjects, though the eye can discern only angular, grimacing, and unformed figures, in the midst of violent colors. The pure visage of the Virgin is replaced by a dirty caricature.[16] . . . This is not a religious art, but an infamous profanation.

There follows an indictment of painters belonging to a "school" led by "the Communist Picasso" and an assertion that "the time has come to unmask the trickery of this spurious art, which is simply the rejection of the human and the refusal of the divine; the art of nothingness where man goes to the point of denying his own image." After an appeal to Roman authority via quotations from *Mediator Dei* and from an article in *Osservatore Romano* by Father Cordovani excoriating the "production of a pathological art, maneuvered by a heretic propaganda," the text concludes by exhorting the faithful not to be misled by the fact that some members of the religious community support such art. Father Régamey and Father Couturier are attacked for the position of their review, *L'Art sacré,* and the Abbé Morel for presenting the "overly suggestive nudes of Rouault" in public lectures and for praising "the madness of Picasso—Communist artist and enemy of God." The document, cryptically

[15] Much of the force of the Tract's attack upon the Richier Crucifix was diluted by the comparison with the saccharine Christ of Limpéas, recognized immediately, even by those not in sympathy with the Assy crucifix, as a "wax manniken" (De Montrond, "Art sacré et theologie," *Etudes,* 84th year, Tome 271, December, 1951, pp. 314–21) in the worst taste of Saint-Sulpice.

[16] A reference to the *Virgin of the Litany* by Léger.

signed "A Group of Catholics," insists that "the directives of the Holy Father are the only authority [in these matters] and they are explicit."

February and March of 1951 saw an insistent campaign against the church of Assy and particularly the Crucifix of Madame Richier. Led by the virulent Charles du Mont through his *Observateur de Genève,* a drive was begun to bombard Monsignor Çesbron, the Bishop of Annecy, with irate letters criticizing the Crucifix and demanding its removal. These letters (their actual number has never been announced) plus considerable pressure from the Vatican (transmitted through private channels) caused the Bishop in April to order the removal of the work which Malraux had called "the only modern Christ before which one can pray." [17]

Reactions from all quarters were quick and violent. Even before the removal had been publicly announced, Jean Cassou quoted a Dominican Father (unnamed) to the effect that "modern art will have had three enemies, Hitler, Stalin, and the Pope." [18] Bernard Dorival spoke ironically of his pleasure in observing that in the domain of art, "our bishops are in accord with the Kremlin, the White House and the late Mr. Hitler." [19] Defending the Richier sculpture as "strong, expressive, powerful, charged with humanity, and palpitating with love," Dorival saw the reason for its removal in the very fact of its being artistically alive.

The action of the Bishop of Annecy was universally represented in the Catholic press as a "response to the wishes of diocesans who could not accept the representation of Christ which Germaine Richier imposed upon them," [20] and who were "likely to be scandalized" by it.[21] In time it became clear that this was not at all the case. It was soon admitted that not one of the oft-

[17] Cited in Walter Bernardi, "Der Streit um Assy," *Rheinischer Merkur,* May 3, 1951 (file of Father Régamey).

[18] Jean Cassou, "Paris: Controversy and Quintessence," *Art News,* April, 1951.

[19] Dorival, "Epurons les églises," *La Table ronde,* June, 1951, No. 42, pp. 160–62. The reference to the White House is probably an allusion to the personal taste of Mr. Truman.

[20] Fumet, "Un Christ d'atelier peut n'être pas un Christ d'église," *Recherches et débats,* July, 1951, No. 15–16.

[21] Marcel, "Lettre à *La Table ronde* sur le Christ de l'église d'Assy," *La Table ronde,* July, 1951, No. 43, pp. 181–82.

mentioned protests against the Crucifix received by the Bishop of Annecy came from a parishioner at Assy.[22] Dorival noted, moreover, that the parishioners of the plateau of Assy, once beyond their first surprise, were happy to pray before "this man of sorrows, so fraternal to their sufferings." [23] Upon the removal of the Crucifix many of them wrote letters of protest that appeared in local and Parisian newspapers and magazines. Typical of the opinion of the parishioners was a letter from an invalid which described the "suffering and pitiful Cruci-fied" of Richier as "our Christ . . . like one of us." Another, addressed to the Bishop of Annecy, expressed the hope "that our Christ will be given back to us. If it cannot be placed over the altar, then let it be placed somewhere else in the church." [24]

The contradiction between the official ecclesiastical version and the actual facts is confirmed by my private poll of forty-three members of the congrega-tion at Assy, of whom only three had reservations about the Crucifix. The Vatican, it appears, tends to create an abstraction called "the faithful," to which it then attributes its own "official" taste and attitude. This mechanism has not gone unobserved in Catholic circles, and there has been some reaction by French Catholics against the manner in which "the feelings of the faithful have been too often taken in hand by the hierarchy, interpreted, commented upon . . . and even used to support [the hierarchy's] favorite writers and artists." [25]

Yet one should not be misled into thinking that, given freedom of choice, the majority of the Catholic public would respond to modern sacred art in a positive manner, any more than the public at large would respond positively to modern secular art. If the stereotyped imagery of Vatican academicism and Saint-Sulpice is abhorrent to specific communities and various groups within the laity, it is by and large acceptable to the taste of the religious public. "It

[22] Régamey, *Art sacré au XXe siècle?* p. 335.

[23] Dorival, "Epurons les églises," *La Table ronde,* June, 1951, No. 42, pp. 160–62.

[24] Cited in Bernardi, "Der Streit um Assy," *Rheinischer Merkur,* May 3, 1951 (File of Father Régamey). During these months the Crucifix, which has since been placed in the mortuary chapel, was located in a chalet behind the church near the rectory. Visitors with a special interest were discreetly led to it. Cf. *Le Figaro littéraire,* August 18, 1951.

[25] Florenne, "Prière pour un agonisant: fin de l'art sacré?" *Mercure de France,* CCCXVII, No. 1073 (January–April, 1953), 54–62.

will do no good to pretend to disguise the truth," Father Régamey has observed. "There is a profound divorce between modern art and a large part of the public. It is in this divorce that the principal difficulty touching upon religious art resides." [26] As the artist no longer speaks to the community at large or even to one class, but, as Malraux observes, to a "select minority whose values [are] the same as his," [27] any valid art solicited by, and corresponding to, the taste of the broad base of Catholic laity would be impossible.

In the period just after the war the Dominican program had involved not merely the commissioning of works, but also the preaching of the new gospel of sacred art. Fathers Couturier and Régamey believed that real advances could be made with the Catholic public, and particularly with the clergy, through education. In an issue devoted exclusively to the art education of the clergy, L'Art sacré enumerated ways in which an enlightened cleric could help an artist to Christian awareness and in general stimulate interest in a vigorous sacred art by explaining the meaning of liturgy and iconography. The clergy itself was to be educated by a program of courses which the Dominicans envisioned both under their aegis and in collaboration with other orders. This emphasis on clerical action, however, tended to become characteristically distorted. It was not long before some theologians saw themselves as the sole medium by which the artists could be fecundated with religious spirit. The Jesuit Father Henri de Montrond went so far as to say that the whole problem of religious art was "a question of theology and it is on the theologian that the future art of the church depends." [28] By 1950, however, the educational aspect of the program had become hopelessly bogged down, and Father Régamey pessimistically admitted that he no longer believed "anything more [could] be seriously done to bring about a real education of taste with respect to the faithful or the clergy." [29]

Though the term "renaissance of sacred art" has often been used in con-

[26] Régamey, "La Querelle de l'art sacré," La Vie intellectuelle, 19th year, No. 11, November, 1951, pp. 3–48.

[27] Malraux, The Voices of Silence, p. 484.

[28] Henri de Montrond, "Art sacré et théologie," Études, 84th year, Tome 271, December, 1951, pp. 314–21.

[29] Régamey, "Réponse à une enquête sur l'art sacré: presentée par Maurice Brillant," La Croix, May 18, 1952, p. 2.

nection with the efforts of the Dominicans, they themselves have shown a re-markable sense of the limits of possibility. "None amongst us," wrote Father Couturier, "pretended to solve all the problems of contemporary sacred art. . . . Essentially, the solution of such problems is beyond all power, even that of the Church." [30] Both he and Father Régamey stated clearly that there could be no true, broadly based religious art at the present time.

To expect a truly sacred art of a society of our materialist type, and especially a Christian art of nations once again become practically pagan, seems to me a chimera. . . . All sacred art implies certain essential elements of a collective and communicative order: rigorously communal forms of sensibility and imagination. And these forms are not produced except in societies of a type radically different from our own, societies in which religion forms a single body with the totality of the life of the group. . . . In the absence of a Renaissance of art really sacred, I believe in the appearance among us, particularly in France, of works of a "re-ligious" inspiration, very pure, but rigorously individualistic and generally acci-dental, works born spontaneously and by chance, here and there . . . that is to say, I believe in miracles.[31]

On June 10, shortly after the appearance of Dorival's scornful critique of the Vatican for removing the Richier Crucifix, and fifteen days before the benediction of Matisse's chapel at Vence, the late Celso Cardinal Costantini launched the Vatican's first direct attack upon Assy in particular and the Sacred Art Movement in general. Early Vatican references to these matters had been oblique; direct assaults had been left to the laity. Costantini's article, appearing in the top center of the first page of *Osservatore Romano* and faith-fully reprinted by Catholic newspapers and magazines around the world, repre-sented the greatest censure sustained by the Dominicans up to that point. "At Assy in the Haute-Savoie," he began,

a caricatural image that is supposed to be a crucifix was placed in a church. In it we no longer recognize the adorable humanity of Christ. . . . It is an indecent [*sconcio*] pastiche . . . an insult to the majesty of God . . . a scandal for the piety of the faithful. The Bishop of Annecy has removed the sacrilegious figure.[32]

[30] Couturier, "Trois églises" (unpublished project for a preface), January, 1954 (file of Father Régamey).

[31] Couturier, "L'Art réligieux moderne," *Le Figaro*, October 24, 1951, p. 3.

[32] Celso Costantini, "Dell'Arte sacra deformatrice," *Osservatore Romano*, June 10, 1951,

Then, quoting the letter of a Protestant convert, the article goes on to attack the "so-called modern movement in art" as a Protestant plot against figurative art.

Cardinal Costantini considers some modern tendencies acceptable—as long as they "retain the sacred character and the good rules of grammar and syntax of artistic speech." "But today," he notes,

certain barbaric novelties, which do not respect decency or form and which arouse horror in the faithful, produce effects as dangerous in the area of art as in that of faith. The highest ecclesiastical authorities have raised their voices against these aberrations . . . and nobody will doubt that the supreme authorities of the Church have an absolute and exclusive competence in judging all that which refers to the Catholic cult.[33]

This was, fortunately, as close to direct papal condemnation as Fathers Régamey and Couturier were to come. In the months just before the Costantini article, and during many months thereafter, they lived in constant fear of such action.

Costantini's attack upon modern art as "Protestant" and his defense of a hypothetical figurative art that obeys mysterious laws of "artistic grammar" are consistent with the Cardinal's academic taste. Emboldened by his article, the Integrists and conservatives multiplied their attacks upon Assy and the Crucifix. Among the more serious critics was Gabriel Marcel, who replied to the Dorival article in *La Table ronde.* Insisting that an art critic (Dorival) may not "in any manner contest ecclesiastical authority or question its right to remove a work from a church," Marcel went on to criticize the Crucifix (which he admittedly had seen only in photographs) as "much like a rickety branch covered with a sort of mould. . . ."[34]

The sharpest reply to Costantini and Marcel appeared in *Carrefour,* where Morvan Lebesque defended the Richier work. With a genuine sympathy for

---

p. 1. Note that a number of his phrases were literally lifted from the Tract of Angers, and further, that even the Bishop of Annecy had not committed himself to these implied moral or esthetic judgments on a work which the Cardinal had, in fact, never seen.

[33] *Ibid.*

[34] Marcel, "Lettre à *La Table ronde* sur le Christ de l'église d'Assy," *La Table ronde,* July, 1951, No. 43, pp. 181–82.

the artistic conceit involved, he imagined the skin and skeleton of Christ to have fused with the Cross.

Here is the final state of man, surprised in a moment in which he is going to return to the earth; it is ultimately an "object," the thing which "has no name in any language" of which Bossuet speaks. Brother to the *écorchés* of the French Renaissance but brother equally to the fleshless cadavers of the concentration camps, the Christ of Assy shrieks the decadence and the malediction of the body.[35]

In his discussion, Lebesque formulated a question that is at the heart of the dispute: "Has an artist," he asked, "the right to paint Christ as he imagines Him, and above all, the right to translate Him into his [the artist's] formal conception?"[36] A month later, after citing Lebesque's question, Cardinal Costantini gave the Vatican answer: "Absolutely not." Elaborating further, the Cardinal noted that

though the artist retains the liberty of compositional conception and certain modes of expression (as long as they are decorous), and the liberty of various techniques (as long as these do not offend the sanctity of the subject), he does not have any liberty at all to deform the venerable character and theological conception . . . of the sacred representations.[37]

Reviewing the decisions of the Council of Trent and other decrees on sacred art, Costantini reaffirmed his faith in the "millennial canons, which have lasted through all the crises and ephemeral artistic modes."

The fall of 1951 was marked by an increasing number of attacks upon modern religious art. Even François Mauriac, who until then had remained aloof from the dispute, was moved to reply to Integrist criticism. "Can art be heretic?" he asked. "Does there exist an orthodoxy except in Moscow?"[38] His question was answered by a final coup of the Integrists: the demand by Gaston Bardet that "the mutilations of the figure of Christ and of the Holy Virgin . . .

[35] Morvan Lebesque, "Le Scandale du Christ d'Assy," *Carrefour,* 6th year, No. 356, July 11, 1951, p. 3.
[36] *Ibid.*
[37] Celso Costantini, "Réponse à diverses critiques," *Osservatore Romano,* August 20, 1951.
[38] François Mauriac, "Des Couleurs et des goûts," *Le Figaro,* December 4, 1951.

56

be condemned by an Index." "In our day of disorientation and interior heresy," Bardet continued, "only recourse to Rome is possible. And it is urgent, before the evil extends more widely, as happened in the case of certain errors of a scientific order. . . . The affair of Assy shows the pressing necessity to create an Index for artistic works." [39] And who is to be "editor" of this Index? The Virgin Mary. "From the representation that a painter makes of Mary," Bardet argued,

one can easily decide whether an artist is sacrilegious. Thus with respect to the Virgin of the *Miserere* of Rouault . . . we cannot hesitate [in considering him sacrilegious]. It was long ago that St. Grignon du Monfort revealed that those who have not the proper love and respect for Mary are Jansenists and Calvinists. Marian testimony can leave no doubt. The Holy Father who moves in Mary knows it better than anyone else. Is it not then Mary who should decide on heresies? [40]

By this time the "querelle de l'art sacré" had caused such furore and re-crimination in Catholic circles that some form of highly authoritative official directive became necessary. The first of these to appear was an eleven-point statement of principles promulgated by the Episcopal Commission for Pastoral and Liturgical Matters of France. In the hierarchy of the French Church the bishops are grouped in commissions, whose role it is to study questions which, in their importance, pass the limits of the diocesan community. One of these, presided over by Monsignor Martin, Archbishop of Rouen, is concerned with questions of liturgy and sacred art. This group elaborated the Directive and submitted it to the Assembly of the Cardinals and Archbishops of France, where it was approved.

The Directive was essentially a compromise, sufficiently general in language (no works or artists are specifically cited) to pacify momentarily both sides in the dispute. The over-all tone was, in fact, unexpectedly liberal, considering the views of many influential members of the French hierarchy, and far more favorable to the Dominican cause than the Instruction that was soon to ema-nate from Rome. Section I [41] recognized that sacred art is "living" and that it

[39] Bardet, "Una Polemica si allarga," *Arte cristiana*, XXXVIII, No. 11–12 (November–December, 1951), 129–30.

[40] *Ibid.* [41] See *La Croix*, May 18, 1952, p. 1.

must "correspond to the spirit of its times in techniques as well as materials." The Commission then noted with satisfaction that "some of the most famous contemporary artists have been invited to work in our sanctuaries and have willingly accepted" (sec. II),[42] and it hoped that they would "know how to impregnate themselves with Christian spirit." Otherwise, the Commission cautioned, "these artists would be unsuited to their tasks" (sec. III). In any case, their works must be understandable by the faithful without (and here the Commission echoes the words of Rome) it being necessary "that one give them long intellectual explanations" (sec. V).

Meanwhile, in Rome, Pius XII had spoken "on the function of holy art" to a group of Italian artists received in audience on April 8. Though the directors of *Fede ed arte* retroactively interpreted this speech as a prelude to the Instruction later delivered by the Sacred Congregation of the Holy Office,[43] there was nothing in the speech to warrant such a conclusion. Limiting himself to philosophical generalities, the Pope discoursed on the "intrinsic affinity of art with religion," noting that the "function of all art lies in breaking through the narrow and torturous enclosure of the finite in which man is immersed while living here below, and in providing for his hungry soul a window on the infinite." Therefore, he reasoned, "the more an artist lives religion, the better prepared he will be to speak the language of art, to understand its harmonies, to communicate its emotions.[44]

In spite of the official character imparted to the critical articles of Cardinal Costantini by his ecclesiastical position as well as by the organ in which these articles appeared, his opinions were technically those of an individual and could be criticized on that level. No such possibility existed, however, with respect to the severe critique which came in the form of an Instruction on holy

[42] This passage was generally taken as at least a limited affirmation of the Dominican program, and Father Régamey registered "immense joy . . . at seeing the authorities of the Church recognize, for the first time in two centuries, the value of the greatest living artists." Régamey, "Directives de l'épiscopat," *L'Art sacré,* May, 1952.

[43] Carlo Paluzzi, "Il Papa agli artisti," *Fede ed arte,* 1st year, No. 4, April, 1953, pp. 115–16.

[44] Pius XII, "The Function of Holy Art" (Papal address), *Catholic Mind,* 50th year, No. 1079, November, 1952, pp. 697–99.

art issued by the Sacred Congregation of the Holy Office on June 30, 1952.[45] This ultraconservative document, signed by Giuseppe Cardinal Pizzardo and Alfredo (now Cardinal) Ottaviani, begins with a short historical review of the ecclesiastical position on sacred art, quoting the second Council of Nicaea, which threatened with severe penalties "those who dared to wickedly invent anything contrary to ecclesiastical institution." It continues with a repetition of the injunction of the Council of Trent against "distorted and confused execution," as well as that of Pius X against anything "which disturbs or even merely diminishes the piety and devotion of the faithful, or which might reasonably be considered in bad taste or cause of scandal." [46] Listing those laws of the Canon applicable to art, and citing texts by Pius XI and Pius XII, the authors of the Instruction insisted that

the objections raised by some that art must be adapted to the necessities and conditions of the present times are of no moment. For sacred art, which originated with Christian society, possesses its own ends, from which it can never diverge, and its proper function, which it can never desert.

This passage gave great pleasure to the Integrist faction and became an important citation in their subsequent criticism.

Next, in order to "preserve the faith and piety of the Christian people through sacred art," the Instruction called to mind certain Canon laws (especially No. 1279) which condemn "unusual images . . . not in conformity with the approved usage of the Church" or those which "represent a false dogma . . . or which would be an occasion of dangerous error to the unlearned." In an oblique rebuke (though not a condemnation) of the Dominicans, the Congregation maintained that artistic commissions should be en-

[45] Sacred Congregation of the Holy Office, "On Sacred Art" (Instruction to Bishops), June 30, 1952. English translation in Catholic Mind, 50th year, No. 1079, November, 1952, pp. 699–702.

[46] It is important to note that the terms "distorted and confused," used by the Council of Trent with respect to the doctrinal sense of the subject matter, are here being applied to the stylistic character of art.

trusted "only to men who are outstanding for their technique, and who are capable of expressing sincere faith and piety." [47]

Though the Instruction contained no new legislation, it was clearly an official critique of the Dominican program. A decisive blow had been struck for the conservative and Integrist forces. "Let them [the Dominicans] govern themselves in the future," the Abbé Auvert reminded, "by recalling the Catholic adage, 'Roma locuta est, causa finita'—Rome has spoken, the matter is closed." [48]

Since 1952 the debate on sacred art has continued—with lessening intensity, but with greater irresponsibility. The triumph of ultramontanism, which the Instruction signaled, freed reactionary members of the clergy and lay Integrists to attack modern art as a Communist-Protestant-Masonic-Jewish-merchant plot against the Catholic Church. Cardinal Costantini, who had already marked a relationship between modern religious art and Communism in his articles in *Osservatore Romano*, added that "there is no reason to be surprised that Communism is pursuing its ends even in the field of art and is trying to desecrate Catholic iconography and render it ridiculous and repugnant." [49] The Bolshevik element in "certain churches of our century" [50] was attacked by the Abbé Auvert, and Paul Scortesco explained the horror of the church of Assy by the fact that "almost all the artists who worked [at it] . . . are Communists. . . . What more could they do if Malenkov asked them to make a building which would ridicule Christ?" [51]

[47] "Technique" in Vatican parlance means "finish" in the classical sense. (See Chapter 1.) "Sincere faith and piety" can in this context be taken only as meaning adherence to Catholicism.

[48] Auvert, *Défense et illustration de l'art sacré*, p. 157.

[49] Celso Costantini, "Signore ho amato il decoro della tua casa," *Fede ed arte* (entire issue), 2d year, No. 2, February, 1954, p. 34.

[50] Auvert, *Défense et illustration de l'art sacré*, p. 135.

[51] Scortesco, *Saint Picasso peignez pour nous*, p. 65. In actual fact, only two (Lurçat and Léger) of the nine important modern artists who contributed to Assy were Communists. A total roster would show two Communists out of seventeen artists.

Assy was not the first church participated in by Communists. In 1943 Oscar Niemeyer, a Communist party member, designed the church of St. Francis of Assisi at Pampulha, Brazil, which was decorated with murals and ceramics by Candido Portenari. The church aroused

But whereas most Integrists overlooked the difference between modern art and the puerile academicism celebrated by the Soviets, Scortesco admitted it and proposed a novel explanation: "Those who know the spirit of obeisance of the Communists judge that we have here a new form of disparagement: it is a question of discrediting the Church by a [modern] art which is the manifestation of an agonized capitalism, thus to be able to demonstrate [later] the necessity of an art imposed by and submitted to the norms of Marxist propaganda." [52]

To Bardet, on the other hand, the "movement representing this sacrilegious art [was] a part of a deceitful internal heresy . . . of this latent Protestantism." "Removal of the Christ of Assy," he insisted, was "the equivalent of a declaration of war against this interior Protestantism just as was the proclamation of the dogma of the Assumption to the Anglo-Saxon Protestants." [53] In his turn Auvert [54] attacked "modern pseudo-art" as an insidious "species of freemasonry —insinuating itself everywhere." The plot was abetted, according to Scortesco, by "Jewish-Masonic merchants [who] took hold of an art which in itself was addressed to no one . . . [and who] for the satisfaction of money, pride, and perversion, presented these acrobatics . . . to the public in ways which rendered them impossible to judge." [55] In view of this, Auvert argued it would be "absurd to enrich [the artists] . . . under pretext of Christian charity," for they are in effect pictorial prostitutes who, like Matisse (and this sentiment is brazenly attributed to the artist himself), "would never have developed his art in the way he did had he not found people stupid enough to buy it." [56]

tremendous animosity in some quarters, the mayor himself suggesting its demolition. See Stamo Papadaki, *The Work of Oscar Niemeyer* (Reinhold, 1950), pp. 93–103.

[52] *Ibid.*

[53] Bardet, "Una Polemica si allarga," *Arte cristiana,* XXXVIII, No. 11–12 (November–December, 1951), 129–30.

[54] Auvert, *Défense et illustration de l'art sacré,* p. 93.

[55] Scortesco, *Saint Picasso peignez pour nous,* p. 30.

[56] Auvert, *Défense et illustration de l'art sacré,* p. 31. Perhaps the most vicious of such calumnies is the quotation attributed to Picasso in Papini's *Libro Nero,* in which the painter dismisses himself as a public prankster living parasitically off "the imbecility, vanity, and cupidity of his contemporaries." Though these remarks were established, shortly after their publication, as complete fabrications, they were widely disseminated in Catholic circles in

If the Dominicans of *L'Art sacré* had been sent reeling by the Instruction, the events of the next two years came near to being knock-out blows for the whole French branch of the Order and, indeed, for the New Gallicanism. Having tried and failed to control the Worker-Priests and the Dominican intellectuals by pressure exerted through the conservative upper echelons of the French hierarchy, Rome decided to intervene directly. In 1953 the Worker-Priests' Mission of Paris was instructed to take in no new recruits. Then Cardinal Pizzardo, who, as Secretary of the Sacred Congregation of the Holy Office, had issued the Instruction, donned his cloak of Prefect of the Congregation of Seminaries and wrote a letter to all archbishops and bishops in France forbidding seminarists to work in mines and factories.

By the end of the year ill feeling had reached such a height that Cardinals Leinart, Gerlier, and Feltin undertook a special journey to Rome. On their return to Paris they announced a compromise solution, which implied that they had quieted Roman fears. Priests henceforward would live only in a presbytery and would do only part-time work. The entente ended soon afterwards, however, with a Papal order disbanding the Worker-Priests as of March of the following year. When Cardinal Piazza, head of the Sacred Congregation of the Religious, subsequently went to France and himself closed down the training seminary for the Mission of Paris, his action was taken as an insult by the entire French hierarchy.[57]

Meanwhile, the Vatican attitude toward the Dominicans had become so

---

France. See *Le Christ dans le bainlieu,* XIX, No. 19 (1952). This type of thinking, though more common and more vicious since the war, is not new. In reviewing the pre-war situation, Father Couturier noted that "though some of the greatest artists of our time have risked in their work not only their most precious gifts but even their reasons for living . . . Catholic opinion and Catholic thought have seen nothing in it but snobism, farces, or marketeering by Jewish merchants and critics." *Art et Catholicisme,* p. 77.

[57] Nevertheless, many of the Worker-Priests continued to preach and say Mass. Cardinal Feltin's office glossed over the issue and nothing was done in Paris to stop them or to denounce their activities. In the hope of resolving this indecisive situation in a favorable way, Cardinal Feltin sent a report on the Worker-Priests to the Vatican in March, 1959. Despite the reputedly more liberal attitudes of Pope John XXIII, Rome instructed the French Church (in September, 1959) to formally finish with the Worker-Priests movement and seek "new forms" of evangelism.

hostile that by 1954 rumors were circulating in Rome that the Order was to be dissolved in France. To avoid this extraordinary action, the General of the Order, Father Suarez, agreed to dismiss from office the Provincials of Paris, Lyon, and Toulouse. Such authoritarian action could have been accepted only in the most dire circumstances, as it runs counter to the basic Dominican practice of choosing officers by election from below. Another part of Father Suarez's compromise that was widely criticized among the French laity and in the non-Catholic intellectual world was the dismissal of four of Paris's best-known Dominicans. Fathers Congar and Chenu (the latter was theological advisor to the Worker-Priests) had to give up their chairs at the Collège de France; Father Feret, a professor at the Institut Catholique de Paris, was removed; Father Boisselot, editor of *Actualité* and director of the Dominican publishing house, Les Éditions du Cerf (which published *L'Art sacré*), was removed from his various posts. Publication of *Actualité* was halted, but it has since been resumed under a lay editor with the Dominicans helping informally.[58]

But the Dominican intelligentsia suffered still another blow. All their books now have to be submitted to special censorship before they may be printed. Permission to publish is no longer given by the usual ecclesiastical authorities in France; it can be granted only in Rome by the Congregation of the Holy Office. Since Dominican influence and prestige resulted largely from their writing, the imposition of this censorship was a major setback and created a most embarrassing situation *vis-à-vis* the nonreligious literary and artistic friends of the Order.

[58] A somewhat similar fate befell *Quinzaine,* a liberal Catholic review which, while in sympathy with the Dominicans, had no connection with the Order. After sanctions from Rome, its editors obtained local ecclesiastical permission to begin again under a new name, *Le Bulletin.*

4. THE PRIMACY OF FAITH

While "religious art" is subject to conflicting interpretations, "sacred art" (i.e., art ancillary to the celebration of the liturgy) can be clearly defined, for it falls exclusively within the province of the Catholic Church itself. It is clarified explicitly through statements by authoritative members of the hierarchy, and implicitly by the art which the hierarchy commissions to decorate its structures. No one can deny the final authority of the Papacy in determining what is acceptable and unacceptable to the Church. Consequently, the technical question of whether the church of Assy and other modern experiments, like those at Audincourt, Vence, and Ronchamp, constitute legitimate sacred art must be answered by the institution itself. As we have seen, that answer is negative.

But though Vatican pronouncements reject the art of Assy in the name of the Canon, a study of the *Codex Juris Canonici* reveals no comprehensive or consistent body of regulations regarding sacred art. We find, rather, a patchwork of largely vestigial rules concerned primarily with iconographic content. These do not define any over-all attitude toward the fine arts, nor do they contain legislation pertinent to many of the problems that have arisen in the course of the recent dispute. As a result, the experiment at Assy has forced the hierarchy to formulate a more thoroughgoing position which, when examined closely, appears to be based less on canon law than on the philosophies, tastes, and biases of the present leaders of the Roman curia, the constant references to the canons in their pronouncements notwithstanding.

SACRED ART AND CANON LAW

Among the myriad laws of the *Codex Juris Canonici* as it was codified in the early part of this century, No. 1279 is the oldest and most important of those regarding sacred art. Its first paragraph dates, in essence, from the Second Nicene Council, which, in resolving problems raised by the iconoclastic controversy, warned that "the composition of religious images is not left to the invention of artists, but is [dependent upon] the laws and traditions of the Catholic Church. The art alone belongs to the painter; the order and disposition to the Fathers." [1] Apart from the iconoclastic controversy, there is no record of this decree or any other legislation on sacred art having been invoked previous to the Reformation. While a cleric like Saint Bernard might rail against this or that aspect of the art of his day, there was nothing resembling an official Vatican art policy in either the Middle Ages or the Renaissance. New styles and new iconographic types were established and went their way without let or hindrance.

It was only with the Counter-Reformation that consciousness of a need for legislation on sacred art became widespread. The twenty-fifth session of the Council of Trent exhorted Bishops to bar from their churches any art that might shock, seem out of place, or smack of the profane. In 1642, Pope Urban VIII, observing that various abuses persisted, reiterated and amplified the statement of the Council of Trent, demanding not only that "unusual" (*insolitus*) images be banned from churches (unless expressly permitted under special conditions by the bishop), but also insisting that all images of holy figures wearing vestments or shown in actions "inconsistent with their orders and with tradition" be restructured correctly or destroyed. [2] This later became

---

[1] Cited in Mariani, *La Legislazione ecclesiastica in materia d'arte sacra*, p. 105. This rather vague dichotomy is still insisted upon by some Vatican critics. They differ, however, in the interpretation of "order and disposition." In a case where the placement, size, posture, and vestments of the figures in a particular scene were determined by a theologian, he would, in effect, be composing the picture. In practice, however, even in the most conservative quarters (the Scuola Beato Angelico, for example) theologians do not initiate suggestions for compositions, but simply exercise the right of review over the artists' work.

[2] C. Costantini and G. Costantini, *Fede ed arte*, I, 184.

65

the basis of paragraph 2 of Canon 1279. Paragraph 3 demands that all images have "due decency and respectability." [3]

It is the proscription of the "unusual" that forms the legislative basis of the Vatican position in the recent debate on sacred art.[4] It has been cited by the Pope and the Holy Office, and was referred to by the Bishop of Annecy when he removed Germaine Richier's Crucifix from the church of Assy. This usage, however, is contrary to the original intent of the term, since it is now being applied to the stylistic distinctiveness of modern painting. Considered in its historical context, the word "unusual" was directed against the iconography or dogmatic content of the image.[5] The question of an "unusual" style has no precedent in church history.

[3] Mariani, *La Legislazione ecclesiastica in materia d'arte sacra,* p. 106. The determination as to whether a given image is "unusual" and thus subject to removal is made by the Ordinary (bishop) of the area in which the church is located. If he feels incompetent to judge in a given instance, he may refer the problem to the appropriate Diocesan Council for Liturgy and Sacred Art. Questions bearing on basic principles may be decided by the National Assembly of the bishops and archbishops of the country involved, but they are in turn subject to the authority of the congregations of the Roman curia. According to canon law and papal decree, the primary legislative body for sacred art in the curia is the Sacred Congregation of Rites, given its authority in these matters by the constitution *Immensa* promulgated by Sixtus V in 1588. In 1908, Pius X clarified its duties, and its special competence was incorporated in 1918 in the *Codex Juris Canonici* as law number 253. Since Gregory XV's Constitution *Inscrutabile,* the Sacred College of the Propagation of the Faith has also had the power to legislate in matters of sacred art, particularly where ecclesiastical activity is on the missionary level or where the hierarchy is incipient.

In the recent debate, however, the role of top legislative authority in matters of sacred art has been usurped by the Congregation of the Holy Office. It is this body, rather than the Congregation of Rites, which issued the "Instruction." The curious shift in authority is worth noting since it is well known that Integrist sentiment is stronger in the Holy Office than in other bodies of the curia, and that its Secretary, Giuseppe Cardinal Pizzardo, is one of the main antagonists of the Dominican movement in France and of modern sacred art in general.

[4] Fundamental to Canon 1279, according to Mariani, is the principle that even religious pictures or sculptures disseminated for private use are under the jurisdiction of the Bishops. Mariani, *La Legislazione ecclesiastica in materia d'arte sacra,* p. 55, note.

[5] ". . . the Holy Council decrees that no one is permitted to erect or cause to be erected in any place or Church, howsoever exempt, any unusual image unless it has been approved by the Bishop; also, that no new miracles be accepted and no relics recognized, unless they

The only other Canon of major importance in the current dispute, No. 1164, prescribes that sacred art must observe "forms received from Christian tradition." [6] The rub here, of course, is that the word "tradition" is open to a variety of interpretations. The Vatican's is summarized by Mariani as "that manner of making . . . an image in attitudes and compositions approved by ecclesiastical authorities . . . who have determined tradition by their explicit acceptance [of certain types] and their oft preventative rejections." [7] According-ing to this view, as it is put into practice, the modern artist may make only minor changes in the body of norms inherited from the first two thousand years of Christian history. It is true that papal authorities insist that "modern art should be given free scope in the due and reverent service of the Church," [8] but the only art that is in fact accepted amounts to no more than reworkings of older forms. The fallacy of the papal position can be understood if it is applied retroactively to the great eras of liturgical art. Had the present con-cept of a crystallized tradition, more or less frozen since the Counter-Reforma-tion, been put into effect earlier, it would have had to reject Romanesque, Gothic, and Renaissance art, each in its turn.

In practice, then, "tradition" is understood by Rome as a body of styles and usages drawn from the past which stand apart from and in opposition to the main currents of the art of the last hundred years. Vatican authorities countenance no breaking out from these bounds in the name of the freedom

---

have been investigated and approved by the same Bishop, who, as soon as he has obtained any knowledge of such matters, shall, after consulting theologians and other pious men, act thereon as he shall judge consonant with truth and piety." *Canons and Decrees of the Council of Trent,* trans. by H. J. Schroeder (St. Louis and London, 1941).

[6] See Régamey, *Art sacré au XXᵉ siècle?* p. 171.

[7] Mariani, *La Legislazione ecclesiastica in materia d'arte sacra,* p. 63.

[8] Pius XII, *Mediator Dei,* p. 76. According to the Cardinals Costantini (*Fede ed arte,* I, 211–12), "one must not think that the Church is against modernity. But it is cautious and prudent, with an experience of nearly two thousand years behind it. It knows how to dis-tinguish modernity from modernism, that which is living and vital from that which is simply convulsive. . . . By modernism we mean the caricature of modernity: those extravagant and arbitrary forms which from time to time are presented to us as art; we mean that anarchical and revolutionary spirit of certain recent artists who compose works in unusual forms. . . . The Catholic religion is the most modern thing that exists in the world."

of the artist. "Liberty, the rights of art, pure art before sacred art? No," says Cardinal Costantini. "Sacred art constitutes a great and comprehensive language with which and through which the soul of the Church speaks with God. The maternal, magistral Church has created this language, speaks it, teaches it, develops it, extends it. The Church and none other." [9]

In the dispute under discussion here only Canons 1279 and 1164 have actually been involved. Others refer either to details or to matters not pertinent to present problems.[10] Moreover, with the exception of the removal of the Richier Crucifix, there has been no condemnation of specific works of art in the name of canon law. In fact, action of this sort has been extremely rare throughout Church history.[11]

GENIUSES WITHOUT FAITH

The central problem raised by the experiments of the Sacred Art Movement has been that of the legitimacy of employing non-Catholic artists. The Dominicans established *quality* as the primary criterion for selecting artists, preferring men of genius—regardless of faith—to those who might be devout but untalented.

It was in reply to frequent criticism of the employment of atheists like Bonnard and Communists like Léger that Father Couturier first gave literary formulation to his missionary position. Ideally, he admitted, Christian art

---

[9] *Fede ed arte,* I, 187.

[10] Among the other canons bearing on sacred art are Nos. 485 (recalling the respect due to the House of God), 1162 (formal authorization of the Bishop required for the construction of a church), 1261 (avoidance of superstitions, theological errors), 1280 (permission of Bishop required to restore older works of art), 1385 (images as well as books may be subject to ecclesiastical censure).

[11] Among the few examples are the condemnation by Urban VII in 1628 of the representation of the Holy Trinity by a single figure with three heads, and in 1633 the so-called Jansenist crucifixion in which the figure of Christ has his arms upraised. Benedict XIV in 1745 declared heretical a group of images in which the Holy Ghost was represented in the form of a young boy. Carlo Borromeo Frank, *Kernfragen kirchlicher Kunst* (Vienna: Herder, 1953), pp. 110–11. Until recently, the single modern instance was a decree issued in March of 1921 condemning an image of the dying Christ by the Flemish painter Servaes for its "too crude realism and its . . . deformations." Mariani, *La Legislazione ecclesiastica in materia d'arte sacra,* p. 113, note.

should be resurrected by geniuses who happen also to be saints, "but under actual conditions, since men of this kind do not exist . . . it would be safer to turn to *geniuses without faith than to believers without talent. . . .* [as Delacroix said] One should always bet on genius." [12] Father Régamey further elaborated this radical position by insisting that although many works by these great artists will not be "exactly Christian," the cleric should gather them in as soon as he considers them "in some way sacred." [13] "In our world in revolution," he suggested, "let us apply the rule fixed by Pius XI and Pius XII with respect to Catholicism and indigenous art: Accept it as long as it is *not contrary to the faith.*" [14]

To reinforce these ideas the Dominicans argued the essentially spiritual character of all great art, an analogy of art and religious faith unfairly criticized in conservative quarters as an "equivalence." [15] They further noted that most of the artists at Assy came from a generally Christian background, and that since the genius of great artists lies so deep within them that it touches the "inner wellsprings of a faith," they might be Christians without realizing it. Remember, observed Father Couturier, that Saint Augustine said of the Church: "Many are outside who believe themselves to be within, and many are within who believe themselves to be without." [16] Certainly the works of these modern artists fall within Father Régamey's astonishing definition that "all is Christian except sin." [17]

There having been no real precedent for such a position,[18] and consequently

[12] Couturier, "Religious Art and the Modern Artist," *Magazine of Art,* XLIV, No. 7 (November, 1951), 268–72.

[13] Régamey, "L'Art sacré, sera-t-il chrétien?" *Recherches et débats,* New Series, I, No. 1 (May, 1952).

[14] Régamey, *L'Art sacré au XXe siècle?* p. 200.

[15] Ochsé, *La Nouvelle Querelle des images,* p. 99.

[16] Couturier, "Religious Art and the Modern Artist," *Magazine of Art,* XLIV, No. 7 (November, 1951), 268–72.

[17] Régamey, "Rome, 1950," *L'Art sacré,* January–February, 1951, No. 5–6, pp. 22–26.

[18] Citing evidence that early Christian decorations in the catacombs were made by pagan painters, Henze and Filthaut (*Contemporary Church Art* [New York: Sheed and Ward, 1956], p. 18) try to legitimize the new position. Considering that the structure of the Roman Church was not yet fully developed, this early Christian practice hardly makes a convincing precedent.

no appropriate legislation in the Canon, the Vatican reacted in a guarded way. Just after the Second World War Rome adopted a "wait-and-see" policy, inasmuch as both the hierarchy and the Dominicans hoped that participation of the great modern masters at Assy, Vence, and Audincourt might lead to their conversions. At Father Couturier's request the Pope gave his blessing to the artists (Catholics and non-Catholics alike) working at Assy (cf. note 3, p. 78).

The first official warning in this connection had come in the Directive of the Episcopal Commission for Sacred Art in France, issued in May of 1952. Knowing that the artists of Assy were, for the most part, non-Catholics, the Commission nevertheless "rejoiced" that the most famous modern masters had been invited to decorate a church and had accepted. But, as we have seen above, the Commission also observed that unless these masters were able "to impregnate themselves with the Christian spirit," they would be "unsuited to their tasks." "Impregnation" is a vague term, and while the Directive obviously looked forward to the possible conversion of the artists involved, it did not explicitly make Catholic confession a *sine qua non* of participation. The ultra-conservative Instruction issued the following month by the Holy Office spoke generally of the need that artists working in churches be "capable of express-ing sincere faith and piety."

But it was not until Christmas of 1955, after the dust of the Vatican-Dominican quarrel had largely settled, that Rome gave the *coup de grâce* to the Sacred Art Movement by specifically condemning the participation of non-Catholic artists in church decoration. In the encyclical *Musicae sacrae disciplina,* Pius XII stated that

the artist who does not profess the truths of the faith or who alienates himself from God in his soul or conduct, must not in any manner occupy himself with religious art: he does not possess, in effect, that interior eye which permits him to discover that which the majesty of God and the divine cult require . . . [the works of such artists] shall therefore never be worthy of being admitted by the Church into its divine edifices.[19]

[19] Pius XII, *Musicae sacrae disciplina,* Encyclical letter of December 25, 1955, French text, *La Documentation catholique,* January 22, 1956, No. 1217, pp. 74–75.

In this same encyclical the Pope also pronounced Rome's final words on the general activities of the Sacred Art Movement. "We have not failed to note," wrote His Holiness,

that during these recent years certain artists, gravely offending Christian piety, have dared to introduce into churches works of a personal nature [*des oeuvres de leurs façon*] totally without religious inspiration and entirely contrary to the correct rules of art. They try to justify these deplorable activities by specious arguments which they pretend to derive from the nature and character of art itself. They say, in effect, that the inspiration by which the artist proceeds is free, and that it is not possible to submit this inspiration to laws and norms foreign to art—be they religious or moral—because one would thus gravely offend the dignity of art and shackle and enchain even the artist guided by a sacred inspiration. . . . However, such expressions of "art for art's sake" . . . constitute a grave offense against God himself. . . .[20]

Fundamental, then, to this newly defined Vatican viewpoint is the belief that faith is primary in questions of artistic inspiration and legitimacy (at least in religious art). By their very participation, the non-Catholic artists at Assy had implicitly questioned this principle. A few contradicted it explicitly, not only as regards Assy, but even with respect to the great religious art of the Middle Ages. As we shall see, Rouault stated that in questions of sacred art "one must begin by loving painting." Chagall, commenting on the qualities that distinguish the great religious works of the past, remarked that "there were good and bad artists even then. The difference did not lie in their piety, but in their painterly ability." [21] Léger told the monks of La-Pierre-Qui-Vire that "it was *not faith* which inspired the artists of the Middle Ages to create great works." "This opinion has shocked people," he continued, "but it is my belief. For me their work is beautiful objectively, in terms of reasons and relationships of a plastic order, and not for sentimental motives. . . ." [22] An awareness of other than religious motivation in sacred art even of the medieval period has provided increasing commentary by historians and critics in recent years.

[20] *Ibid.*, p. 74. [21] Cited in Erben, *Marc Chagall*, p. 12.
[22] Léger, "Sens de l'art moderne," *Zodiaque*, II, No. 18–19 (January, 1954), 36–40.

THE PRIMACY OF FAITH

FAITH AND MEDIEVAL RELIGIOUS ART

"The historical coincidence of certain phases of religion and art," writes Herbert Read, "leads to an easy generalization which, however, is not confirmed by closer scrutiny. Indeed, the more we consider the question, the more ready we become to dismiss as a popular fallacy the idea that religion promotes art." [23] Meyer Schapiro in turn observes that

the wide-spread idea that medieval art was the work of monks or profoundly religious lay artisans inspired by a humble attitude of selfless craftsmanship and service to the Church rests on the assumption that this art is through and through religious and that the people of the Middle Ages esteemed art only as it was useful, devotional and directly imbued with spiritual conceptions in accord with the traditional teachings of the Church. The monuments and the writings . . . tell us otherwise. . . . These texts abound in esthetic judgments and in statements about the qualities and structure of the work. They speak of the fascination of the image, its marvelous likeness to physical reality, and the artist's wonderful skill, often in complete abstraction from the content of the object of art.[24]

The popular myth of the artist-monk and the concomitant notion of the primacy of religious motivation in the creation of the great works of the Middle Ages has also been attacked by G. G. Coulton. He traces modern dissemination of this idea to wishful thinking and uncritical acceptance of statements in Montalembert's *Monks of the Occident*. In *Art and the Reformation* Coulton demolishes Montalembert's thesis,[25] concluding that "the fashionable doctrine of the present day as to the relations of medieval art and medieval religion is not only far from the truth, but mischievously remote, resting on a superficial confusion." [26] ". . . monks who did any kind of artistic work, at the most favourable times and places, were a small minority in the community; and, if we take all the times and places together, the monastic

---

[23] Herbert Read, "Art and Religion," *Listener,* XVI, No. 395 (August 5, 1936), 256–258.

[24] Schapiro, "On the Aesthetic Attitude in Romanesque Art," in *Art and Thought.*

[25] Coulton, *Art and the Reformation.* A special appendix, pp. 505–15, is devoted to the work of Montalembert and later writers subscribing to his views.

[26] *Ibid.,* p. 23.

72

artist was quite an exception." [27] "And even if we confine ourselves to [the art of] the churches, we have no right to assume more religion in the man who cut and laid the stones than we assume of militarism in those who raised the towers and battlements." [28]

The problem of ascertaining the role of religion in the genesis of medieval art is not solved, however, simply by the discovery that the artists were not necessarily practicing religionists or even pious men. The individual artist was, in fact, very much a function of the cultural milieu and, as Schapiro concludes,

the creation of medieval art did not require deeply religious artists but rather artists who had been formed within a stable religious milieu, and whose craft had been developed in tasks set by the Church. . . . Hegel said very justly that in an age of piety one does not have to be religious in order to create a truly religious work of art, whereas today the most deeply pious artist is incapable of producing it.[29]

Since the Reformation, but more markedly since the French Revolution, the Church has been increasingly suspicious of artists. And rightly so, as the convictions of the latter have been more and more in conflict with ecclesiastical belief. Advanced contemporary artists being for the most part indifferent, if not antagonistic, to all forms of dogmatic religion, the Church has had to deal with them with great circumspection. The Church at Assy represented a calculated risk. Would the results contain expressions incompatible with the religion? To the Vatican and most conservative Catholic critics it does—thus the cries of heresy.

[27] *Ibid.*, p. 32.   [28] *Ibid.*, p. 209.
[29] Schapiro, "On the Aesthetic Attitude in Romanesque Art," in *Art and Thought.*

Part II. ARCHITECTURE AND DECORATIONS OF THE CHURCH OF ASSY

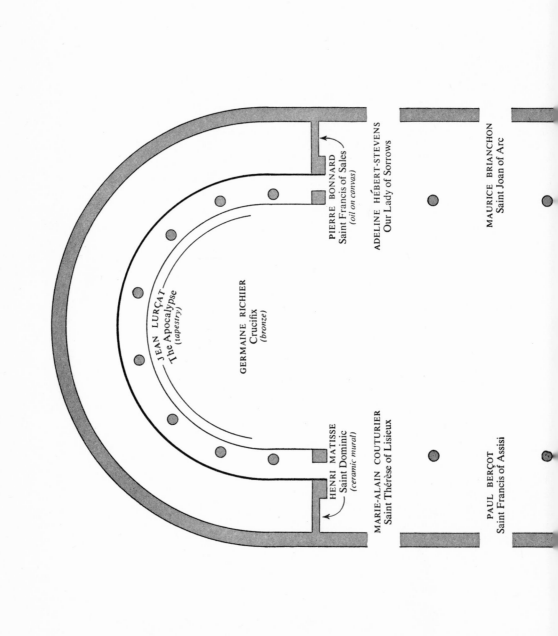

PIERRE BONNARD
Saint Francis of Sales
(oil on canvas)

ADELINE HÉBERT-STEVENS
Our Lady of Sorrows

MAURICE BRIANCHON
Saint Joan of Arc

JEAN LURÇAT
The Apocalypse
(tapestry)

GERMAINE RICHIER
Crucifix
(bronze)

HENRI MATISSE
Saint Dominic
(ceramic mural)

MARIE-ALAIN COUTURIER
Saint Thérèse of Lisieux

PAUL BERÇOT
Saint Francis of Assisi

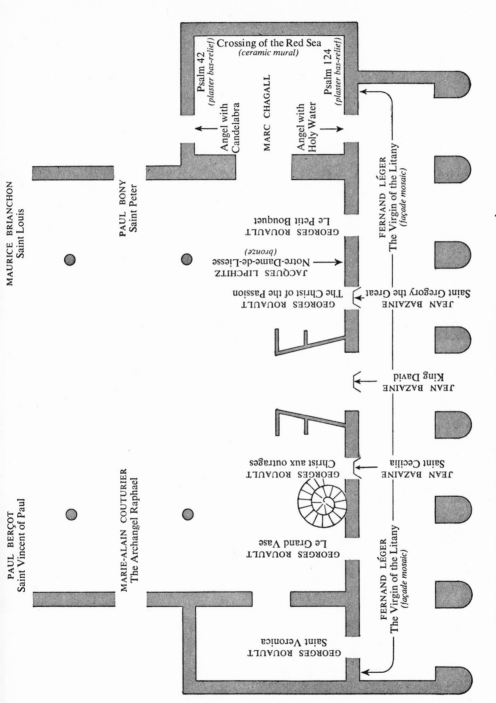

MAURICE BRIANCHON
Saint Louis

PAUL BONY
Saint Peter

Crossing of the Red Sea
(ceramic mural)

Psalm 42
(plaster bas-relief)

Psalm 124
(plaster bas-relief)

MARC CHAGALL

Angel with
Candelabra

Angel with
Holy Water

PAUL BERÇOT
Saint Vincent of Paul

MARIE-ALAIN COUTURIER
The Archangel Raphael

GEORGES ROUAULT
Le Petit Bouquet

JACQUES LIPCHITZ
Notre-Dame-de-Liesse
(bronze)

GEORGES ROUAULT
The Christ of the Passion

JEAN BAZAINE
Saint Gregory the Great

FERNAND LÉGER
The Virgin of the Litany
(façade mosaic)

JEAN BAZAINE
King David

JEAN BAZAINE
Saint Cecilia

GEORGES ROUAULT
Christ aux outrages

GEORGES ROUAULT
Le Grand Vase

FERNAND LÉGER
The Virgin of the Litany
(façade mosaic)

GEORGES ROUAULT
Saint Veronica

PLAN OF DECORATIONS, THE CHURCH OF NOTRE-DAME-DE-TOUTE GRÂCE AT ASSY

The photographs for Figures 5, 16–18, 37, 39, 41, and 42 are by Merlin, Assy; those for Figures 10, 12B, and 13 are by Paul Bony; those for Figures 29–36 are by Adolph Studley, New York. Figure 12A is reproduced through the courtesy of the Museum of Modern Art, Paris, and Figure 38 through the courtesy of the Museum of Modern Art, New York, photograph by Sunami. Figures 19 and 20 are reproduced through the courtesy of Jean Lurçat, and Figure 52A appears through the courtesy of Germaine Richier. The color plate of the definitive maquette for Fernand Léger's *Virgin of the Litany* and Figures 21–25 are reproduced through the courtesy of Mme Léger. The color plate of Bonnard's *Saint Francis of Sales,* which appears as frontispiece, is reproduced with the permission of Pierre Cailler, Geneva.

1. NENNO BARABINO, *Madonna and Child*

2. TYPICAL SAINT-SULPICE CHRIST

3. ANGELO
MARELLI,
Maesta
APSE MOSAIC,
SAN GIORGIO
ALLA VITTORIA,
REGGIO CALABRIA

4. THE CHURCH OF NOTRE-DAME-DE-TOUTE-GRÂCE AT ASSY
    MAURICE NOVARINA, ARCHITECT

5. WEST FAÇADE
   DOOR BY JOSEPH PARRACINO, MOSAIC BY FERNAND LÉGER

6. INTERIOR, LOOKING EAST
   TAPESTRY BY JEAN LURÇAT

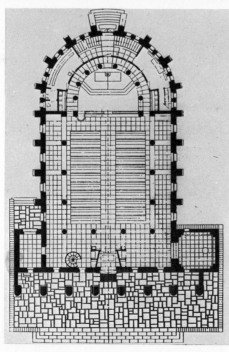

7. MAURICE NOVARINA,
   ARCHITECTURAL PLAN

8. MARGUERITE HURÉ,
Loaves and Fishes
STAINED GLASS WINDOW,
CRYPT

9. CONSTANT DEMAISON, *Moses*
CARVED ROOF BEAM

10. GEORGES ROUAULT, *Christ aux outrages*
    A. FIRST CARTOON, OIL ON PAPER

B. SECOND CARTOON, OIL ON PAPER

11. GEORGES ROUAULT, *The Christ of the Passion*
     STAINED GLASS WINDOW, WEST FAÇADE
     EXECUTED BY PAUL BONY

12. GEORGES ROUAULT, *The Christ of the Passion*
     A. OIL ON CANVAS, MUSEUM OF MODERN ART, PARIS
     B. WINDOW DURING PROVISIONAL REASSEMBLAGE

13. GEORGES ROUAULT, *Le Grand Vase*
   A (LEFT): OIL ON CANVAS,
      COLLECTION OF THE ARTIST
   B (RIGHT): CARTOON FOR
      STAINED GLASS WINDOW
      IN WEST FAÇADE

14. GEORGES ROUAULT,
    Saint Veronica
    OIL ON CANVAS,
    COLLECTION OF THE ARTIST

15. GEORGES ROUAULT, *Saint Veronica*
STAINED GLASS WINDOW, MORTUARY CHAPEL
EXECUTED WITH FRAMING DESIGN BY PAUL BONY

16. JEAN LURÇAT, *The Apocalypse*
DETAIL OF THE DRAGON

17.   JEAN LURÇAT, *The Apocalypse*
      DETAIL OF THE WOMAN (ABOVE) AND THE ARCHANGEL MICHAEL

18. JEAN LURÇAT, *The Apocalypse*
     DETAIL OF PARADISE (LEFT) AND THE DRAGON

19.　JEAN LURÇAT, *The Apocalypse of the Mal-Assis*
GOUACHE STUDY, COLLECTION OF THE ARTIST

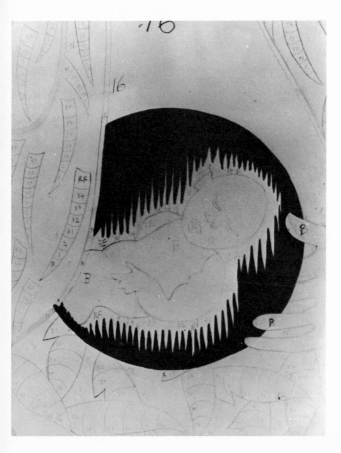

20.　JEAN LURÇAT, *The Apocalypse*
CARTOON, DETAIL OF THE CHILD

21. FERNAND LÉGER, *The Virgin of the Litany*
WATER-COLOR STUDY FOR THE FIRST STATE

22. FERNAND LÉGER, *The Virgin of the Litany*
WATER-COLOR VARIANT OF THE FIRST STATE

23.   FERNAND LÉGER, *The Virgin of the Litany*
      WATER-COLOR STUDY FOR THE SECOND STATE

24.   FERNAND LÉGER, *The Virgin of the Litany*
      WATER-COLOR STUDY FOR THE THIRD STATE

25. FERNAND LÉGER, *The Virgin of the Litany*
     WATER-COLOR STUDY FOR THE FOURTH STATE

26. FERNAND LÉGER, *The Virgin of the Litany*
     FAÇADE MOSAIC

27. FERNAND LÉGER, *The Virgin of the Litany*
A. DETAIL OF THE MOSAIC SURFACE

B. DETAIL OF
   THE MADONNA

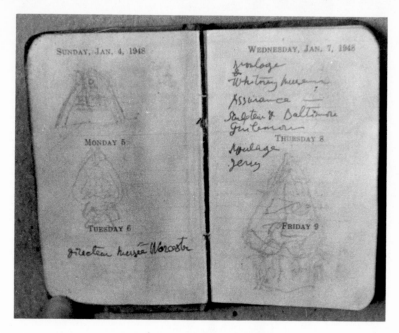

28. JACQUES LIPCHITZ, *Notre-Dame-de-Liesse*

A. FIRST PENCIL SKETCHES

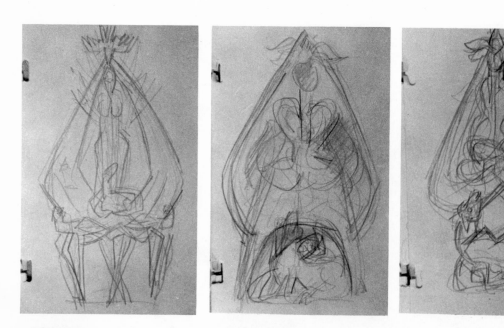

B. DRAWING I   C. DRAWING III   D. DRAWING VIII

29. JACQUES LIPCHITZ, *Blossoming*
BRONZE

30. JACQUES LIPCHITZ, *Spring*
PREPARATORY INK STUDY

A. MODEL I, BRONZE

B. MODEL II, BRONZE

31. JACQUES
     LIPCHITZ,
     Notre-Dame-
     de-Liesse

C. MODEL III, BRONZE

D. MODEL V, BRONZE

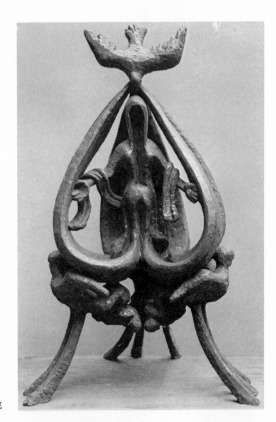

32. JACQUES LIPCHITZ,
Notre-Dame-de-Liesse
A. LARGE MAQUETTE, BRONZE

B. THE ARTIST WITH FULL-SCALE
PLASTALINE MODEL
LATER DESTROYED BY FIRE

33. JACQUES LIPCHITZ,
     The Virgin in Flames
     BRONZE

34. JACQUES LIPCHITZ,
     Lesson of a Disaster
     BRONZE

35.   JACQUES LIPCHITZ, *Notre-Dame-de-Liesse*
BRONZE, FRONT VIEW OF DEFINITIVE VERSION

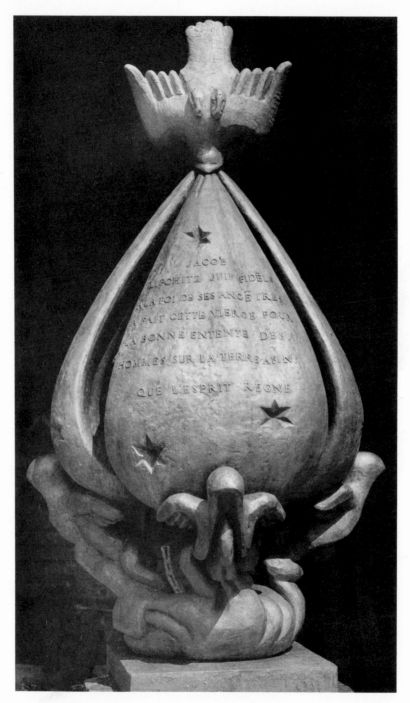

The inscription on the sculpture reads:

JACOB
LIPCHITZ JUIF FIDÈLE
A LA FOI DE SES ANCÊTRES
A FAIT CETTE VIERGE POUR
LA BONNE ENTENTE DES
HOMMES SUR LA TERRE AFIN

QUE L'ESPRIT RÈGNE

36. JACQUES LIPCHITZ, *Notre-Dame-de-Liesse*
BRONZE, REAR VIEW OF DEFINITIVE VERSION

37. MARC CHAGALL, *The Crossing of the Red Sea*
     CERAMIC MURAL, BAPTISTRY

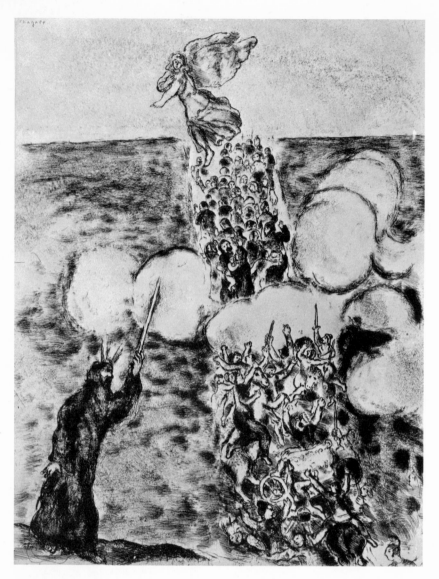

38. MARC CHAGALL, *The Crossing of the Red Sea*
ETCHING

39. MARC CHAGALL,
The Crossing of the Red Sea
CERAMIC MURAL, DETAIL

40. MARC CHAGALL, *Crucifixion*
CERAMIC PANEL

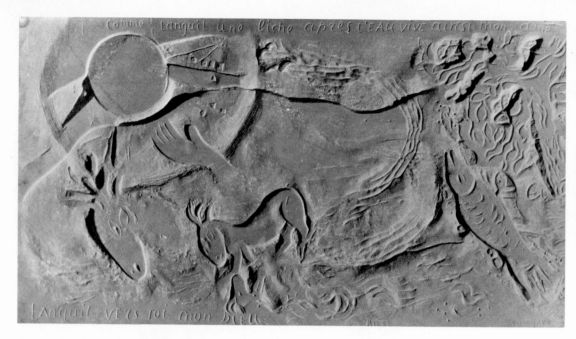

41. MARC CHAGALL, *Psalm 42*
PLASTER BAS-RELIEF, BAPTISTRY

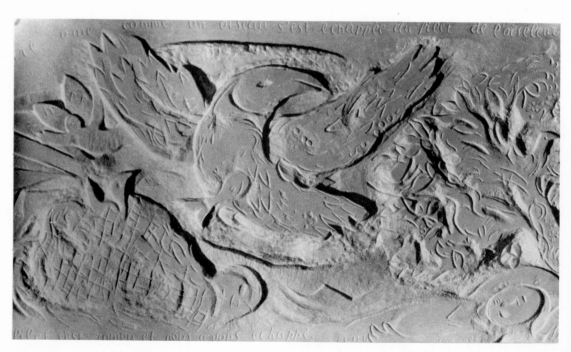

42. MARC CHAGALL, *Psalm 124*
PLASTER BAS-RELIEF, BAPTISTRY

43. MARC CHAGALL,
The White Crucifixion
OIL ON CANVAS

44. MARC CHAGALL,
UNTITLED
COLOR LITHOGRAPH

45. PIERRE BONNARD, *Saint Francis of Sales*
     DETAIL OF FOREGROUND

46. HENRI MATISSE, *Saint Dominic*
SKETCH FOR FIGURE 47 WITH
THE MODEL, FATHER COUTURIER

47. HENRI MATISSE,
Saint Dominic
CERAMIC TILE,
ALTAR DECORATION

48. PAUL BONY, *Saint Peter*
STAINED GLASS
WINDOW,
SOUTH AISLE

50.　PAUL BERÇOT,
　　　Saint Francis of Assisi
　　　CARTOON

49.　PAUL BERÇOT, *Saint Francis of Assisi*
　　　STAINED GLASS WINDOW, NORTH AISLE

51. JEAN BAZAINE,
Saint Gregory the Great
CARTOON

STAINED GLASS WINDOW, TRIBUNE

52. GERMAINE RICHIER, *Crucifix*

A. PLASTER MAQUETTE

B. UNIQUE BRONZE CAST,
TEMPORARILY INSTALLED
IN MORTUARY CHAPEL

53. GERMAINE RICHIER, *Crucifix*
UNIQUE BRONZE CAST *in situ* AT ALTAR

5. THE STRUCTURE

Early in 1937 Edouard Malot submitted to Father Devémy a series of preliminary drawings for a church, but these were rejected by the Canon in
favor of plans by Maurice Novarina, a Savoyard architect, who had already
built the churches at Vongy (disfigured by decorations that were added later),
and at Le Fayet, the decoration of which was in the hands of Alexandre
Cingria's Group of Saint Luke.[1] Novarina had distinguished himself by creating churches whose structure and materials harmonized with the physical
environment. Canon Devémy particularly liked Notre-Dame-des-Alpes at Le
Fayet, whose low enveloping forms, holding strongly to the earth, are ready
to brave the tremendous snows and winds of the mountains. Here Novarina
had used a great wooden roof extending far beyond the walls for protection,
a feature which he derived from the local chalet style and which he was to
make a conspicuous characteristic of the church at Assy (Figure 4). This
type of religious architecture, building upon regional traditions, was singled
out in 1938 for special praise by Father Couturier, already editor of *L'Art
sacré,* who spoke of it as "a signal example of what sacred art should be
. . . an art common to the place and time in which one lives." Much was to
be expected, he added, from Novarina.[2]

[1] Though the plans of the church of Assy are signed by M. Malot as well as Novarina,
the former had no part in the creation of the design. His co-signature appears to be a matter
of prestige.

[2] Couturier, "Deux églises Savoyards," *L'Art sacré,* 4th year, No. 29, May, 1938, pp. 117–21.
An inventive though not deeply gifted architect, Maurice Novarina has since been inextricably
linked to the development of modern religious art in France. His most notable church, after
Assy, was that of Audincourt, for which Bazaine did a façade mosaic and Léger his great

THE STRUCTURE

In keeping with the landscape of the Mont Blanc massif, dominated as it is by cliffs and forests, Novarina decided to build the church of stone and wood. The rough green granite blocks forming its walls were cut from a local quarry, and the rose-tinted marble used for the interior pavement was brought from nearby Combloux. The Canon told the architect that he would like "something inspired by a great stone style like the Romanesque," and Novarina went to work adapting this historical mode to the environment and to the local chalet style of the houses. Some of the practical necessities which had to be considered were met by the inherently "functional" character of this chalet style. The low walls and sweeping roof are designed to support the weight of the tremendous winter snows, while the sharp pitch of the roof encourages the heavy deposits to slide off. In order to protect the walls from the piling up of drifts, the eaves overhang a considerable distance.

At an altitude of 1,000 meters it is exceedingly cold in winter, and as the congregation was made up largely of convalescents, the problem of heating was paramount. The low roof, which considerably reduces the internal volume, makes comfortable heating possible, and circumvents the difficulties that plague attempts to heat some of the older mountain churches where the ceiling is warm and the congregation cold. In this connection, Novarina also decided to build a crypt, which, being smaller, would be more intimate and still more easily heated. The crypt was to be used for weekday services during the winter, when attendance at Mass is lower.

Work got under way at Assy in May, 1937, when the chosen site was leveled and excavation for the crypt was begun. Financial support came largely from friends of Canon Devémy among the patients at the various sanatoria, many of whom were wealthy, and from gifts by Pius XI in 1937 and Pius XII in 1939. These gifts have often been deceptively cited with the implication that they represent Papal approval of the experiment at Assy.[3] It should be

series of stained glass windows. Novarina subsequently gave up his regional style and is now working more effectively in a mode inspired by Le Courbusier.

[3] E.g., the Canon Devémy in his public lecture at Angers. Cf. "L'Église d'Assy et l'art sacré," *Courier de l'ouest,* January 6, 1951, p. 1; Couturier, "L'Église d'Assy," *Arts,* April 16, 1948, p. 1; "The Assy Church," *Life,* June 19, 1950; and elsewhere. In a note to the editor of *Liturgical Arts,* Father Couturier enlarged upon references to the papal gift by observing that

noted that both gifts antedated the earliest participation at Assy of any genuinely modern or non-Christian artists.

Novarina oriented the church in the usual manner, its apse facing east, as required even for modern churches, except when rendered impossible by the topographical conformation.[4] But curiously, the whole purpose of this orientation is nullified by the fact that at Assy, as is not infrequent elsewhere in France, the clergy has returned to the old custom, derived originally from synagogue worship, of celebrating the Mass facing the congregation. This practice renders the structuring of the liturgy less hieratic and makes the dialogue of the Mass more intimate. At Assy the priest now faces west, despite the policy generally maintained by the Dominicans that "it is certainly the priest celebrating the holy sacrifice, rather than the congregation, who should be turned towards the east *even if he is facing the congregation.*"[5] In order to resolve just such conflicts the *Bulletin paroissial liturgique* of 1939 had suggested that the orientation of a church in which Mass is to be celebrated in this way should be reversed, in keeping with the earliest Christian usage, the apse to the west.[6]

The architecture of Assy is in no way revolutionary, and the only novel element, the open porch of the west façade, is perhaps the least successful aspect of the work. This porch is created by a 5-meter overhang of the gabled roof, supported (Figure 5) by eight columns. Formed of rusticated granite

---

on his visit to the Pope the Holy Father gave his blessing to the modern artists working at Assy, but admitted that "he would have done the same for others." Note on Assy, *Liturgical Arts,* XIX, No. 2 (February, 1951), 30–31.

[4] Cf. Oreste Pantalini, *Arte sacre e liturgia* (Milan: Enrico Hoepli, 1932), p. 99.

[5] Régamey, "Note sur l'orientation," *Cahiers de l'art sacré,* 1945, No. 1, p. 30.

[6] *Bulletin paroissial liturgique* (Paris: Les Éditions du Cerf, 1939). Such an assertion, contrary to the policy traditionally maintained by the Vatican, is characteristic of the independence with which the liturgists of the Gallican Church have confronted practical problems.

Vatican objection to the priest celebrating the Mass facing the congregation has recently led to a decree (Acta Apostolice Sedis XXXIX, 8 July 22, 1957, pp. 425–26) requiring the tabernacle to be placed on the main celebrating altar. Maurice Lavanoux observes that, as a result, "the mass versus populum, while not specifically indicted, is rendered practically impossible or at least extremely difficult if the usual form of the tabernacle is preserved." Editorial, *Liturgical Arts,* XXVI, No. 2 (February, 1958).

79

courses, the columns (two of which are engaged to spur walls attached to the body of the church) spring from a stone platform raised four steps above ground level. Though the overhanging roof undoubtedly needed support for the winter months when it carried a heavy load of snow, the eight columns used for this purpose by Novarina seem both in number and proportions dissonant with the rest of the building. They are far too wide, in structural as well as esthetic terms, for the light wooden roof above them. Yet, paradoxically, the central columns are too narrow for their own height. The esthetic failure of the arrangement of this outer porch and, even more, the fact that the columns partially obstruct the view of the Léger mosaic have led to the suggestion that they be removed.[7] This, however, might be an injustice to the Léger work, for it was conceived to be seen behind them.

The spur walls mentioned above are 20.6 meters (67 ft. 7 in.) apart and rise to a height of 3.2 meters (10 ft. 6 in.), thus establishing the base and the sides of the decorative field of the façade. The top of this field is demarcated by the gabled roof, which rises to a height of 10 meters (32 ft. 9½ in.) in the center. Six small, round-arched windows with granite borders perforate the façade on the arcade level, and three more, without borders, are located in the tribune. These windows—few in number, widely spaced, and small in size—are functions of special problems of fenestration peculiar to churches built high in the mountains. Since stained glass windows are not very resistant to the high wind pressures that develop, they cannot be grouped contiguously as in Gothic churches, nor can they be large in size like those Matisse designed for Vence. They must fill isolated apertures in an otherwise heavy wall. Such an arrangement makes for a somber interior, articulated here and there by jewels of light.

The large wooden façade door, handsomely designed by Joseph Parracino, who also created the interior furniture, leads into a kind of narthex area 4 meters (13 ft. 1½ in.) deep, bounded on the left side by the entrance to the mortuary chapel and on the right by the steps down into the baptistry. The

[7] Richard Douaire, "Pilgrimage to Assy, and Appraisal," *Liturgical Arts,* XIX, No. 2 (February, 1951), 28–30.

portal proper, extending 2 meters (6 ft. 6¾ in.) into the narthex, is flanked on left and right by confessionals. Two engaged and ten free-standing columns separate the central nave from the two side aisles. They are granite monoliths, 2 meters high, which, in keeping with the Spartan character of the interior, have no column capitals. Round arches of granite spring directly from the tops of the columns, supporting granite walls that rise to the tribune level. There, in the west gallery, the organ and choir stalls are located. The north and south galleries, truncated by the gabled roof, have room only for some extra chairs and are used only on special holidays, when the congregation is unusually large. They are lit by mansard or attic windows cut into the gabled roof, four on each side.

Four larger windows light the uncomfortably narrow aisles which terminate in the east in subsidiary altars, the northern one being that of the Holy Sacrament. These altars are set into the large masonry wall that separates the sanctuary from the nave. Eight more granite columns, supporting rusticated Romanesque arches, complete the articulation of the interior by continuing the rhythm established in the nave around the semicircular sanctuary (Figure 6).

The large pink marble altar is in table form, like those of earliest Christianity, and rests on a single central support. This is not uncommon in France, particularly in regions where the Liturgical Movement has been strong. Such an altar stresses the understanding of the Eucharist as a "communal meal," as opposed to the sacrificial aspect underlined by the sarcophagus-shaped altars. The former are related to the increasing liturgical intimacy common in some quarters of the Gallican Church, reflected in the turning of the priest towards the congregation and the tendency to translate the Mass into French. Long held objectionable in Vatican quarters,[8] such table altars were specifically condemned in the Papal Encyclical *Mediator Dei*.[9]

A wooden wall, fashioned in a rectangular grille motif, separates the

[8] Celso and Giovanni Costantini, *Fede ed arte,* II, 134, had spoken of the single support table altars as "difficult to admit, for they do not lend themselves well to the liturgy. . . ."

[9] Pius XII, *Mediator Dei,* p. 36.

arches of the apse and the ambulatory, from which one descends into the crypt. Here the materials and articulation are much the same as in the church above, with pavement and ceiling of the rose-gray granite of Combloux and monolithic granite columns without capitals bearing rusticated Romanesque arches. The area of the crypt equals exactly that covered by the choir and apse, whose rhythm and form it recapitulates in a lower story cut 2.4 meters (7ft. 10½ in.) into the earth.

The baptistry located in the basement of the campanile (see Figure 7), is lit by the southernmost window of the façade (with which it is continuous in the west), and by another window in the east wall of the tower. The base of the bell tower projects 1.8 meters (5 ft. 11 in.) southward beyond the spur wall to make possible a square baptistry, 4.8 meters (15 ft. 9 in.) on each side, in contrast to the mortuary chapel, 3.6 meters (11 ft. 9¾ in.) wide, which balances it to the north of the narthex. In accordance with the symbolism of the liturgy, which requires, in memory of the original practice of immersion, that the floor of the baptistry be located lower than that of the nave,[10] three large steps separate the interior of the baptistry from the nave proper.

Though the baptistry seems quite detached from the nave owing to its incorporation with the campanile, such complete separation as is represented, for example, by older baptistries like that of the Cathedral of Florence, is no longer liturgically acceptable. These run contrary to the requirements of the Roman rite of 1925, which demands that the place of the preliminary baptismal ceremony and, above all, the baptistry itself open clearly into the church proper.[11]

The campanile, rising 32 meters (105 ft.) from the platform, provides a vertical foil for the low-slung body of the church, the gabled form of which echoes the rhythm of the mountain range behind. There is little variation or invention in the profile of this tower; indeed, the projection at its summit of a sound-blind, which resembles the grill of a confessional, creates an unpleasant sense of top-heaviness. This impression is intensified by the sudden

[10] Cf. A. Cassi Ramelli, *Edifici per il culto* (Milan: Edizione Vallardi, 1953), p. 62.

[11] Régamey, "Le Lois de l'église sur l'art sacré," *Cahiers de l'art sacré*, 1945, No. 1, p. 6.

truncation of the tower by the tiny gabled roof that sits upon it like a hat many sizes too small.[12]

Brought to international attention by the later history of its decoration, the architecture of the church has been subjected to critical inspection of a kind it was not created to endure. The opinions of critics have ranged from that of Duthuit, who attacked it as a "hybrid of an Assyrian temple, a Swiss chalet and a steel factory," [13] to that of Dorival, who, while addressing certain reproaches to the architect, praised the "frankness of the maquette" and the "perfect adaptation to the landscape." [14] The most copious praise for the architecture comes from critics of "modernistic" taste within the orbit of the Church. Victor-Henri Debidour, for example, gains leverage to attack the decorations of Léger and Bonnard by singing the praises of the architecture, all of which, particularly in the interior, he finds "of the first order." [15] Needless to say, the critical temper of the Dominican Fathers has not been compromised by this celebration of the *juste milieu,* but with respect to Assy diplomacy has held them to cryptic statements such as that the architecture is "far from faultless." [16]

[12] The campanile has been more severely criticized than any other part of the architecture; the critic Frank Elgar, for instance, likened it to a pigeon roost. "L'Église d'Assy, une magnifique tentative manquée," *Carrefour,* 6th year, No. 313, September 12, 1950, p. 9.

[13] Georges Duthuit, "Documents," *Transition, Forty-nine,* 1949, No. 5, pp. 125–26.

[14] Bernard Dorival, "L'Église d'Assy ou la resurrection de l'art sacré," *Médecine de France,* 1950, No. 18, pp. 29–32.

[15] Victor-Henri Debidour, "Autour de l'église d'Assy," in *Problèmes de l'art sacré,* ed. Debidour (Paris: Le Nouveau Portique, n.d.), p. 289.

[16] Couturier, "La Leçon d'Assy," *L'Art sacré,* September–October, 1950, No. 1–2, pp. 16–20.

6. THE STAINED GLASS WINDOWS

THE ROUAULT WINDOWS

It was almost an accident that Georges Rouault's window of the *Christ aux outrages* became the first work by the century's greatest Catholic artist [1] to enter a church. Unlike the four other Rouault windows, later commissioned specifically for the church of Assy, the *Christ aux outrages* was created as an exhibition piece. The glazier Jean Hébert-Stevens, who had been experimenting since 1925 with the translation into stained glass of various modern (or, better, "modernistic") styles, organized an extensive exhibition at the Petit Palais in the months of May and June, 1939. For this exhibition Rouault, Gromaire, Bazaine, and others offered window cartoons, which were realized in the Hébert-Stevens atelier under the control of the painters themselves. Of the various artists whose contributions were solicited, only Braque declined.[2]

In his youth Rouault had worked as an apprentice in the atelier of a glazier named Hirsch, but neither then nor at any time until 1939 had he faced the task of designing a window himself. In 1937 the architect Henri Vidal had

[1] Though Rouault's parents were Catholic, his father is said to have left the Church in bitter resentment over the condemnation of Lamennais. The young Rouault was sent to Protestant schools and only converted to Catholicism in his twenties. Much of the Gallican spirit of revolt and independence exemplified by the father's attachment to Lamennais was carried over into the son's religious painting.

[2] Though not out of lack of interest or sympathy. He was later to familiarize himself with the technique and at the suggestion of Father Couturier designed (1954) a set of three windows for the church of Varengeville, his (Braque's) summer home. See John Richardson, "Le Nouvel 'Atelier' de Braque," *L'Oeil,* June 15, 1955, No. 6, pp. 20–26, 39.

84

asked him to create a window for the church of Tavaux-Cité in the Jura. But, at the time, Rouault was busy trying to complete a group of canvases required of him under the oppressive terms of the Vollard contract, and he could not accept the Vidal offer. By 1939, however, his time was literally more his own, and he furnished Hébert-Stevens with cartoons, painted in oil on paper, for three windows: (1) a seated *Christ aux outrages,* executed by Hébert-Stevens, later acquired by the Museum of Modern Art, Paris; (2) a *Crucifixion,* executed by Hébert-Stevens, ultimately not shown in the exhibition because of dissatisfaction on Rouault's part, but since reworked and now installed in the Church of La Salette near Grenoble; (3) a second seated *Christ aux outrages* (Plate 1), executed by Paul Bony. This was the one selected by Canon Devémy.

Of the four Rouault windows executed by Bony expressly for Assy in 1946–49, only one, the *Grand Vase,* was made from a cartoon. The rest were translations of paintings selected by Rouault and Father Couturier for their suitability. Tired and anxious to complete a number of nearly finished canvases, Rouault could not summon up the effort required to prepare special cartoons for these four, and, in fact, executed the cartoon for the *Grand Vase* only after it was clear that the painting of that subject that had been selected was of proportions unsuitable to Assy.

It is thus not surprising that the *Christ aux outrages* of 1939, which was preceded by a cartoon and the execution of which was most attentively supervised by the painter, should be Rouault's most distinctive window and the one on which any critical discussion of the painter as a glass designer should be centered. Rouault had actually provided two very similar cartoons for this window. Both the first (Figure 10A), done in the size of the window to be executed, and the second (Figure 10B), done in roughly one-fourth scale, show Christ seated facing right, his lower arms resting on his thighs. Through the prison window at the right is a vista leading to a distant cross. The major difference between the two cartoons is the presence, in the larger, of a round arch border at the top (clearly defined on the right, but only suggested on the left). Bony elected to work from the smaller cartoon, which is the superior composition, particularly in its expressive details. Here the curve of Christ's back is accentuated by its contrast with the straighter line of the cape (a polarity missing in the large cartoon where both lines are curved), and the contour lines of the chest and stomach are surer, their analogies to the shapes in the head more developed.

It will be recalled that the width of the *Christ aux outrages* was by chance exactly that of the space reserved in the west façade at Assy. But as the window was rectangular in its original form, it had to be adapted to the round-arched aperture in the wall by the addition of some extra panels at the top. Bony executed this alteration late in 1939 with the approval of Rouault, whose larger cartoon (which was not used) had in any case included this motif, suggesting its congruence with the rest of the design.

The window as executed makes a quite different impression from the cartoon, though not so markedly different as a comparison of black and white photographs suggests. It is primarily when the window is seen against a strong light and the contrast between the dark "leading" and the translucent glass panels is maximized, that a sharpness and projection quite foreign to the spirit of the cartoon are produced. The resultant loss of subtlety is only partly compensated for by the increased luminosity of the glass panels.

The colors are unexpectedly true to the tonality of the cartoon, though they vary in their pitch depending on the lighting conditions. The background of the chamber in which Christ sits is composed of sections of blue, tending here and there towards purple, and blue-green, giving way in spots to a light white-green. Christ's body, in tones of yellow tempered with green and pink (right shoulder and stomach area), is set off by small patches of his rich crimson robe. The halo, a golden yellow, provides the richest single accent.

The "leading" fragments the image into many small irregular panels ranging from roughly one inch to ten square inches in size. It generally follows the contours indicated by Rouault, but here and there technical necessities forced Bony to make unexpected and unhappy additions, such as the almost horizontal strip in the right upper arm. These extra leadings tend to give the body of Christ a patchwork character not present in the cartoon. In medieval windows, the leading patterns often function in opposition to the figural composition, but the resultant fragmentation leads to an intentional and rich two-

86

dimensional decorative effect. In the Rouault window some of the cohesiveness of the cartoon is sacrificed with no such corresponding gain.

One might have imagined that Rouault, more than other artists, would have created cartoons revealing special consciousness of the possibilities and limitations of stained glass, cartoons which would have accordingly differed in structure from his oil paintings. This, however, is not the case. Rouault's window cartoons cannot be distinguished in any way from the main body of his work.[3] Of course, this fact can be easily (and wrongly) rationalized by falling back on the recurrent critical notion that Rouault's painting style is itself based upon the art of stained glass. His dealer Vollard, for example, quoted Rouault as saying,

I have been told before that my painting reminded people of stained glass. That's probably because of my original trade. . . . My work consisted in supervising the firing and sorting of little pieces of glass that fell out of the windows they brought us to repair. This latter task inspired me with an enduring passion for old stained glass.[4]

Waldemar-George has noted Rouault's experience in "dexterously repairing medieval windows" and added that "only the technique of stained glass can give the key" to his style.[5] Jean Grenier "recognizes [window] leadings" in Rouault's contours,[6] and Joseph Pichard insists that while working in the Hirsch atelier Rouault "was assimilating, without realizing it, impressions which were later to partly determine his painting"[7] The view favoring "the apparent relation of Rouault's contours to window leading" was also supported by James Thrall Soby in his Museum of Modern Art monograph.[8]

[3] On the other hand, Matisse (at Vence) and Léger (at Audincourt) seem to have given special attention to the peculiarities of the medium and varied their work accordingly.

[4] Ambroise Vollard, *Recollections of a Picture Dealer* (Boston: Little, Brown, 1936), pp. 213–14.

[5] Waldemar-George, "Georges Rouault, peintre sacré et maudit," *La Renaissance,* XX (October–December, 1937), 5–30.

[6] Grenier, "Idées de Georges Rouault," *L'Oeil,* April, 1957, No. 28, pp. 30–41.

[7] Pichard, "L'Oeuvre de Rouault," *L'Art d'église,* January, 1953, No. 1, pp. 3–7.

[8] James Thrall Soby, *Georges Rouault* (New York: Museum of Modern Art, 1947), p. 8.

THE WINDOWS

This attractive and deceptively simple thesis, however, is not substantiated by a careful study of the esthetic and historical facts. Apart from the questionable authenticity of the Vollard citation,[9] a glance at the academic windows that were being created and repaired by ateliers like Hirsch's would immediately raise doubts as to their influence on the integration of Rouault's style.[10] Moreover, the painter himself has stated that the older windows he was able to see while an apprentice glazier "were rather of the Renaissance than of the twelfth or thirteenth centuries."[11]

More convincing than these historical factors is the actual superficiality of the resemblances between Rouault's paintings and medieval stained glass. Rouault's paintings and the window cartoons based on them are both fundamentally *unlike* medieval windows. A careful analysis reveals that in the handling of color, shading, leading, perspective, and fragmentation, Rouault's techniques are only remotely related to those of the medieval glaziers and are in many ways directly opposed. If one were to insist that he was learning a lesson about medieval glass while an apprentice at Hirsch's studio, one would have to admit at the same time that he learned it rather badly. The sources of Rouault's style are to be found rather in a primitivizing of the chiaroscuro tradition of Rembrandt and more immediately in the art of Gustave Moreau.

A juxtaposition of the *Christ aux outrages* with any of the panels of the great west windows at Chartres (Rouault's favorites) will reveal the unexpected differences. In the Rouault window the linear black leadings almost exclusively define the contours of the figure or setting, thus emphasizing the projection of these forms in the figure-ground relationship. This effect is further heightened by the chiaroscuro modeling (e.g., the arm or stomach area), which gives volume to the forms.

The glazier at Chartres,[12] constrained to employ leading on contours where

[9] Vollard became somewhat notorious for attributing to painters remarks that tended to substantiate his (Vollard's) personal theories.

[10] Lionello Venturi observes, moreover, that in the work done following Rouault's apprenticeship no stylistic element recalling stained glass is present. *Georges Rouault* (2d ed.; Paris: Skira, 1948), p. 16.

[11] Georges Rouault, "Anciens et modernes," *Le Point,* 6th year, No. 34–35, March, 1947, pp. 48–54.

[12] Though they are usually held up as the greatest examples of "Gothic" stained glass, these

color changed, used many additional and structurally unnecessary leadings to fragment the color panels into small, black-margined areas independent of the objects represented and thus of any figure-ground relationship. These extra leadings are introduced with a "studied randomness," no two moving in the same way. Though the folds of drapery, facial features, and other details were painted in enamel, they were never modeled in chiaroscuro.[13] The light-dark play within any one color in the Chartres windows is due to variations in thickness of the glass resulting from the "muff" and "crown" methods of blowing. Thus the tonal variation is largely "accidental," and though the glazier, with his sure eye, joined pieces whose tonal range cohered, these light-dark variations were autonomous.

As we retreat from the Chartres windows, the subject matter is consequently drowned in a surge of rich ornamental color, which disengages itself from the figures. This annihilation of spatial projection and tactility through fragmentation and disengaged light-dark play proceeds not only from the decorative propensity of the Chartres artist, but also from his desire to give a flat appearance to glass panels that were visualized, not so much as windows, as replacements for the earlier decorated masonry walls.[14]

Rouault's *Christ aux outrages* has no such disengaged decorative level. The leading and modeling all participate in a figure-ground relation which begins with the discrete and tactile figure of Christ and continues in the perspective vista on the upper right—a spatial "break through" which the Gothic artist sought studiously to avoid, even to the point of markedly blunting orthogonals. As we retreat from the Rouault, the initial figure-ground relationship remains

---

windows, created some time before the second great fire of 1194, are as close stylistically and even historically to the Romanesque. It is in any case with the monastic art of the earlier period that Rouault, a tortured and ascetic recluse, feels his real affinity.

[13] Some thirteenth-century glass realized by other ateliers of the Île-de-France did occasionally use enamel to model in low relief, but these practices were, even there, marginal to the general esthetic of the windows.

[14] The English word "window," derived from the Old Norse *vindauga,* "wind eye," suggests an aperture made for visual purposes, through which the elements may pass. The fixed, translucent, but opaque *vitraux* of the cathedral are entirely opposed in character. Even in transmitting light they serve as transforming agents which maintain the distinction between the interior of the church and the world outside, an opposition foreign to the sense of the word "window."

fixed. This is in keeping with the sense of the Rouault window, not as a glass wall, but as a puncturing of the surface (the window is deeply set) where we read the image as a perspective extension of our own space. The Gothic image, on the other hand, is of another world, not continuous with the space of the spectator.[15]

Moreover, Rouault's sense of color differs markedly from that of the older glaziers. Even against the bright sun his colors at Assy are opaque and predominantly somber. At Chartres the absence of the intermixture of black and the frequency of bright colors (large areas of yellow and smaller areas of secondary light tones) effect an over-all tonal purity and transparency reflecting the joy of the "good news."

What sets the Rouault windows apart from those of older times, even more, perhaps, than their thoroughgoing three-dimensionality and "dirty" coloring, is the absence of any continuous tonal and rhythmic relationship between them and the interior wall surfaces in which they are embedded. In late Gothic and early Renaissance churches the two-dimensional integrity of the inner wall skin was often maintained, even in spite of the presence of perspective devices in individual windows, by virtue of endowing the whole series with some unifying tonal value or structural motif, which was also adjusted to the character of the separating masonry. In this way, as the spectator retreated from the windows, the perspective illusion disappeared, and elements constituting the continuous system of the wall became dominant. Of course, such a structuring presupposes a consciousness of the architectural role of the windows, which Rouault did not have, as well as a possibility for the architect and glazier to elaborate their plans in concert in advance, a situation prohibited by the sporadic integration of the decorative scheme at Assy.

The four windows executed by Bony from 1946 to 1949 were based upon

[15] In their disengaged fragmentation the twelfth-century windows are paradoxically closer to the esthetic of a modern style like Impressionism than that of Rouault, though the process is reversed. In Impressionism the discrete image, seen at a distance, breaks down into many "detached" or "random" color sensations as we approach the canvas. At Chartres we see the discrete image only when close to the window, and this breaks down into tiny varied sensations of color as we retreat. But these sensations cohere in over-all ornamental or geometrical groupings which are foreign to the free distribution of the Impressionist brush strokes.

oil paintings and realized in one-to-one scale. The best of them is the *Christ of the Passion* (Figure 11), very similar to the *Christ aux outrages,* copied from a painting now in the Museum of Modern Art, Paris (Figure 12A). It was placed in the west wall of the church to balance the earlier window (see plan). The painting used as a model happily included the round arch motif, but, as its height was somewhat short of that required for the fenestration of Assy, Bony added a horizontal band in three pieces to the bottom of the window over which Rouault wrote the word "Flagellation." It is impossible to compare the color fidelity of this predominantly yellow, red, and green window with its model, for Rouault reworked that painting in a more blue tonality some years after the realization of the window.

In translating this painting into glass, the major problem lay in rendering the textural richness of the heavy impasto characteristic of Rouault's later style, an impasto which varies with the figures and objects in a kind of low relief. The painterly richness of the original is quite foreign to the medium of stained glass, so much so that Bony resorted here more than in any of the windows to a form of painting on glass. So as not to interrupt the sensitive play of chiaroscuro, the leading was minimized, and the individual panels of glass were enlarged, some to over sixty square inches.

The two windows based on floral still lifes and placed, like the Christs, so as to balance each other on the north and south sides of the portal, were both derived from paintings containing round arch framing motifs. Rouault lengthened the first composition for the purposes of Assy's fenestration by adding a panel across the bottom on which he wrote the phrase "J'ai été maltraité et opprimé." [16] Uninventive in composition, dull in color, and lacking the rich fragmentation of the other windows, it is the least appealing of the group.

The second floral still life, the *Grand Vase* (Figure 13A), was also lengthened by a text panel, this one reading "Et il n'a pas ouvert la bouche." [17] However, the first results were unhappy, as the elongation of the compositional

[16] A slight revision of the first sentence of Isaiah 53.7: "He was oppressed and he was afflicted. . . ." The text fragments were added to both floral windows to associate them with the two Passion windows.

[17] Conclusion of the opening sentence of Isaiah 53.7: ". . . yet he opened not his mouth."

field threw the forms of the vase and flowers too much out of adjustment. Rouault finally solved the problem by spontaneously repainting the still life in the form of a working cartoon (Figure 13B) in which the shapes of the vase, and more particularly the bouquet, are better harmonized with the presence of a lower panel.

The oil of Saint Veronica (Figure 14), used as a model for the window of the mortuary chapel, raised special problems and seems from the technical point of view to have been a highly questionable choice.[18] The painting, then in the private possession of Rouault who allowed me to inspect it, is in a blue-gray range of very delicate "valeurs" and with darks that never become black. The impossibility of avoiding black in the window (at least where the opaque leading occurs) created a difficult situation for Bony, and in spite of his considerable efforts, the finished window (Figure 15) contains marked contrasts which not only annihilate the "valeurs" of the original but vitiate the rich textural variations of its impasto.

Since the painting is a small rectangular panel, Bony created a large Rouaultesque border design on all four sides to bring it up to size.

In order to approximate Rouault's chiaroscuro and painterly textures in the Assy windows, Bony had to employ an elaborate set of techniques. Modern colored glass is pressed in sheets of consistent thickness and is free of the impurities and accidental variations which gave old glass tonal richness and opacity. To achieve the desired density and diversity, Bony exploited the rarely used technique of laminating different colors. In a green panel formed of laminated blue and yellow sheets of glass, either side can be "attacked" with acid so as to produce blue, yellow, or any of the intermediate tones.[19] This technique was employed extensively in the *Christ aux outrages,* and it accounts for the greater richness of that window. In one instance (the head of *Veronica*) four sheets were laminated, but as in all such cases one layer was white. Figure

---

[18] A first unsuccessful version of the window may still be seen at the atelier of M. Bony.

[19] Medieval glaziers resorted to lamination only in the case of red, where the glass was "flashed" (the hot "crown" or "muff" dipped into white glass and reblown) to create a laminate of red and white. This was necessitated by the excessive opacity of the red which, if blown to normal thickness, would have been far too dark. The method of acid attack was, however, unknown to the medievals.

12B shows the window of the *Christ of the Passion* during provisional reassemblage just after the laminated panels on the top had been attacked by acid so as to allow a painterly emergence of the golden halo from the green ground. The same process has been used to establish some contours of the head. The lamination-acid treatment produces considerably different tonal effects from those of medieval windows where variations occur in a light-dark range within one color, not between them.

Whereas enamel was used by medieval glaziers only to outline features, drapery forms, and occasional props, Bony has used light grisailles (green, red-brown, and blue) to build up textures in a painterly manner. In addition, in order to achieve the desired density of tone, he fired the panels three and often four times.

Despite Bony's studious efforts, the windows at Assy are ample demonstration of the fact that Rouault's painterly genius is compromised by translation into stained glass. The more impersonal method of the glazier is a poor vehicle for an art celebrating subtle and intimate qualities of touch. To the extent that Bony's efforts constitute an improvised form of painting on glass, he was making good Bonys, perhaps—but bad Rouaults.

"My father was highly pleased," said Rouault's daughter and confidante Isabelle, "finally to see one of his works in a church." The painter's satisfaction was twofold. First, it was, if only in a limited way, a form of ecclesiastical recognition, and second, it provided what Rouault considered the only proper locale for stained glass. He had not liked the installation of the windows in the exhibition at the Petit Palais in 1939, and when the Canon Devémy was in the process of installing the *Christ aux outrages,* Rouault wrote to him expressing satisfaction that the thick walls of the church would make an excellent setting for the glass, and that he liked to think of the window "emerging from a soft light." As the glass is set in the outer edge of the thickness of the wall, the ten-inch depth of the arched reveal creates a repoussoir of soft light that acts both as a "frame" and as a bridge between the image and the dark inner walls of the church.

The placement, at long last, of a Rouault work in a Catholic church elicited

93

little jubilation in ecclesiastical circles beyond the Dominicans. Following the prompting of the Vatican, general clerical feeling toward the painter has, if anything, hardened. Such apprehension is an old story to Rouault. Before the Second World War the Vatican took little notice of him, and French prelates were almost invariably critical of his work. Their attacks led Waldemar-George to write in 1937 that "in casting its anathema on Rouault, the Church has not only betrayed its interests, but failed in its task." [20]

Rouault's art received little more support until just recently from the more enlightened lay members of the Catholic Revival. Only Maritain, who considers his art to be "at the summit of religious and hieratic painting," [21] spoke out in his defense. One might have expected Rouault's friend and spiritual mentor, Léon Bloy, long a major catalyst of the movement, to have shared Maritain's enthusiasm. But though Rouault drew inspiration from Bloy's medievalism, the writer found Rouault's version of it incomprehensible. Bourgeois in his artistic tastes, Bloy could only appreciate "finished" pictures, and once confided to Rouault that as far as he was concerned, "art ended with the Olympia of Manet." [22] When Bloy went to see Rouault's paintings at the Salon des Indépendents, he was horrified [23] and soon wrote an open letter to the painter accusing him of being "exclusively drawn to the ugly" and of painting "in a vertigo of hideousness." "If you were an obedient man of prayer, a Communicant," Bloy added, "you couldn't paint such horrible pictures. . . . It is time to stop." [24]

Since the last war, as the "querelle de l'art sacré" has developed around the church of Assy, a decisively negative Vatican position on Rouault has emerged. One of two prints (from the Miserere series) which was to have been

---

[20] Waldemar-George, "Georges Rouault, peintre sacré et maudit," *Le Renaissance,* XX (October–December, 1937), 5–30.

[21] Maritain, Foreword to the Catalogue of the Rouault Retrospective Exhibition, Museum of Modern Art, New York, 1953.

[22] Jean Steinmann, *Léon Bloy* (Paris: Éditions du Cerf, 1955), p. 324.

[23] He came out stamping his foot and saying angrily: "I demand to see the Dependents."

[24] Steinmann, *Léon Bloy,* p. 352. It should be kept in mind, of course, that Bloy was speaking of Rouault's early works. These are more rough in technique and more raw in sentiment than his post-World War I paintings.

included in Rome's gigantic 1950 Jubilee exhibition of religious art was rejected,[25] and Rouault's Madonnas and <u>Crucifixions</u> were considered generally as falling within Pontifical reservations on sacred art.[26] Gaston Bardet was ready to put them on his projected index.[27] Cardinal Costantini later cited a *Madonna and Child* of Rouault among a collection of "horrors" which formed part of the "anti-catholic offensive." [28]

The Vatican stand was spelled out in detail by Michele Guerrisi, who described Rouault's art as "born not of authentic religious feeling, but of archaism. . . . His *apparent* religiosity is without charity, and knows no mystical illumination, just as it knows no artistic catharsis." Citing and rejecting Venturi's conjecture that clerical denial of Rouault's art stemmed from the absence of conventional physical beauty in his figures, Guerrisi affirmed decisively on behalf of Vatican circles that the works displease "because they are without *artistic* beauty."

He [Rouault]—as a painter—is not a heretic, but neither is he orthodox: he is simply an exalted iconoclast with respect to the tradition of figuration, and *a clever idolator of post-impressionist geometry*. In the seat of Catholicism we do not intend to allocate to him any work of art, but neither will we condemn him to the Inferno—a tragic and serious thing.[29]

In France, Fathers Couturier, Régamey, and the Abbé Morel, all of whom were personally close to Rouault, labored to make him acceptable to the Catholic community—with limited success. Many intellectuals among the French clergy admit Rouault's greatness but are none the less troubled by his art. "What astonishes us at first," writes Jesuit Father Jean Onimus, "is that these most authentically religious and Christian works seem . . . aggressive and

[25] Régamey, *Art sacré au XXe siècle,* p. 396.

[26] Corrado Mezzana, "Rome 1950," *Arte cristiana,* XXXVIII, No. 7–10 (July–October, 1951), 110–12.

[27] Gaston Bardet, "Una Polemica si allarga," *Arte cristiana,* XXXVIII, No. 11–12 (November–December, 1951), 129–30.

[28] Celso Costantini, "Signore ho amato il decoro della tua casa," *Fede ed arte* (entire issue), 2d year, No. 2, February, 1954, pp. 33–63.

[29] Guerrisi, "L'Arte religiosa e la crisi del gusto contemporaneo," *Fede ed arte,* 1st year, No. 3, March, 1953, pp. 77–84. Italics added.

cruel." [30] Such clerics are disturbed by the fact that Rouault's Christ is seen always as a suffering victim. But the tenuousness of the dividing line between agony as a private emotion and its transcendence in the sacramental Passion forces most such ecclesiastics to consider Rouault a marginal figure. "His work is at the point of separation, a little like that of Bernanos and Graham Greene. One sometimes hears the satanic chuckle in the shadows." [31] There is no question, in any event, that there still are everywhere clerics and over-zealous faithful to whom Rouault's faith and art are suspect.[32]

Rouault himself has nothing but disdain for the characteristic Christian art of modern times. Asked what he thought of the "art" of Saint-Sulpice, he replied: "It does not exist." [33] But he considered the more serious academic religious art of the turn of the century a dangerous threat to him, and for some years at the beginning of his career he shied away from religious sub-jects out of fear of creating works "into which a sullen convention might have slipped." [34] While refusing to paint delicate figures of seraphim and Madonnas acceptable to the Church, he created a form of religious art in reverse, a new iconography of saints and devils made up of clowns, prostitutes, and judges.

For Rouault, the function of the religious artist is "to spend his whole life finding the appropriate and sincere means of expressing his temperament and gifts," [35] obeying throughout "only his interior order." [36] Such a credo con-trasts sharply with the principle of submission established by the Church and fully accepted by "in-group" Catholic religious artists like Praxitele Zographos, who maintains that "only the hierarchy is qualified to recognize the religious possibilities of genius" and that a bad painter is more desirable and more truly religious than renowned masters (like those of Assy) "if he is capable of

[30] Jean Onimus, "L'Art cruel," *Études,* 86th year, Tome 277, June, 1953, pp. 344–55.

[31] *Ibid.*

[32] Régamey, "L'Art sacré, sera-t-il chrétien?" *Recherches et débats,* New Series, I, No. 1 (May, 1952).

[33] Rouault, "Réponse à une enquête sur l'art sacré: presentée par Maurice Brillant," *La Croix,* May 11, 1952, p. 2.

[34] Cited in Jacques de Laprade, "Notes sur Rouault," *Le Point,* 5th year, No. 26–27, August–October, 1943, pp. 59–75. ". . . ou une convention sournoise se serait glissée."

[35] Rouault, "Climat pictural," *La Renaissance,* XX (October–December, 1937), 2–4.

[36] Cited in Régamey, "La Querelle de l'art sacré," *La Vie intellectuelle,* 19th year, No. 11, November, 1951, pp. 3–48.

submitting his style and technique to a single director, and to the desires of the priest." [37]

Rouault speaks like any secular modern painter when he says: "One must begin by loving painting—and then, when one loves painting, one becomes clairvoyant." [38] Such a concept of the primacy of painting is not only apostasy in Vatican eyes, but is contrary to the attitudes which prevailed in the ages of faith.

But if Rouault's attitudes on art are antipodal to those of the Church, his aims and those of the ecclesiastics share a common goal, for Rouault's "only ambition" is some day to paint a Christ "so moving that those who will see him will be converted." [39] The painter has always acted, moreover, with great deference and humility towards the Church, and has never criticized the clergy despite the countless vicissitudes he has suffered at their hands. "One can be religious," said Rouault of them sympathetically, "and feel nothing [with respect to genuine religious art]. One can pray to better feel it, but there is always the question of a gift. Perhaps particular gifts are necessary above all in that which concerns the sacred." [40]

Seen from the point of view of the needs of the Church, there is much in Rouault's art which is unsatisfactory and legitimately suspect. For though he is the greatest Christian artist of our time, his *oeuvre* lacks the essentially communal character which forms the basis of religious, particularly Catholic, experience. He is "of the race of solitary painters," [41] something of a misanthrope personally, and his work is wholly devoid of the joy which the "good news" has inspired in religious painters of the past. Cardinal Costantini is correct when he complains that in Rouault's work "the Christ of the Resurrection tends to be passed over in silence." [42] Sacred art, that is, art for the church building in which the community relives the sacrifice of Christ, must have a

---

[37] Praxitele Zographos, "Les Rapports du peintre avec Dieu," *Tuileries,* May, 1951, No. 8.

[38] Rouault, "Réponse à une enquête sur l'art sacré," p. 2.

[39] Daniel Theôte, "Intimate Moments with Rouault," *Tricolor,* May, 1944, No. 2, pp. 65–98.

[40] Rouault, "Réponse à une enquête sur l'art sacré," p. 2.

[41] Abbé Morel, "Rouault parmi nous," *Cahiers de l'art sacré,* 1946, No. 3, pp. 4–7.

[42] Cited in Auvert, *Défense et illustration de l'art sacré,* p. 61. The limited character of Rouault's iconography, devoid of images of transcendence, would prevent him from having more than a fractional role in a large-scale church decoration.

suprapersonal character that one is hard pressed to find in Rouault. It is para-doxically much stronger in the *oeuvre* of a painter like Léger, where, however, the community celebrated is not the religious one.

Rouault's oblique relationship to the Christian community is that of the mystic, and mystics have always been suspect in the Church. Like the secular modern artist, Rouault not only breaks with tradition, but he discovers, as Nicolas Calas observes, that the social role of modern art, even within Christianity, is to be antisocial. Edgar Wind apprehends something of Rouault's apartness in his characterization of his art as nonsacramental, "one might say almost anti-sacramental." [43]

[43] Edgar Wind, "Traditional Religion and Modern Art," *Art News*, LII, No. 3 (May, 1953), 18–23, 60–63. Though this description is rather apt, its validity suffers from the fact that Wind sought to support it by some doubtful references to the Papal Encyclical *Mediator Dei*. In misquoting and isolating these passages from context, Wind naturally misinterpreted them. Noting the curious omission of the wounds in Rouault's crucifixions (either the wounds are eliminated or the sections of the body in which they would appear are segmented, usually by the frame), he asks how this must be judged in the light of the Encyclical's warning (in Wind's version) that "he wanders from the right path . . . who commands that images of our Divine Redeemer on the Cross be made so that His body does not show the bitter wounds he suffered." This statement would seem to condemn all Rouault's crucifixions, not to speak of most of his other images of Christ. But when we turn to the approved English text of the Encyclical, we find: "One would be straying from the straight path . . . were he to order the crucifix so designed that the divine Redeemer's body shows no trace of His cruel sufferings." Pius XII, *Mediator Dei*, p. 36. The specific phrase, "bitter wounds," is missing here and, more important, we discover that the Pope is not talking about the crucifixion, but about the crucifix, which stands beyond even the sacred image in being a liturgical object. It goes without saying that Rouault's images are not crucifixes, nor were his crucifixions made as works of liturgical art. As devotional images their aim is not to foster participation in the sacrifice, but to provide an object conducive to meditation, to private spiritual exercises the importance of which is insisted upon elsewhere in *Mediator Dei*. The introduction of the wounds would have given Rouault's images a narrative immediacy, destroying the icon-like meditative distance he always wished them to maintain.

According to Wind's reasoning, moreover, Rouault's art would be unacceptable to the Vatican because it does not participate adequately in the sense of suffering insisted upon by the Encyclical. ("His bitter sufferings constitute the principal mystery of our redemption and it is thus only fitting that the Catholic faith should give it the greatest prominence. This mystery is the very center of divine worship since the mass re-presents and renews it every day and since all the sacraments are most closely united with the Cross." *Ibid.*, p. 67.) But

Not all critics, of course, agree that Rouault's art is private in character. Herbert Read, or example, speaks of his "public style" in which "subtleties are subordinated." Rouault's subjects, Read continues, "could be enlarged to the size of a poster, a mural, a stained glass window, and only gain in the process." [44] But the diminished artistic content of the windows at Assy prove Read wrong, I believe, and we can be sure that the loss occasioned by enlargement into a poster or mural would be even greater. An intimate stroke-by-stroke richness of texture and color is Rouault's forte. His groupings and his posing of figures depend for their expression on nuanced gestures and slight inclinations. As a composer he has added nothing new. His division of the canvas is traditional, and he lacks the breadth and boldness necessary for large-scale art. "His painting is a personal act," Malraux concludes rightly, "which in no way concerns the spectator." [45]

THE AISLE WINDOWS

The six stained glass windows designed by Father Couturier, Maurice Brianchon, Paul Bony, and Adeline Hébert-Stevens, are mostly well-intentioned clichés of modernity, unworthy of special attention. Bony's *Saint Peter* (Figure 48) is typical of the group. It suffers from the kind of pseudo-abstraction that does not comprehend genuine plastic values. The spotting of colors has no structural relationship to the choice of forms. The space of the image is uncomfortably inconsistent, for if the border pattern is flat, the figure and the fishnet he holds seem to project out into the space in front of it. Moreover, the colored glass panels of the face, hands, arms, and other points have been partially painted over in grisaille in such a manner as to create chiaroscuro modeling for the figure. The shapes of the glass panels are unimaginative and

---

we have seen that it is in part precisely the excess and intensity of agony on which conservative criticism of Rouault is based. Furthermore, if we look at the Papal statement Wind cites in the context of the Encyclical as a whole, we discover that it is *not* directed towards modern art, but constitutes a warning against an increasing tendency in Catholic art and literature to sacrifice the historical Christ of the Passion in favor of a "pneumatic" or glorified Redeemer.

[44] Herbert Read, "Georges Rouault," in *A Coat of Many Colors* (London; Routledge, 1945), p. 309.

[45] Malraux, "Rouault," *Formes,* December, 1929, No. 1, pp. 5–6.

repetitious, the meaning of abstraction having been misunderstood here, as in so much "modernistic" art, as simplification.

Of these aisle windows, only the two by Paul Berçot merit their place in the church. In contrast to the other artists who designed windows, including Rouault and even Bazaine, Berçot grasped the peculiar character of stained glass. His windows alone are not simply compromised paintings. Berçot's *Saint Francis of Assisi* (Figure 49) is a joyous pastel puzzle. Though he loses control here and there and overcomplicates his groupings, the shapes of his green, orange, yellow, and purple panels are far more interesting and diversified than those of Bony. Whereas the latter relied largely on straight lines, Berçot developed the arabesque, and if his windows suffer from their proximity to Matisse's ceramic, they nevertheless share the same buoyance, unpretentiousness, and sincerity.

Berçot eliminated altogether the chiaroscuro modeling that characterizes the other stained glass windows at Assy. Such tonal variations as are found in panels like the one at the neck of the *Saint Francis* are the result of using grisaille for purely textural variations. Like the (more accidental) tonal variations in medieval windows, Berçot's are independent of modeling and consequently give the image no spatial projection. The cartoon (Figure 50) for the *Saint Francis* reveals the artist as the only window designer at Assy to work from a non-painterly context, clearly marking every leading and leaving nothing to be "translated" by the glazier during the actual execution.[46]

The three windows in the tribune executed from Bazaine's cartoons by Marguerite Huré were conceived at a time when the artist was in a period of transition from semifigurative Cubism to the nonfigurative painting that has established his name during the last decade. These windows do not show Bazaine at his best. Though he took his task very seriously, investigating the problems of the metier of stained glass and consequently modifying his painterly conceptions somewhat, a comparison of the *Saint Gregory* cartoon with the

---

[46] Berçot did the grisaille work himself in Bony's shop. The windows were first executed in simple flat tones according to the cartoon. At this point Berçot elected to give textural variation and brushed on grisaille in different patterns over a few of the panels. This procedure explains certain signal variations between the cartoon and the finished window.

finished window (Figures 51A, 51B) reveals that he was not sure where to indicate leading, with the result that many of the juxtapositions of tender color planes in the cartoon (as in the face) emerged in the window crudely isolated from one another by black lines.

Except for Rouault, Bazaine is the only artist of international reputation represented at Assy who is a practicing Catholic. A man of considerable intellectual stature and author of numerous articles on modern painting,[47] he has collaborated steadily with the Dominicans of *L'Art sacré*. His mosaic façade and glass baptistry for the church at Audincourt (for which Léger did his great stained glass windows) show his art at a more fully ripened stage.

[47] These have been gathered in a small book entitled *Notes sur la peinture* (Paris: Éditions du Seuil, 1953).

101

7. THE TAPESTRY OF LURÇAT

Jean Lurçat's monumental tapestry (see plate), based on the apocalyptic vision from the twelfth chapter of the Book of Revelation, is easily the most popular work in the Assy ensemble. Its compositional breadth, decorative colors, tasteful abstraction, and easy readability combine to create a quantitative appeal with which the more intensely individualistic efforts of artists like Rouault, Lipchitz, and Richier cannot compete.

Such adverse criticism as the tapestry has sustained has been inspired more by Lurçat's public profession of Marxism than by the qualities of the work. Yet the very sympathies that underlie his Communism led him to the restrained, collective, and architectural style which makes his tapestry one of the most appropriate decorations in the church.

In view of Lurçat's political persuasion and the nature of his pre-war iconography, it seemed astonishing when, shortly after the cessation of hostilities, he undertook his largest tapestry to that date for a Catholic church.[1] But Lurçat's wide circle of friends included a few outstanding clerics, among them Father Couturier—and therein, of course, lies the story.

In 1939, shortly before the outbreak of war, Lurçat had a long conversation with Couturier, during which the priest endeavored to persuade him to essay a sacred theme, observing that religion provided a "collective" iconography of the sort that was especially suitable to tapestries, and that a church

---

[1] The tapestry at Assy is 54 square meters. Lurçat has since made a larger one for the Palace of the Council of Europe at Strasbourg. Shortly after the completion of the Assy work he made a second tapestry on a religious theme, a smaller one commissioned by his friend the Marquise de Lubersac for her private chapel.

building was one of the few architectural settings that needed such decoration. Protesting a basic apprehensiveness towards the project, Lurçat resisted. "Suppose," he said, "you wanted me to make a Christ. I would simply make a man whereas you would expect me to make a God." But to demonstrate that his refusal did not stem from "petitesse d'esprit," Lurçat offered to train any Catholic artist chosen by Couturier in the subtleties of tapestry-making. He even suggested a collaboration, in which the religious artist would do the figures and Lurçat the rest—a curious plan, for though such divisions of labor existed in the past, they came about in response to technical rather than spiritual deficiencies.[2]

The question did not arise again until 1944, when Lurçat, who was drawing tapestry cartoons while operating a clandestine radio for the Resistance in Saint-Céré, received a letter from Canon Devémy, a complete stranger to him, suggesting he do a large tapestry for the choir of Notre-Dame-de-Toute-Grâce at Assy. The artist replied that he did not consider himself a proper choice for such a commission as he was not in the least religious, and added that he had already discussed such matters with Father Couturier (though not specifically with regard to Assy). "I knew nothing about this church," he recalled, "and when Devémy requested a tapestry of the Virgin, an image of Saint-Sulpician art came to my mind."

But Lurçat did not reject the commission outright, and the matter simply remained suspended for over a year until he met with Father Couturier, who had returned to Paris soon after the end of the war in Europe. The latter urged him to accept the assignment and, recognizing the inappropriateness of the theme of the Virgin, suggested that he do a tapestry based on the vision of John. Lurçat agreed, and also accepted Couturier's suggestion to do contiguous panels representing Paradise and the Jesse Tree. When Lurçat remarked that he would be unable to represent God convincingly in the Paradise panel, the priest replied simply: "Leave Him out."

[2] It was the supra-individual nature of such a collaboration that especially appealed to Lurçat, the same quality he relishes in his association with the weavers (as Léger did with the artisans who realized his mosaic). The fantasy of a new *artisanat*, which seems to inspire many French Communist artists, appears, like its inspired nineteenth-century prototype, to be somewhat confused and antihistorical.

THE TAPESTRY

What had happened between 1939 and 1945 to cause Lurçat to revise his generally negative attitude toward making a church tapestry? The answer lies in a rapprochement of interests, brought about by the war, between some Communists and clerics (at least the younger and more liberal ones). Though it came to be increasingly exploited by the Communists in the first years of peace, the Resistance had transcended divisions of a religious or political order.[3] And Lurçat was especially aware of the effective work Father Couturier had done for the movement in America. This fact weighed heavily in his final decision to do the tapestry for Assy.

Since 1945, however, in the spreading aura of disillusionment, the liberal branch of the priesthood in France has been forced to give ground. The repression of the Worker-Priests and the "exile" of Dominican intellectuals like the medievalist Father Chenu, a friend of Lurçat, have done much to reopen the inevitable breach between the Church and the Socialists. Lurçat would not be inclined today to create such an ecclesiastical work, he says, and his willingness at the time depended on unique historical circumstances and on the inspiring liberalism and rare purity of faith of Father Couturier. As was the case with Léger, Lurçat's effort was in part the discharge of a deeply felt debt.

Once Lurçat had agreed to make the tapestry, events moved swiftly. He was given a token payment, and the cost of the wool and the weaving were guaranteed by friends of Canon Devémy with the aid of a generous grant from the French Ministry of Fine Arts. (This was personally arranged by Robert Rey, Minister of Fine Arts and an admirer of Lurçat's work.)

Lurçat visited Assy and spent five days studying the architectural setting and the lighting conditions of the sanctuary. Though modern tapestries are often hung as small ornaments on larger walls, functioning decoratively in the same manner as easel paintings,[4] Lurçat conceives of them ideally as

---

[3] On the outside wall of the Dominican convent of St. Pierre in Paris, in which Father Couturier lived, is a bronze plaque commemorating a group of member priests who were executed by the Germans for "acts of patriotism."

[4] The unfortunate confusion of the arts of tapestry and easel painting dates back to Jean-Baptiste Oudry's directorship of the Gobelins. It persists even in the tapestries of such moderns as Braque, Rouault, and Picasso. In the 1920s Madame Cuttoli commissioned the now

inseparable from architecture, as decors that "stop only at the angles of walls, chimneys, and windows." [5] For him architecture forms the only natural setting, determining the shape of the field of the tapestry and to some extent the disposition of its masses. He found the interior at Assy an excellent setting, owing to its simplicity and severity.

Lurçat decided to cover the entire wall surface of the choir-apse area; consequently, the tapestry begins just above the arches and rises to the ceiling, except for its upper corners where vertical rectangles were cut away to allow for the clerestory windows which light the choir (Figure 18). Since the horizontal dimension of this field is disproportionately long, Lurçat, who often has difficulty in sustaining rhythms in his compositions, decided to divide the surface into four distinct zones. The largest (upper center) has a black ground and runs horizontally, parallel to a narrow belt of white ground below it. These two are then enclosed by large vertical fields of red (left) and green (right). This broad division and simple color arrangement established the mood of forthrightness and bold reduction to decorative essentials which persists throughout the elaboration of the tapestry and is a mark of Lurçat's style.

Subjects of symbolic character, like the apocalyptic scene chosen for the main panel, especially recommend themselves to tapestry, where literalness and detail are out of place and where imaginative settings permit the elimination of the horizon line with its perspective illusion, the presence of which tends to interrupt the decorative continuity of a two-dimensional mural art. Moreover, the theme of the Apocalypse has a special significance for Lurçat, as the integration of his mature style owed much to his "discovery" in 1937 of

---

famous tapestries by these painters as well as others by Matisse, Léger, Miro, and Lurçat. What came out were copies of pictures, slow to execute, more costly than original paintings, and without their nuance and finesse. Though the occasional tapestries of most of these artists still remain within the concept and style of an easel painting, the efforts of Madame Cuttoli stimulated Lurçat (and Léger) to search for an answer to the problem of a true tapestry. See Claude Roy, *Jean Lurçat* (Geneva: Pierre Cailler, 1956), p. 28.

[5] Of course, the artist can put this idea into practice only when an important work is specifically commissioned. Most of Lurçat's work is done in normal rectangular shapes and sold to chance buyers through art dealers. When hung, these tapestries have about the same decorative character as a bold abstract painting hung in the middle of a wall.

the magnificent Apocalypse of Angers, a tapestry completed in 1382 for the Duke of Anjou. Though the medieval work retains the horizon line and some perspective details, its antirhetorical character, its simple organization of forms, its cohesiveness on the level of two-dimensional decoration, and, above all, its limitation of the palette to some twenty tones acted as catalysts in Lurçat's search for a counteragent to the prosaic academicism and equation with easel painting that had brought about the decadence of tapestry.

By 1939, his definitive style clearly established, Lurçat began to elaborate his answer to the Angers work, a tapestry which was to be a presentation of "the Apocalypse of *our* times." [6] This was the *Apocalypse of the Mal-Assis,* the unfinished cartoon of which was destroyed by the Germans when they raided Lurçat's studio in 1944. A gouache study, still extant (Figure 19), shows a barren landscape, above which an explosion of cosmic magnitude takes place. Its impact shatters three large chairs, the only foreground objects, which are the "thrones" of the *mal-assis* (uneasily seated), the economic and spiritual exploiters of the people.[7] Peace came not long after the destruction of the cartoon of this secularized apocalypse, and with it the theme was resurrected, this time within the framework of a religious iconography. Once Lurçat had committed himself to do the Assy tapestry, no eligible subject could have been more congenial. He could treat it as a symbolic struggle of good and evil.

Lurçat began to design his Assy cartoon directly in full scale, basing the main panel on John's vision of a heavenly woman threatened by a great red dragon. At the right (Figure 17) of this zone sits a female figure encircled by a giant flaming radiance (denoting that she is "clothed with the sun") and accompanied by a moon "under her feet." The crown of twelve stars described in the text as "upon her head" are treated less literally, being distributed in an astral area compromising the upper region of the circle of the sun. This field of twelve large stars is also enriched by four recessively colored smaller ones, which are not mentioned in the text but which Lurçat introduced to act as foils for the larger stars and to more fully decorate the space.

Saint John says that the woman is "with child," and Lurçat has represented

---

[6] Pierre Hirsch, *Jean Lurçat et la tapisserie* (Paris: Victor Michon, 1946), p. 11.

[7] As he worked on the cartoon during the war, Lurçat came to think of these as members of the hierarchy installed by the conquering Nazis.

this condition by showing the infant within a sphere held directly before the woman's abdomen by her right hand. In her left hand the woman triumphantly holds aloft a globe (not present in the text) which we necessarily read in connection with the circular enclosure of the child and which thus may be taken to be the world that He will save. The woman (traditionally considered the Virgin), the center of liturgy and humanity in the vision, is rather uninventively drawn, with an oversimplified schematism of features that renders her face a caricature (this passage is, not insignificantly, the weakest part of the work).

The predominantly gray dragon occupying the left side of the panel is, on the contrary, one of Lurçat's handsomest inventions (Figure 16). Here the artist began by rejecting outright the color red (retained at Angers) which the text designates for the beast, since (depending on the shade) it would have conflicted with, or bled into the red Paradise panel at the left. This decision is consistent with Lurçat's attitude elsewhere in the work, whereby esthetic judgments take precedence over iconographic accuracy.[8]

John tells us also that the dragon had "seven heads and ten horns, and seven crowns upon his heads." Lurçat carefully follows the text in the number of heads (making one dominant and envisioning the others as outgrowths of the various tails [9]) and goes the text one better in the number of horns.[10] There are many precedents for Lurçat's elimination of the crowns (the Angers tapestry being one), but none for the emblematic cipher he has placed on the body of the beast. It was interpolated by the artist as a symbol of death and malice: Against a blue-green ground the weathered skull of a dead animal is explored by a lizard.[11]

[8] When medieval artists did not conform to the texts, their departures were often determined by needs or aspirations of an extra-esthetic order.

[9] Meyer Schapiro has pointed out a possible source for this arrangement in a monster on the lower band of the lintel (under the right arm of Christ) of the Beaulieu tympanum. Also, three grotesque human heads emerge from the summits of the coils of a serpent at the feet of St. Benedict at Souillac, but here they seem to issue from holes in the serpent and do not grow out in the manner of the Assy and Beaulieu compositions.

[10] This, as distinguished from other departures from the text, seems to have been wholly accidental. Lurçat did not even recall it. However, one cannot imagine such insouciance with respect to iconographic detail in the work of a Catholic artist.

[11] Lurçat studied medieval bestiaries in order to obtain such symbols. He has published a short popular monograph on the bestiary in tapestry testifying to the importance of these

THE TAPESTRY

Below the main black-ground panel with its figures of gray, brown, and pink is a horizontal white-ground field (Figures 16, 17) containing a scene in which the Archangel Michael triumphs over the dragon. Here many iconographic motifs, such as the impaling of the beast, were freely invented by Lurçat. In a shift from the more static heraldry of the upper zone, he introduces a narrative structuring that makes possible a continuity of shapes across the whole field, linking left and right to a degree not attained in the scene above. On the right, the tan body of Michael has been rendered two-dimensionally, a pair of interlocking circles representing his halo (red with small pointed radiances) and his shield (green and light blue with flame-like radiances), have been superimposed on his figure. These flame-like and circular motifs assimilate Michael to the astral forms in the composition above him. His spear penetrates the chest of the dragon and emerges on the far side, severing on its way a number of the monster's subordinate heads (seen flying through space on the left). One of these heads and the end of the dragon's tail form a link to the brown semicircle of the earth on the far left of the panel. This is decorated with stylized trees and a tortoise with a shield-shaped shell. As with Michael on the right, Lurçat attached the earth to the scene above, this time by carrying down the crescent shape of pink containing the "third part of the stars in heaven."

The large red vertical panel bordering the tapestry on the left (Figure 18) is anchored by a circle, again symbolizing the earth, which is subdivided into four fields escutcheoned with emblems of the four "kingdoms" (reading clockwise): the vegetable (grasses and flowers), mineral (rocks), man (upper half of human figure), and animal (ox head and sparrow). From this disk rises a foliate tree entwined with a serpent, which identifies the environment as Paradise. On the right is an exquisitely decorative sequence of animals, including butterflies, ducks, turtles, and birds, culminating in a crowing cock, heroic symbol of rebirth, and more particularly of the Resistance, that dominates Lurçat's private bestiary and is the most familiar subject in his tapestries.

The green vertical panel on the right of the tapestry likewise contains foliate decoration, here in the form of a Jesse Tree, in tan and black with leaves of

texts and illustrations as a source of his private symbolism. See Jean Lurçat, *Le Bestiaire de la tapisserie du moyen âge* (Geneva: Cailler, 1947).

108

brown elaborated by red edges and white veinings. The bearded figure of Jesse, shown from the waist up, anchors the panel and forms the counterpart of the circle of the earth in the left vertical field. Heads with expressions of intense anguish are hung like masks on the tree, but in spite of the existence of a similar motif in oriental literature and art,[12] its use here belongs to the private fantasy of Lurçat. He makes no attempt to identify these heads with figures from religious iconography, and the tree does not culminate in the traditional figure of Christ.

The choice of the twelfth chapter of the Apocalypse for the main panel and, even more, the divided character of the composition as Lurçat conceived it, resulted in a strange and untraditional apse decoration. Normally, at the visual and iconographic apex of a church we find a climactic figure of the faith, generally Christ (often as the Pantocrator) and sometimes, as in Canon Devémy's original plan for Assy, the Madonna in majesty. In any case, the centralized image represents a consummation of the dogmatic drama spelled out in detail elsewhere in the church. The spiritual and esthetic unity expressed by such apse decorations is missing in the Lurçat tapestry, where the middle is empty and the two protagonists of good and evil are represented in almost equal size and importance to the sides of the axis. At Assy we do not have the sense of all experience resolving into a single cohesive scheme, but rather a suggestion of eternal conflict between two opposing forces. A medieval artist would never have placed such a theme in the apse of a church, and even if he had, we may be sure that he would have devised some compositional arrangement clearly demonstrating the triumph of the woman.[13] Though Lurçat himself considers the empty middle "a weakness of the composition," it resulted in part, he says, from his unwillingness to accept the implications of making the woman larger and more central.[14]

[12] This is the Wak-Wak tree whose blossoms were heads. Some Arabic sources describe the heads as wailing. See Gabriel Ferrand, "The Wonderful Wak-Wak Tree," *Encyclopedia of Islam,* fasc. R, pp. 1106–7.

[13] This was true in the Angers tapestry and in the smaller narrative versions of the subject. In the thirteenth-century English Apocalypse, Morgan Library MS/524, fol. 30v, the woman is made large and raised to a dominating, though not central, position in the field.

[14] Canon Devémy suggests quite a different explanation for the divided character of the composition. Recalling that he had asked Lurçat for a work that would remain *au second*

THE TAPESTRY

The Catholic critic Victor-Henri Debidour [15] insists that at Assy "it is the beast that triumphs," but his view is not sustained by the narrative arrangement of the scene or by the relative proportions and disposition of the protagonists. He is correct, however, in so far as the dragon is a fascinating and brilliantly drawn creature (if slightly smaller) in contrast to the pedestrian representation of the woman. Lurçat laughs at the notion that the beast triumphs ("For me, hope always exists"); at the same time he admits that the beast interests him more than the woman. "Remember," he says,

that the men of my generation . . . have been expert at making monsters; this is what we love. In the late twenties I happened to glance at a number of *Cahiers d'art* and was struck by the monstrous aspect of the art of our epoch. . . . All this goes back to the period around the First World War. We were baptized at Verdun. Just as soon as we had gotten over that, came the war in Spain, and hard on its heels the Germans.[16]

Perhaps the Catholic critic Yves Sjöberg is closest to the truth when he argues that "in this composition of binary rhythm, [Lurçat] places in balance the principle of good . . . and the spirit of evil, in the form of a dualism that recalls Manicheanism more than the Catholic triumph of Mary over Satan." [17]

The method Lurçat employed in the realization of the Assy tapestry, a system he established in the late 1930s, consists of outlining all shapes and placing shorthand color references inside the isolated sections. The reference numbers and letters form a private code known to the weavers and stand for the palette of but forty-four colors within which Lurçat does all his work.

---

plan in the decorative scheme and not dominate the altar, he considers the open center of the tapestry Lurçat's response to the necessity of isolating the altar crucifix so that from the nave it will be seen against an unfigured ground.

[15] Debidour, "Autour de l'église d'Assy," in *Problèmes de l'art sacré,* p. 297.

[16] It was at the very time Lurçat was designing the Assy beast that he had to travel to Germany to recover the body of his son, captured while working for the Resistance and killed by the Germans on the last day of the war.

[17] Yves Sjöberg, *Mort et resurrection de l'art sacré* (Paris: Grasset, 1957), p. 125.

It is not without a certain irony that the founder of the Dominican Order should have been distinguished in the crusade against the Albigenses whose heresy revolved around a belief in dualism, a belief of Eastern origin not unrelated to Manichaeanism.

A detail of the child from the original cartoon (Figure 20) shows only the black painted in. The white color of the infant is indicated by the letter B and the ochre of the ground above his circle by the number 16.[18]

This self-imposed limitation of the palette serves many purposes. First, it eliminates the normal margin of color error that occurs when a painterly cartoon is translated into tapestry,[19] since the standardized colors are known beforehand to Lurçat who draws his cartoons with them in mind. But, most important, it gives the tapestry a flat, decorative boldness (chiaroscuro is impossible) and simplicity necessary in works of large size, where the multiplication of colors and nuances results in a "graying out" and an impression of fragmentation and triviality (as in the academic "machines").

With this system Lurçat singlehandedly rescued tapestry from the decadence into which it had fallen through its confusion with the art of painting, a decadence which had begun in the Renaissance and become increasingly marked in the eighteenth century. By 1740, for example, the weavers at the Gobelins factory were using 373 tones; in 1780 they employed 587. The situation had come about in part through the influence of the painter Jean-Baptiste Oudry, named Inspector General of the government tapestry factories in 1733, who instructed tapestry designers to give to their works "all the spirit and intelligence of paintings, in which [art] alone resides the secret of making tapestries of true beauty." [20] To achieve this questionable goal craftsmen at Gobelins were using one thousand tones by the middle of the nineteenth century in translating cartoons made by painters who gave no attention whatsoever to either the special possibilities or the limitations of tapestry. After Chevreul discovered the means of dividing the seven fundamental colors

[18] The seventy or so weavers of Aubusson who execute the tapestries of Lurçat work from a common table of references standardized in 1939. Numbers 1–6 denote grades on the yellow scale; 7–11, tones of gray; 12–16, a scale of ochres, and so forth. Certain colors are indicated by letters, e.g., RF is deep cadmium; Fl, bronze green.

[19] One of Lurçat's first tapestries, *The Harvest,* made before the color system was standardized, differed enormously from the cartoon. Forty-five nuances were dyed to match those of the painted cartoon. Each batch of wool was *almost* the color of the cartoon. But forty-five times "almost" accounted for the tremendous difference. Since then Lurçat has always chosen the colored wools first, basing the cartoon on their values. See Roy, *Jean Lurçat,* p. 30.

[20] Cited in Roy, *Jean Lurçat,* p. 50.

into 14,400 nuances, this enormous scale was put at the disposal of the designers at Gobelins and Beauvais. An almost maniacal exploitation of nuances followed, so that by 1930, when Lurçat was experimenting in the art, three thousand tones were in general use. Since there is a practical minimum to the amount of wool that can be dyed any one color, it was necessary to dye almost seven hundred kilograms in order to obtain just twenty kilograms of a particular off-shade. Tremendous waste thus began even before work on the tapestry proper had commenced—a waste that resulted in astronomical prices for the finished product.

Lurçat's limited and standardized palette not only reduced wool costs but made it possible to recover the cadence of execution established in the thirteenth and fourteenth centuries (one square meter per worker per month, as compared with fifteen to twenty square centimeters per worker per month standard since the eighteenth century), thus further reducing costs and making tapestry more popularly available.[21] But most of all, his limitation of means reinforced the sense of tapestry as a more rude than delicate product, a rough surface where contrasts, general structure, and arabesques rather than the nuances impress the spectator's sensibility. This method, says Lurçat, prevents him from "falling back unconsciously on his training as a painter, chancing chiaroscuro, glazed effects, and plastic processes unrealizable in tapestry."[22]

Perhaps the reasons for the popular success of Lurçat's tapestry at Assy and its consonance with the architectural ensemble are to be found in its collective symbology and simple language. These qualities seem no longer possible in the art of painting, which has become intimate both in its subjects, even the symbolic (as in Surrealism) having assumed a private character, and in its facture. Monumental themes, familiar as late as David and Delacroix, now seem out of place in painting. Tapestry, however, lends itself to such collective reductions of ideas and values. If these often seem banal (and would seem even more so in easel painting), it is nevertheless in this very banality that

[21] In 1956 the retail cost of a Lurçat tapestry was only 110,000 francs, or a little over $250 per square meter. Before the First World War tapestries often cost well over $1,500 per square meter.

[22] Roy, *Jean Lurçat*, p. 60.

tapestry's greatest possible strengths reside. For to the extent that the common-place and collective can be intensified by genius, a truly monumental art will be engendered. In spite of the limitations I feel in regard to the Assy tapestry —its compositional awkwardness and overly decorative character—it has a certain grandeur, a grandeur which the critic René Lacôte rightly insists is to be discovered in the "banality which [Lurçat] renders in its *astonishing primal freshness*." [23]

[23] René Lacôte, "Jean Lurçat et l'avenir de la tapisserie française," *Arts de France,* January, 1951, No. 34, pp. 62–63.

8. THE FAÇADE MOSAIC OF LÉGER

Public and ecclesiastical astonishment, due more to his Communism than to the character of his art, greeted the announcement that Fernand Léger was designing a mosaic mural for the church of Assy. Yet this orientation toward the collective, stronger in Léger than in any other outstanding modern painter, accounts at once for the architectural character of his painting and his interest in the Dominican program.

Given to verbalizing easily on art and other matters, Léger was most explicit in his anticlericalism prior to the Second World War. His "cult of the object" was the core of a materialism rich in poetry, but it naturally precluded any rapprochement with traditional Christianity. For Léger the pure experience of art replaced the "shopworn formulations" of religion. "Your mission," he proclaimed to a gathering of architects in Athens in 1933,

is that of substituting for the sentimental and outmoded church an equivalent work, beautiful in itself, and capable of liberating humanity from the interference of the religions. . . . [We need] a new *cult of the beautiful* that will not be made of vague promises or a problematic future life, but of beautiful, rational, and finite objects one may touch with the hand. . . . The highest power of man consists of understanding the world, virtue, and beauty without the vulgar aid of symbol and the recourse to hidden divinities of the cult of the supernatural such as the Church has foisted on a timid and fearful majority. But this shadowy religion is in its turn in decline.[1]

By the time he delivered that lecture Léger had implemented his position with an esthetic system comprehending, in addition to easel painting, a "second

[1] Fernand Léger, "Discorso agli architetti," reprinted in *Casabella continuita,* September–October, 1955, No. 207, pp. 69–70.

and monumental mode of plastic expression." This was mural painting. Its esthetic was to be bold and simple as befits a public art, and it was to be a function of the disposition of its architectural setting, respecting live surfaces and acting but to overcome dead ones. Color was reinterpreted as an adjunct of architecture, and walls were to be covered by "flat tones organized in a generally abstract composition." [2] By "abstract," in this formulation, Léger meant nonfigurative; in his easel painting he continued to apotheosize objects. Léger located the most important distinction between the mural style and the easel painting in the fact that "mural painting loses its origin of individual creation. It enters into the domain of the collective." [3] Here the artist must forego his absolute independence and submit himself to the rigors of collaboration with the architect and artisan.

Léger considered *La Ville* of 1919, composed primarily with pure flat tones, to be the origin of the "plastic revolution" which led to his architectural decorations. Thereafter, it was possible without chiaroscuro or mixing of colors to obtain a sense of depth and dynamism. Symptomatically, it was in the field of publicity that the new possibilities were first exploited. "The pure tones of blues, reds and yellows escaped from this picture and inscribed themselves on posters, in shop windows. . . . Color was free. It had a completely new action independent of objects, which before this epoch, were charged with containing and holding it." [4]

In the period from 1921 to 1925 Léger's friendship with leading modern architects led to a preliminary practical application of his theories of a new rapport between color and architecture. The Paris Exposition of 1925 offered an opportunity to present these ideas to the public at large. Here Léger was shown (through models) in collaboration with Mallet-Stevens in a "Project for an Embassy" and with Le Courbusier in the "Pavilion of the *Esprit Nouveau.*" But architecture requires money to become a reality, and since neither the French Government nor the other institutions that might have

---

[2] Pierre Descargues, *Fernand Léger* (Paris: Éditions Cercle d'Art, 1955), p. 80.

[3] Léger, "Réflexions sur l'intégration de la peinture et de la sculpture dans l'architecture," *I Quattro Soli,* I, No. 1 (January, 1954), 8.

[4] Léger, "L'Architecture moderne et la couleur," *Formes et vie,* 1951, No. 1.

employed Léger saw much value in his ideas, these never left the drawing board. The great transformations and realignment of values generated by the Second World War had to intervene before this became possible.

Though Father Couturier had long admired Léger's work, he came to know his fellow countryman personally only during their wartime exile in America. The priest sensed a deep correspondence between the aims of Léger's art and the architecturally oriented needs of church decoration. "Since the medieval period," he wrote, "walls have never been covered with this simplicity, these noble striking colors, these large forms of a familiar solemnity." [5] In his turn, Léger was much taken by the vigorous friar, whose ideas on religious experience and religious art were so independent and strikingly argued. The artist "quickly discerned, in this energetic and good person, his high quality as a man and artist." [6] Friendship with Couturier did much to modify Léger's views on the religious community, and, though he never pretended to religious belief, he did temper his previous anticlericalism to the extent that collaboration in a sacred monument became possible. Father Couturier hoped that through personal contact with the dogmas and great subjects of Christianity Léger might be inspired to create a "great work," and the artist assured him that when they returned to France, they would "do a church together," [7] a vague project but one which at the end of the war was suddenly realized.

Having been brought up in an extremely religious environment (so much so that he reacted against it as he grew up [8]), Léger brought somewhat more background to his participation at Assy than Father Couturier had first imagined. His father having died when he was very young, Léger had been sent to a religious school at Tinchebray by his mother ("a holy woman who spent many hours of her life . . . praying . . . for me"). [9] Now, nearing

[5] Couturier, "Léger et le moyen âge," in *Fernand Léger: La Forme humaine dans l'espace* (Montreal: Éditions de l'Arbre, 1945), p. 16.

[6] "Letter from Léger," *L'Art sacré,* March–April, 1954, No. 7–8, p. 6.

[7] Descargues, *Fernand Léger,* p. 126.

[8] Léger, "Sens de l'art moderne" (interview), *Zodiaque,* I, No. 18–19 (January, 1954), 36–40.

[9] Descargues, *Fernand Léger,* p. 7.

seventy, he was to speak to clerics of his respect for those who have need for religion, and particularly of his admiration for the great saints. But he never relented in his conviction that the Church, i.e., religion adopted socially and "organized in liaison with the dominating bourgeoisie," is still "too far from Christ." "I do not feel the need for moral support," he proclaimed to the monks of La Pierre-qui-vire. "I love the dangerous life, the one which we [modern painters] lead." [10]

It was natural that Léger's interest in the "transformation of the wall through color" should have led him to study Byzantine mosaics, and it was his increasing fascination with this medium that determined its choice at Assy. Ever since his trip to Italy in 1924 the one-time architectural assistant had deeply admired Byzantine art, particularly the integration of its architecture and decoration. "With the Byzantines," Léger observed, "architectural sense went before everything else. . . . They did not use the third dimension. And thus instead of destroying the wall they respected it." [11] Yet in spite of Léger's interest in the Byzantine and passing characterizations of him as a "byzantine mosaicist," [12] the gaiety, brightness, open organization, and frank absence of mystery of the Assy façade reveal him as quite opposite to the Byzantines in spirit. [13]

Léger realized that the medium of mosaics has been rendered almost obsolete by modern social evolution inasmuch as our architecture is no longer

[10] Léger, "Sens de l'art moderne," *Zodiaque*, II, No. 18–19 (January, 1954), 36–40.

[11] Léger, "Byzantine Mosaics and Modern Art," *Magazine of Art*, XXXVII, No. 4 (April, 1944), 144–45. Here Léger's views seem somewhat inadequate. If the Byzantines did not destroy the two-dimensional integrity of the wall through a perspective device, they did tend to compromise its plasticity by dematerialization through light. Often, moreover, their fields of decoration were antiarchitectural in arrangement, as, for example, in the choir and apse of San Vitale, Ravenna.

[12] E.g., Descargues, *Fernand Léger*, p. 59.

[13] In fact, the individuation of shapes and other qualities in the Assy mosaic link him more to the Romanesque than other historical styles and account, perhaps, for the happy integration of his façade mosaic in a church of neo-Romanesque architectural character. Léger prefers the twelfth-century French to the Byzantine. "Those [Romanesque] artists," he said admiringly, "loved their métier, and they created a magnificent collective work." "Sens de l'art moderne," *Zodiaque*, II, No. 18–19 (January, 1954), 36–40.

constructed with an eye to permanence and durability, so important in older times when it constituted an assertion of the perpetuity of institutions. Thus it was not surprising that his interest in this medium would eventually lead him to consider decorating a church building, the symbol of a relatively static institution in an otherwise dynamic civilization, and thus one of the few likely locales for an enduring monumental work.

In the 1930s Léger's interest in mosaics had been further stimulated when Auguste Perret [14] showed him new materials, including opaque tesserae of very intense colors, more in the scale of Léger's palette than those previously available. Léger considered other limitations of the medium surmountable and even conducive to a high form of art since they discourage facility and cleverness. "The more restricting the medium, the more difficult the artist's invention—but the more stimulated." [15]

But though Léger had "always wanted to execute a great mosaic mural," [16] it was only during his sojourn in the United States, and partially as a result of his germinal contact with Father Couturier, that the possibility began to come alive.

In 1945 Father Couturier decided on the church of Assy as the site of Léger's first religious collaboration. But it was not until the following year that previously negotiated projects were set aside, and Léger was given the entire western façade to decorate. "At last, a wall," he exclaimed as he finally

[14] The name of Auguste Perret is inseparable from the revival of religious architecture in France. At a time (1923) when sacred painting was still *en pleine décadence,* Perret built one of the first concrete churches, Notre-Dame-de-Raincy, a magnificent edifice "which is incontestably the prototype of modern religious architecture." Pichard, *L'Art sacré moderne,* p. 40. Most recently, he figured as architectural consultant for the Dominican chapel in Vence decorated by Matisse.

In connection with Notre-Dame-de-Raincy, Perret worked out a wall system composed of thick translucent pieces of colored glass embedded in concrete. This was the origin of the method used (1950–52) by Léger for his windows at Audincourt.

[15] Léger, "Byzantine Mosaics and Modern Art," *Magazine of Art,* XXXVII, No. 4 (April, 1944), 144–45. But while mosaics discourage facility and cleverness, they also preclude a personalized manipulation of the matière and an esthetic refinement which less group-oriented modern painters would not care to sacrifice.

[16] *Ibid.*

118

stood before the church. But his joy was tempered by the dismaying discovery that the field of the façade was partially hidden by the eight large granite columns supporting the overhanging roof. Léger reconciled himself to these, however, and to the nine small windows perforating the façade. He diagrammed the placement of the pillars and the manner in which they cast shadows during different hours, planning to take this into consideration in working out his cartoon.

Father Couturier and Canon Devémy had selected the litany of the Virgin as the subject for the mosaic. This was appropriate for the church, which is dedicated to the Virgin,[17] and for Léger, because the text refers to various symbolic objects. Besides, as the painter himself observed, a multiple rather than a unified subject would be more easily adapted to a field broken up by columns. After discussing the text with Canon Devémy, Léger took the plan of the façade and a diagram of the locations of the pillars and windows and returned north to his studio at Gif-sur-Yvette where he began work on the studies.

The field at Léger's disposal was 20.6 meters (67 ft. 7 in.) long across the base, with its gabled top reaching a height of 10 meters (32 ft. 9½ in.) at the apex. The left and right sides of the field are demarcated by spur walls, rising to a height of 3.2 meters (10 ft. 6 in.), which come forward to join the outer columns. Just above the rusticated granite border running along the base and around the door are six small windows, evenly spaced so as to fall opposite the intercolumniations. At the tribune level, roughly two-thirds the center height of the field, are three small windows spaced so as to fall between the four central columns.

Léger curiously disregarded a major asset of the text in the earlier states of the design by not showing the objects used as metaphors for the Virgin in the litany. Both the water-color sketch (Figure 21) and the maquette for the First State consist of an irregular mountainous landscape spanning the entire width of the field. Here Léger thought to assimilate the façade to the alpine

[17] As the congregation of Assy is composed largely of convalescents, the concluding prayer of the litany is most appropriate. Here the intercession of the Virgin is beseeched to insure "perpetual health of mind and body."

119

environment which the gabled roof also recapitulates. Simple forms of green foliage sprout from four tiers of hills, and above the portal a symmetrically featured and coiffed Virgin peers out of an ornamental radiance. On the right, the sun, with long and sharply pointed rays, rises above the landscape. Six motifs from the litany of the Virgin (the *Tour d'Ivoire* [Tower of Ivory], *Vase d'Honneur* [Vessel of Honor], *Étoile du Matin* [Morning Star], *Arche d'Alliance* [Ark of the Covenant], *Maison d'Or* [House of Gold], and *Port du Ciel* [Gate of Heaven]) are represented only by printed titles, which are distributed rather symmetrically across the field, four superimposed on the landscape and two on the sky. The possibilities of lettering, so skillfully exploited in Léger's canvases about the time of the First World War, are here strangely neglected, and, indeed, the whole design does not show him at his best.

The most significant compositional change revealed by the water-color study for the Second State [18] (Figure 23), in contrast to the First State and its variant [19] is the hieratic reaffirmation of the Virgin through the higher placement of her head (now without the medallion) and the correspondingly lower and decentralized location of the sun. The irregular arabesques radiating from the Virgin are more complicated here than in the variant, and they have a brighter and more richly diversified color scheme, containing two tones of blue, dark and light orange, yellow, green, brown, and white. For the first time in these sketches, a long straight line has been introduced, serving here as the horizon which truncates the rising sun at the left. In both the First State and the variant there are no straight lines of any length; no doubt Léger felt there that he had to contrast his forms to the rigid articulation of the columnar grid cutting across the surface of the mosaic.

The sketch for the Third State (Figure 24) introduces a wholly new conceit. The major iconographic elements of the previous formulations—Virgin,

[18] A water-color variant of the First State exists (Figure 22), in which the locations of the sun and the Virgin's head have been exchanged.

[19] The larger gouache maquettes for the first four states correspond in all details to the water colors except where otherwise specified. They are more tightly painted and contain no *pentimenti*.

120

FERNAND LÉGER, *The Virgin of the Litany*
DEFINITIVE STUDY FOR THE MOSAIC, WEST FAÇADE

landscape, sun, and titles of the litanies—have all been eliminated. Only the irregularly overlapping curvilinear areas remain, and these have been enlarged in size and dispersed so as to cover the entire surface of the field. They are demarcated either by narrow black lines or by two types of black and white striped border patterns that wind their way across the field like giant snakes. Gargantuan stalks and blossoms fan out over the flat color areas to half the height of the façade. But since these flowers are associated with small forms by the viewer, the entire façade seems considerably dwarfed. It was no doubt this error of scale, of a type familiar in ancient Egyptian architectural decoration, that led to the total rejection of this Third State.

In the Fourth State (Figure 25) Léger returned to the motif of the Virgin in a full circle medallion (as in the variant) centrally located above the door (as in the First State). Here, for the first time, he experimented with a formulation using less than the whole field of the façade. An abstract pattern of parallelograms fans out from points on a vertical central axis. These color panels are alternately yellow, blue, and a grid pattern of blue and white. The whole composition is bordered in orange. The residual area of the field was to be left in the original whitewash surface of the façade.

Converging on the Virgin are four segmented medallions, patterned like those of the First State and located symmetrically on the blue and yellow fields. Their segmentation, caused by the successive overlapping of the planes, gives a slight sense of forward projection to the Virgin's medallion. Léger has here abandoned not only the iconography of the Litany (as in the previous state), but also the cosmic and natural symbols, in favor of isolating the Madonna.

Though this Fourth State is striking in its simple radiant pattern, it is unlikely that it would have harmonized well with the columns of the porch, and its insistent symmetry seems rather dry in comparison with both the earlier and final states.

The definitive maquette (see plate) is far more intense in invention than any of the previous designs. Though the Madonna remains in a central medallion, the irregular polygonal panels that constitute the remainder of the composition counteract the symmetry of the field in their "random" placement. The notion of employing only part of the façade was carried over from the Fourth State, but, in place of the regular radiating pattern, giant colored polygons now spread upward and outward across the surface like an expanding puzzle.

For the first time, the objects celebrated in the litany are imaged alongside their printed titles. Executed in white and set in the various colored polygons are (on the left) the *Rose Mystique, Vase d'Honneur, Trône de la Sagesse, Étoile du Matin,* (on the right) *Arche d'Alliance, Miroir de Justice,* and *Tour de David.* To these symbols, all of which were present as titles in previous states, a foliage design representing the *Jardin Fleuri* has been added. The irregular silhouettes of these objects (even the sides of the *Tour de David* have been bowed out) provide a piquant contrast to the straight-edged contours of the color panels.

These representational elements play a secondary role, however, and the primary impression of the definitive state is nonfigurative. Admitting the presence of such figuration only exceptionally in mural art, Léger insisted that the objects represented in such cases would have to be "integrated in the abstract nonfigurative spirit . . . for they are a secondary consideration, and it is the abstract conception that remains dominant. Such figuration is introduced then uniquely as an element of variety." [20]

Perhaps the most striking characteristic of the definitive state of the mosaic is the subtle variety in the shapes, colors, and distribution of the forms. Though Léger reinforces the symmetrical and hieratic character of the façade field in his axial placement of the Virgin, he disperses the remainder of the shapes, no two of which are alike, with a taste for freedom and asymmetry. The entire design is delicately asymmetrical, being weighted to the left side of the central axis where the percentage of façade area covered by mosaic is greater than on the right. Of the eighteen color panels, the orange one above the Virgin's head is roughly on the center axis, nine are to the left of that axis, and only eight to the right. Léger compensated for this quantitative asymmetry by placing slightly brighter and more expanding colors in panels to the right of the axis (light blue as opposed to dark blue) and by giving them more broken and hence more visually engaging silhouettes. So marked

[20] Léger, "Sens de l'art moderne," *Zodiaque,* II, No. 18–19 (January, 1954), 36–40.

is the individuation of shapes that in spite of the straight-edged character of the color polygons, not one of them proves to be a regular geometrical form.

Only the definitive composition shows Léger at his best. The artist himself admitted to "romanticizing and softening [his] usual composition" [21] in the earlier sketches. Since Father Couturier had a major role in the final determination, the result at Assy is testimonial to his taste. "His judgments on the sketches [for the façade]," wrote Léger, "were rapid and correct." [22]

The creation of the definitive maquette marked the end of Léger's collaboration with Couturier and signaled the beginning of a new one with the artisans of the Maison Gaudin in Paris, who actually executed the mosaic. Léger recalled his fruitful association with the artisans with somewhat exaggerated and perhaps politically inspired nostalgia. "I knew nothing of the technique of mosaic," he overmodestly proclaimed.

I learned from the workers and put my confidence in them. They found extraordinary nuances of blue for me. They were happy really to do something, not to be just executors but to participate in the creation of a work. They telephoned me all the time: "Monsieur Léger, come and see—we have found this, we have found that." And it was always marvelously right. Ah, the French workers! [23]

The artisans demonstrated how the use of tesserae of but one shade throughout a single-colored panel would result in dryness, and Léger agreed that the polygons would have to be "vibrated" through the introduction of a number of tesserae of neighboring "fugitive" tones. He decided to distribute these in straight lines at irregular intervals, forming patterns of squares and rectangles (Figure 27A). Such tesserae are always lighter than the local color. In the blue-green, for example, they are a lighter yellow-green; in the orange, a yellow-orange; and in the yellow, a light lemon. At the normal distance from the façade the spectator is, of course, unaware of them.

In May, 1949, the mosaic was shipped to Assy and installed. For purposes of transportation and installation the tesserae were pasted face down on the reversed working cartoon, which was then cut into manageable sections. After

[21] "Notre-Dame-de-Toute-Grâce" (An interview with Léger), *Vogue* (Paris), March, 1948 (Léger File, Museum of Modern Art).

[22] Letter from Léger, *L'Art sacré*, March–April, 1954, No. 7–8, p. 6.

[23] Descargues, *Fernand Léger*, p. 127.

the tesserae had been inserted section by section into the rapid drying cement of the façade, acid was used to remove the paper from the front face and the glass was polished.

As might be expected, a number of minor changes took place while the definitive maquette was translated into the cartoon which served for the finished work (Figure 26). The white cement bands containing the black tesserae titles of the symbolic objects were widened, and the title *Fontaine Scellée* was placed on the side of the orange panel at the top center of the mosaic. Since this symbol is not imaged, the isolation of the title suggests that Léger considered the field as unbounded and capable of expansion. Thus the figuration of the *Fontaine Scellée* would hypothetically appear in a panel beyond the boundaries of the present composition.

Most of the changes made in the working cartoon relate to the design of the Virgin's head and her medallion (Figure 27B). In the definitive maquette she is surrounded by a halo of gold rays on a white ground, which is in turn inserted concentrically in a larger medallion form. This medallion form consists of a meandering pattern and an alternation of black and white rectangles, recalling elements in the First and Fourth States. Some time in the course of the actual execution of the mosaic Léger made new drawings for the head of the Virgin and the medallion. The mosaicists recall the existence of these drawings, but there is no record of them. It is probable that they were destroyed by Léger.

Whatever the number of and fate of these drawings, they resulted in a new design in which the Virgin's halo was bordered by a meandering pattern from which emanate large curvilinear flaming forms whose tips touch the outer boundary of the medallion. The visage of the Virgin, which had remained simple and relatively inarticulate in the sketches and maquettes, is here conceived with a powerful sense of linear decision and a delicate asymmetry of features, contrasting with the rigid frontality of the head. The hair, which hung loosely in all the previous designs, is now caught, peasant fashion, in a kerchief knotted at the neck. It falls lower on the Virgin's right side, an emphasis reinforced by the lowering of the Virgin's right eye and eyebrow and the slight contraction of its size.

124

While the tesserae of the color panels are glass, those of the central medallion are colored marbles. The ground is white marble, and the patterns are delineated in black. A slightly pink marble has been used for the face.

The pure bright colors of the mosaic have a tremendous visual impact, particularly when viewed against the winter snows. And though these colors have been attacked by a leading conservative authority on church art as being those of children's crayons,[24] it is precisely in this naïveté and frankness of handling that the spirituality of the mosaic resides. Its pure color chords rupture continuity with the surrounding natural world and call the spectator to a different, more intense level of experience. In contrast to the faded color modulations familiar in traditional church art, Léger provides a color scheme that is eminently robust and healthy, qualities not without importance in a church created for a congregation of the sick.[25]

Critical reaction to the Léger mosaic has been predictably partisan. With the exception of the Dominicans of *L'Art sacré,* most writers within the Church have reserved for it a scorn second only to that lavished on the Richier crucifix. To Debidour, for example, the whole work is "indefensible." [26] Scortesco [27] considers the head of the Virgin "a blasphemy," and Ochsé is content to dismiss her as a "vulgar and not too intelligent call-girl." [28] Members of the Assy congregation, on the other hand, rank the mosaic with the tapestry of Lurçat and the windows of Rouault as one of the finest works of the ensemble, and the curé tells us that it is especially popular with the local shepherds who come down from the mountains with their flocks and stand before the colorful façade "touts contents." [29]

[24] Debidour, "Autour de l'église d'Assy," in *Problèmes de l'art sacré.*

[25] The peculiarly hardy and salutary character of Léger's art is no doubt related to his peasant origins and a childhood spent close to the land. Christian Zervos, "Fernand Léger," *Cahiers d'art,* 8th year, No. 3–4, 1933, pages unnumbered. Léger long speculated about the therapeutic possibilities of color, and "polychrome hospitals" and the "cure by colors" ("Architecture moderne et la couleur," *Formes et vie,* 1951, No. 1, pp. 24–28) occupied him in the last year of his life.

[26] Debidour, "Autour de l'église d'Assy," in *Problèmes de l'art sacré.*

[27] Scortesco, *Saint Picasso peignez pour nous,* p. 61.

[28] Ochsé, *La Nouvelle Querelle des images,* p. 103.

[29] Descargues, *Fernand Léger,* p. 128.

9. THE LIPCHITZ VIRGIN

The story of Jacques Lipchitz's monumental sculpture of *Notre-Dame-de-Liesse* begins with the Retrospective of his work held in Paris (Galerie Maeght) in 1946. There the astonished sculptor was approached at the opening by a representative of the church of Assy who suggested that he make a Madonna for the church. When he asked: "Do you know that I am a Jew?" the cleric replied, "If it doesn't bother you, it doesn't bother us."

Pleased by this attitude, Lipchitz decided to consider the project, and during the following months, as he traveled through France in search of pieces left behind in his hurried wartime flight to the United States, the idea of creating a Virgin for a Catholic church intrigued him more and more. It was early in 1947, after he had returned to New York, that Lipchitz first spoke with Father Couturier, who was then on a return trip to the Americas.[1] He had known the priest slightly before the war and had great sympathy with his experiment at Assy.

When Couturier raised the question of a sculpture of the Virgin, Lipchitz replied that he would be willing to do it, but only under certain conditions. He had given the matter a great deal of thought since the first proposal, and wanted to place a special inscription on the piece. Should this be agreeable to the Dominican, further negotiations could take place. The text of the inscription, now on the posterior of the sculpture, reads: "Jacob Lipchitz, Jew, faith-

---

[1] This meeting with Father Couturier and the establishment of the commission took place in the United States in 1947 and not during Lipchitz's trip to France, as suggested by Larrea ("An Open Letter to Jacques Lipchitz," *College Art Journal*, XIII, No. 13 [Summer, 1954], 251–88) and Segy ("The Meaning of Jacques Lipchitz' Sculpture"; typescript).

126

ful to the religion of his ancestors, has made this Virgin to foster understanding between men on earth that the life of the spirit may prevail." [2]

Father Couturier took the inscription under advisement, not wishing, evidently, to authorize such an arrangement independently. Four months later he sent Lipchitz a very enthusiastic letter, not only accepting the inscription, but praising the spirit that dictated it. There followed a series of negotiations in which it was established that the sculpture was to be mounted on a baptismal font for which Lipchitz was provided with approximate dimensions. The sculptor informed Father Couturier that he preferred not to accept money for the piece and for this reason he would have to sandwich the work between his regular commissions. The church was to pay only the foundry costs, and three casts were authorized.[3]

For many months Lipchitz busied himself with other work, hoping all the time that some idea would develop that might serve as a starting point for his Madonna. But nothing came. Then one day early in January, 1948, while riding in the New York City subway, he had a "vision" which provided the nucleus of the Virgin of Assy. Having no sketch pad with him, the sculptor took out a tiny address book and made two small pencil sketches (Figure 28A). The first of these, on the lower part of the left page (the drawing above it is unrelated), established the basic "tear" shape of what was to become the Virgin's canopy, and introduced the sacrificial lamb below. In the drawing

[2] "Jacob Lipchitz, juif fidèle à la foi de ses ancêtres, a fait cette Vierge pour la bonne entente des hommes sur la terre afin que l'esprit règne."

[3] An interesting series of events is connected with the second cast, events which to us may may seem simply fortuitous, but which to Lipchitz, for whom the entire creation of this Virgin is permeated with a sense of mystery, had a special significance. Not long after his participation at Assy was publicly announced, he received a strange letter from a lady in Texas asking if it might he possible to have Lipchitz's Virgin for a private religious celebration. The piece not yet having been created, Lipchitz replied that it was, of course, impossible. The exchange of letters, however, led eventually to the purchase of the second cast by this lady, who turned out to be a descendent of Robert Owen, and who presented it to the Utopian Socialist village of New Harmony. That the piece should have found such a home especially pleased Lipchitz, and the phrase "New Harmony" seemed to him at the time an apt description of his own spirit. The third cast will soon be placed in the monastery founded by St. Colomba on the Scottish Isle of Iona.

at the right the animal was moved to the interior of the canopy, its place being taken by a series of vague supports, later to become the Archangels. Upon his return to the studio, Lipchitz proceeded to make a series of eleven pencil drawings (Figures 28B, 28C, 28D) developing this first idea to a point approaching the five small-scale models that preceded the large sculpture.[4]

The tear-shaped canopy, which evolves into what Lipchitz refers to as the "three parts of heaven," is the nucleus of the conceit and remains the single consistent element throughout the metamorphosis of the vision. The shape is associated with Lipchitz's conviction that for the Catholic, the world is what Lipchitz calls a Marian vision of "a vale of tears." One understands easily the poetic process by which, as the first vision clarified, the Virgin emerged from the center of the tear-shaped form.

But just as in Lipchitz's life periods of suffering have been transcended by others of optimism and joy, so from the reading of the canopy as a tear, we progress to a new association: the flower bud. The artist himself has observed the relationship between the Virgin of Assy and the bronze called *Blossoming* completed in the year 1942 (Figure 29). Here the curved parts of the "tear" or "inverted heart" shape seem like petals of a blossom opening to reveal a pistil in the process of being anthropomorphosed into a woman's body. The breast and arms are clearly identifiable, and the dual stems below the blossom can be read as legs. Since the Virgin has been traditionally associated with flowers, it was logical that Lipchitz's Virgin should have evolved unconsciously from earlier experiments in floral anthropomorphism.

Still another linkage with the floral motif may be perceived by comparing the Virgin of Assy with the ink study (Figure 30) for *Spring,* a small bronze completed in 1942.[5] Here the petal segments are closed at the top, and the shape is very similar to that of the Virgin's cartouche. In the center, furthermore, may be seen developing the nucleus of the vague anthropomorphic form present also in the earliest sketches for the Assy work, before the shape and pose of the Virgin were clarified.

[4] These drawings are extensively reproduced and analyzed in the Columbia University doctoral dissertation on which the present book is based.

[5] Cf. *The Drawings of Jacques Lipchitz* (New York: Curt Valentin, 1944).

128

Associations to spring, growth, and budding carry us naturally to the idea of birth, so inseparable from the Mother of God. In this connection it is significant that the shape of the canopy of the Assy Virgin is related, as Segy observes,[6] to the lower part of *Cradle I,* a sculpture dealing with the idea of maternity and inspired by the birth at that time of Lipchitz's daughter.

It is in *Cradle I* also that the dove, so important for all but the earliest versions of *Notre-Dame-de-Liesse,* is first encountered. This symbol, which Lipchitz calls "a feeling of happiness," leads by association through other of the sculptor's works to a suggestion of the personage absent from *Notre-Dame-de-Liesse* but inseparable from the concept of the Virgin Mother: her Son. The shape given the dove at Assy is a most familiar one in the last twenty-five years of Lipchitz's sculpture, and its strange recurrence is without question connected to a mysterious and hallucinatory experience in which the artist was deeply moved by a cloud in the form of a bird with outstretched wings.[7] Lipchitz used this vision as the starting point for a number of sculptures joining mother and son, from the birdlike *Mother and Child* of 1930 to that of 1941, a monumental bronze in which the wings of the bird have been transmuted into the outstretched arms of the mother.

Many associations to maternity anticipating the Assy Virgin were present, then, in the evolution of Lipchitz's sculpture as far back as 1929, and the elaboration of this theme in recent years was given impetus by the sculptor's marriage, the birth of his child, and the resultant happiness.[8] The commission for the Madonna could not have come at a more propitious moment. As the consummation of a long, many-leveled process developing within the oeuvre of the artist, it became a work whose simple forms contain an intense concentration of symbols.

By the time Lipchitz had completed the drawings, the main iconographic constituents were clearly established: The dove of the Holy Ghost flying earthward catches in his beak the tripartite "canopy" of the heavens, supported

[6] Ladislas Segy, "The Meaning of Jacques Lipchitz' Sculpture" (typescript), p. 212.

[7] This event is described in Juan Larrea, "An Open Letter to Jacques Lipchitz," *College Art Journal,* XIII, No. 13 (Summer, 1954), 251–88.

[8] The title chosen by Lipchitz for his work at Assy, "Our Lady of Joy," is symptomatic in this connection.

from below by Archangels, and from the center of which emerges the Virgin, her hands outstretched in a gesture of reception. These elements remain constant throughout the five small models, dating from 1947 to 1950, which were made primarily to experiment with the relationship of sculptures to variously shaped baptismal fonts (Figure 31).

These models were succeeded by the large maquette (Figure 32A), a photograph of which was sent to the Dominican Fathers, whose approval it met. Though made without a baptismal font, this sculpture was equipped for such location by its long curved legs of proportions resembling those of Model I (though the forms here are narrower and have a lighter and more graceful appearance).

Throughout the year 1951 Lipchitz was occupied with translating this maquette into the full-scale definitive Plastaline model to be used for casting (Figure 32B). But in January, 1952, as he was making final corrections, his studio was completely gutted by fire. This misfortune involved much more than *Notre-Dame-de-Liesse,* for the fire destroyed many finished sculptures and casts, and overnight Lipchitz saw the labor of many years torn from his *oeuvre.*

It is typical of the man that he rose above the tragedy. With the aid of friends he was able to build his present studio at Hastings-on-Hudson and to resume work. In retrospect, the positive spiritual impact of the fire has proved greater than the loss involved, and Lipchitz's meditations on the disaster have been steeped in mystery. One of its by-products was the magnificent *Virgin in Flames* (Figure 33), more beautiful than the definitive work, which the sculptor created not long after the fire. While contemplating the charred ruins of his studio, Lipchitz imagined how his Plastaline model must have looked as it was consumed in flames. The *Virgin in Flames* shows the Plastaline model standing on the rectangular work table (the remains of which Lipchitz studied very carefully) while flames break out from all its parts. Larrea associates this vision with Lipchitz's Old Testament heritage and calls the sculpture the "flower of the burning bush." The sculptor agrees with his assertion that the fire was "a most incomprehensible chance or sign event, a baptism of fire as the people of Israel experienced it under the unextinguished resonances of

130

the Prophet Zachariah, in the German crematories." [9] "I did it to remember," said Lipchitz of the *Virgin in Flames.*

When he resumed work on a Virgin for Assy, Lipchitz sensed that the piece could never be the same. Long troubled by the necessity of omitting the sacrificial Lamb, he now took the fire as a kind of heavenly omen and came to the conclusion that the Virgin "did not want to be born without the Lamb." Shortly afterward he received a communication from Father Couturier announcing that the sculpture would not be put in the baptistry, as Chagall had offered a ceramic mural that would be hidden by the large Lipchitz piece. For Lipchitz this was happy news for it freed him from the restrictions imposed by the font, and again he read it as a kind of omen in favor of returning the Lamb to his sculpture.

It was in May, 1953, when Lipchitz had settled in his new studio, that he resumed work on a second large Plastaline model which, cast in bronze, was delivered to the church on July 16, 1955. Aside from the inclusion of the Lamb, this definitive piece (Figures 35, 36) differs in many minor respects from the Plastaline model destroyed in the fire. Emerging clearly now from under the hood of the Virgin is a nose handled so as to suggest that the remainder of the physiognomy is lost in the shadow. The wings of the Archangels below have been simplified and somewhat shortened so as not to detract from the figure of the Lamb on whose curved prone body the feet of the Archangels now rest. The Lamb is arranged so that his head is in the front central axis of the piece, turned upwards toward the Virgin, with eyes closed and neck outstretched as if at the moment of his sacrifice. The delicate asymmetry, present already in the earliest models (the left side of the Virgin's canopy is slightly higher and slightly narrower), has been retained, and the surface of the canopy is articulated with six-pointed stars of David cut angularly into its thickness.

While the decision to let Chagall design the baptistry decoration freed Lipchitz from the restrictions imposed by the baptistry font, it also raised a serious question as to where a monumental piece of this order could be satisfactorily located within the church. Lipchitz would have liked the *Notre-Dame-*

[9] Larrea, "An Open Letter to Jacques Lipchitz," *College Art Journal,* XIII, No. 13 (summer, 1954), 251–88. A second sculpture related to the fire is the *Lesson of a Disaster* (Figure 34).

de-Liesse to be in an intimate architectural setting, perhaps in a chapel constructed especially for it, with simple whitewashed walls which he hoped would in time be covered by *ex votos* of the faithful. As he worked on the sculpture, he imagined it lit by flickering candles and surrounded by people in prayer. Father Couturier thought the sculpture might be placed in the choir to the left of the altar, but soon after its arrival at Assy Canon Devémy and Novarina decided to place it in the south section of the narthex (see plan), not far from the entrance to the baptistry, where it is framed by two Rouault windows. It thus symmetrically balances the spiral staircase leading to the tribune on the north side of the narthex.

Though Lipchitz is a religious Jew, he says that he experienced the image of the Madonna as intensely as any deriving from the Old Testament. This does not mean he is a pantheist or insensitive to differences between religions. He once roundly criticized Father LaFarge at a religious art seminar for suggesting that a Buddhist sculpture which filled him [LaFarge] with religious feeling might be well placed in a Catholic church. Religions, Lipchitz argued, are built on definite philosophies, and the Christian and Buddhist points of view are at odds. In the case of Judaism and Christianity, however, he does not admit such a distinction. While making his Virgin, he felt "really concerned with the Catholic point of view," but this was easy to feel because "we belong to one Judeo-Christian Western tradition. For me it's the same thing, a kind of direct continuation." [10]

But from the beginning Lipchitz was concerned that his participation in the church of Assy, intended as an act of universal good will, would be misunderstood as a repudiation of his own religious views. The degree to which conversions from amongst the Jews were publicly exploited, and the manner in which Matisse, who remained an atheist until his death, was reported in certain circles as having been converted,[11] aroused in Lipchitz a fear for the

---

[10] The element which especially attracts Lipchitz in Catholicism is the importance given the figure of the Mother. Fundamental in the *oeuvre* of the sculptor, the maternal theme is relatively neglected in the Old Testament.

[11] Cf. p. 157. The falsification of Matisse's sentiment in regard to his Chapel of the Rosary are cited and discussed in Alfred Barr, *Matisse: His Art and His Public* (New York: Museum of Modern Art, 1951), p. 287.

132

integrity of his position. This anxiety prompted him to make the inscription a condition of his acceptance of the commission. His fears seemed confirmed when *L'Art sacré* falsely reported [12] that Lipchitz had *asked* to be allowed to participate at Assy instead of having been *invited* to do so by church officials.

Unlike most of the other participants at Assy, Lipchitz kept the congregation, its character, and its needs in mind throughout the creation of his work. This concern accounts in part for his belief that religious art should be "readable"—though not necessarily at first glance. Accordingly, he pressed the realism of *Notre-Dame-de-Liesse,* he says, "as far as my esthetic permits." He considers it "eminently legible."

This emphasis on readability is bound up with Lipchitz's belief in the importance of subject matter in religious art and, for that matter, his increasing sense of its importance in all aspects of art. In his early Cubist style, and in fact up until the years 1926–27, the formal element was paramount. With the *Joie de Vivre* of 1927 came the real beginning of the stress on subject matter which for the sculptor represents a more direct attachment to his human audience.

The process of Lipchitz's art is bound up with a sense of participation in the spiritual. "When working," he says, "I am linked to the entire cosmos. By rhythm I am linked to time, by volume I am linked to space, and by the subject-matter I am linked to human beings, to their sufferings and joys. And through the feeling of creation I am bound to our Lord himself. From this comes the fascination of work and also the feeling of responsibility."

[12] *L'Art sacré,* May–June, 1950, p. 8. Father Couturier subsequently sent his apologies for the error.

10. THE BAPTISTRY DECORATIONS BY CHAGALL

Marc Chagall's decision to undertake the decoration of the baptistry of Notre-Dame-de-Toute-Grâce was in part the outgrowth of his long friendship with Jacques and Raïssa Maritain and, through them, of a more recent acquaintance with Father Couturier. Chagall came to know the Maritains in the 1920s, a time when French art and culture were going through a period of conservatism, even reaction, partly in response to the disorder engendered by the war. If the conservatism in the air was reflected in Picasso's turning from the ascetic Cubism of 1909–13 to more decorative forms of abstraction and even to neo-Classicism, for other artists and intellectuals it took the form of a receptiveness to religion.[1] Men who had been leaders of the pre-war avant-garde were converted or reconverted to Catholicism. Max Jacob and later Severini and Satie were baptized, but perhaps the most notable convert was Jean Cocteau, whose acceptance of the sacraments constituted a personal triumph for his friend Maritain.[2]

[1] Historical and psychological causes of a similar order no doubt account in part for the relative conservatism and widespread religious interest prevalent in the West since the Second World War. It seems significant that the initial revival of Catholic art was heralded during the First World War by Cingria and then realized in action by various groups of modernistic religious artists in the following decade. Again, during the Second World War, the Dominicans established the program which led to Assy, Audincourt, Vence, and Ronchamp in the years just after the war.

[2] In 1926 considerable attention was drawn to the renascence of Catholicism among French intellectuals by a public exchange of book-length annotated letters between Jean Cocteau and Jacques Maritain. In his *Lettre à Jacques Maritain* (Paris: Stock, 1926), Cocteau recounted

134

Though Chagall had painted a *Calvary* in 1912, references to religion in his painting previous to the late 1920s bore the marks of a private nostalgic folklorism rather than a conscious confrontation of religious themes. Nevertheless, the Maritains and others who were concerned with the renewal of religious art considered Chagall the prototype of the true religious artist. Jacques Maritain published an article on him in 1929,[3] and Mme Maritain later wrote poems on his work. During the Second World War she published a short poetic account of his life and art.[4]

The decade of the 1930s saw Chagall's interest in religious themes increase. With Vollard he agreed to undertake a large-scale series of etchings illustrating the Old Testament,[5] and in this connection made a trip to Palestine and adjacent areas in 1931. "I found the true spirit of the Bible on that trip," Chagall said, "and at the same time a greater consciousness of my own being. The land and the air of the East are impregnated with wisdom."

As Chagall worked on his Bible, religious symbols and references multiplied in his painting. Just before and during the Second World War these centered around a series of Crucifixions. Since then themes of joy have largely replaced those of suffering. Deep involvement with the Bible during the past decade led to a proliferation of Old Testament themes in the form of sculptures, reliefs, paintings, stained glass windows, and the large ceramic mural completed late in 1956 for Assy.

Much has been said by others about Chagall's religiosity, very little about it by the painter himself. The presence of Jesus in many of his pictures has given currency to the notion that he is moving towards conversion. Though Chagall firmly denies this, it has remained a hope among his Catholic friends. As early as 1929 Jacques Maritain pointedly called the humility of

---

the circumstances and background of his conversion. Maritain's *Réponse à Jean Cocteau* (Paris: Stock, 1926) was a commentary on Cocteau's conversion and an informal exposition of the neo-Thomist theory of religion and art, elaborated more completely in *Art and Scholasticism*.

[3] Jacques Maritain, "Chagall," *Sélection,* Cahier 6, June, 1929, pp. 27–29.

[4] Raïssa Maritain, *Marc Chagall* (New York: Maison Française, 1943).

[5] Cf. Marc Chagall, *Illustrations for the Bible*. Introduction by Meyer Schapiro. Additional text by Jean Wahl (New York: Harcourt, Brace, 1956).

Chagall's art "a virtue almost Christian," [6] and René Schwob, a Jewish convert to Catholicism, wrote cryptically that the painter "nourishes, almost without knowing it, a violent nostalgia for the eternal." [7] It is only in this eternal, he continued, "where humanity realizes itself in the flesh of Christ," that Jews "can find that harmony and order which their art lacks." [8]

"Though I have much sympathy for religious people and have long had good friends of all faiths," Chagall has said, "I am not conscious of any belief on my part, Jewish or Christian, though other people are free to speculate on this aspect of my imagery as they have done in connection with other elements in my pictures, about which I myself have nothing to say." On an earlier occasion he had been more explicit: "I am not now, and never have been, religious. Moreover, I felt that religion meant little in the world that I knew, even as it seems to mean little today." [9]

Chagall's religious imagery is thus not an expression of belief or an affirmation of dogma, but an expansion of a poetic vocabulary of a private order, in which religious symbols take their place with lovers, wandering pedlars, fantastic animals, and other creatures of the painter's universe. Living in the Western world, we cannot avoid coming in contact with Christianity and its central figures, whatever our own beliefs. Christ is a poignant part of the landscape of everyday experience. But in the same way that we can read, write, and speculate on the Bible as a great contribution to man's spiritual life and as a literary and historical document, so we can detach the figure of Jesus from the structures of dogma built up around him and consider him in a private way. Chagall has used the material of religion to enlarge his private symbolism, but his art does not elaborate on the concepts of religion

[6] Jacques Maritain, "Chagall," *Selection,* Cahier 6, June, 1929, pp. 27–39.

[7] René Schwob, *Chagall et l'âme juive* (Paris: Correa, 1931), p. 40.

[8] *Ibid.,* p. 113. Chagall is much troubled by such wishful thinking, which seems particularly widespread among Jewish converts to Catholicism, of whom Raïssa Maritain and René Schwob are the most notable. The first time I spoke with him, he insisted on making certain that I was not a convert before he would talk about his work at Assy. He fears that his contribution there will be appropriated by the Church for propagandistic purposes.

[9] James Johnson Sweeney, "An Interview with Marc Chagall," *Partisan Review,* XII, No. 1 (Winter, 1944), 88–93.

nor has it expanded its imagery. "For me," he has said, "Christ was a great poet, the teaching of whose poetry has been forgotten by the modern world." [10]

Maritain speculates that Chagall "does not know very exactly which dogma, Jewish or Christian," his Bible proposes.[11] The fact is that it proposes no dogma at all. The very word is abhorrent to the painter. "Dogma means separation," he insists, "and separation means conflict, struggle, hate and war." [12]

Chagall's flight from France and his wartime sojourn in New York brought him into closer contact with certain members of French culture in exile than would probably have been the case otherwise. This was especially true in regard to Father Couturier, with whom he became quite friendly. Thus, when, in 1948, after his return to France, the latter spoke to him of the project at Assy, and Maritain urged his support, Chagall was happy to contribute.

As Chagall was Jewish, at least in heritage, it was decided to offer him the baptistry to decorate. With Father Couturier he journeyed to Assy to study the layout. In the baptistry there was one large wall unbroken by a window, for which Chagall decided to do a mural. It was obvious, however, that such a mural would be largely concealed by the baptismal font already undertaken by Lipchitz. Consequently, Couturier, in a consultation with Canon Devémy and the architect Novarina, decided to relocate the Lipchitz sculpture elsewhere in the church, though this fact was not communicated to the sculptor until some time later.

The focus of the baptistry decor was to be a mural of the Crossing of the Red Sea (Figure 37), a scene of salvation through water, which has been treated since early Christian times as a prefiguration of the sacrament of baptism. For the windows Chagall planned scenes of an angel holding a jug of holy water (west side) and an angel with candelabra and flowers (east side), both to be realized in grisaille in order to provide sufficient light for the

[10] Lecture by Marc Chagall delivered at the University of Chicago. English translation included in *The Works of the Mind,* ed. by Robert Heywood (Chicago: University of Chicago Press, 1947).

[11] Jacques Maritain, *Art and Poetry,* p. 21.

[12] Walter Erben, *Marc Chagall* (London: Thames and Hudson, 1957), p. 19.

mural. For the same walls, somewhat below the windows and towards the side, the painter projected two small subordinate panels, the themes of which were left undecided. Later, in 1953, after Chagall had made up his mind to realize the mural and panels in ceramic tile, he executed a small *Crucifixion* (Figure 40) for one of the side walls, but this piece was subsequently put aside when he decided to substitute two low reliefs (Figures 41, 42) with subjects based on Psalms 42 and 124.

The choice of these subjects from the Psalms was appropriate. The opening line of Psalm 42, which Chagall engraved freehand along the top and bottom of his relief, reads: "As the hart languishes for the water of the brook, so my soul languishes for Thee, O Lord." The motif of longing for water relates the scene directly to the baptismal theme. But water, in such baptismal prefigurations as the Red Sea and the Flood, is also fearful and destructive, and it is in this manner that it figures in the text of Psalm 124. Here the Psalmist is saved from "the waters that overwhelmed" him and the "stream which had gone over" his soul by the intervention of the Lord. Verse 7, which Chagall engraved on the second relief, reads: "Our soul is escaped as a bird out of the snare of the fowlers." The theme of water, thus picked up from the previous relief, becomes enriched by the metaphor of the bird (also associated with salvation through baptism in the story of Noah) in such a manner as to expand the animal series of the other relief (beasts and fish) and rejoin, in this single instance in the baptistry, Chagall's private symbolism, in which the bird is a recurrent motif.[13]

The decision to realize the Crossing of the Red Sea in ceramic tiles was made sometime after 1950, when Chagall moved from Orgeval to Vence. In this town, near the ceramic center of Vallouris, he began experimenting

---

[13] Usually associated in Chagall's work with themes of love and joy, the bird makes a surprising and enigmatic appearance in the gouache of the *Descent from the Cross* (1947). Here the otherwise human figure holding the body of Christ is endowed with a bird's head and bears a striking resemblance to the bird-man "Loplop," the central figure in Max Ernst's private symbology. One is tempted to relate its presence here to the fact that the eagle is the symbol of the Apostle John. Such an interpretation is risky, however, and probably smacks more of art history than the intuitional creative method of Chagall allows.

under the direction of the Master Potter Serge Ramel. During 1951–54 Chagall produced only small ceramic works, which he considered experiments leading toward the mural that he hoped to undertake. He wrote of these as "a sort of foretaste; the outcome of [his] life in the south, where one feels so strongly the significance of this craft." "The very earth on which I walk," he continued, "is luminous. . . . I have wanted to use [it] like the old artisans." [14]

The use of ceramic tile and sculptured low relief has turned out to be a mixed blessing. *The Crossing of the Red Sea* is far more legible in the penumbra of the baptistry than a painted mural would have been, since the hard polished surfaces of the tile pick up the maximal amount of light. [15] However, the very low relief of the side panels makes their forms almost indistinguishable. It would have been far better for Chagall to have painted, or at least tinted, these.

Though *The Crossing of the Red Sea* was begun in 1952 and finished in 1956, the composition is based on the etching Chagall made of this subject (Figure 38) for his Bible prior to 1939. [16] The etching shows Moses standing, staff in hand, at the left, forming the side of an elongated triangle, the other side of which is composed of Egyptians and, above them, Jews. At the apex of the triangle is the Angel of the Lord pointing to the Promised Land be-

[14] Chagall, "Ceramics," a note dated Vence, September, 1952, printed in the catalogue of the Chagall Exhibition at the Curt Valentin Gallery, New York, November, 1952.

[15] Though the surface is bright, the colors themselves are quite pale, consisting mostly of light yellow (the Egyptians, costume of Moses), light blue (waves), and white (Angel) against a sea of darker blue. The handling of the color in general lacks the subtlety and the gemlike saturation that Chagall achieves in his oils.

[16] Some question has been raised with respect to the dating of the plates for the Bible. While the gouaches for the color lithographs are largely recent, the etchings were probably all executed before 1939, at which time stacks of them were put in storage in Paris. Though Chagall has indicated, on a few occasions, that some of the etchings are recent, William Lieberman, curator of prints at the Museum of Modern Art, dates them all prior to 1939. He assures me, however, that if any of them are later, they would be the ones in irregular or smaller format. Thus the dating of the large vertical *Crossing of the Red Sea* would not be open to question in any case.

139

yond. All these constituents are mentioned in the Bible text, and, as is the case with the other etchings of this series, Chagall's private symbolic lexicon has been omitted.[17]

The Assy mural repeats all these figures in their same position. It adds to them, however, by filling the spaces left open in the etched composition with a cast of characters drawn less from the Bible (or religious imagery in general) than from the familiar private iconography of the painter. On the horizon at the upper right a small boat has been introduced, and above it, a vision of the Crucifixion. To Christ's left, a group of forlorn men and women are led by a wandering Jewish pedlar, sack over his shoulder and staff in hand. At Christ's right is a woman in mourning and a grandfather's clock from which emerges an arm holding an open book. Above the seas to the left of the column of Jews floats a young couple, embracing, and at the horizon line, just under the arm of the Angel of the Lord, the figure of the Wandering Jew is repeated. At the extreme left, a fish rises from the sea to observe King David floating through the skies, harp in hand.

Chagall has always resisted interpreting his various symbols and protests vehemently (partly in reaction against his having been called at times a "literary painter") that he employs his familiar *dramatis personae* simply to satisfy formal demands. "I fill up the empty spaces in my canvas *as the structure of my picture requires,* with a body or an object according to my humour." [18] But any number of subjects can be manipulated to fill up the space of a canvas in accordance with formal needs, and Chagall's explanation does not do justice to the far from accidental choice he has always made. The various elements of his fantasy, however, are not linked according to a literary or storytelling device, but follow the chain of private associations.

---

[17] This seems to be consistently so in the illustrations for the Bible. Though, as Schapiro observes (Introduction to Chagall, *Illustrations for the Bible*), there are anachronisms, like the star of David, stemming from Chagall's unsophistication in matters of history and ethnography, we never find in the etchings those private symbols which invade the same scenes as they are realized in the Assy mural or in the large Biblical paintings that have occupied Chagall for the last five years.

[18] Sweeney, *Marc Chagall* (New York: Museum of Modern Art, 1946), p. 15.

When we survey the subjects Chagall has used at Assy to "fill up" the open spaces present in the etching—Crucifixion, clock, pedlar, boat, couple, fish, and King David—we find a group subtly linked, as we shall see, by an unquestionable logic. But this logic does not grow predictably from the narrative of the Biblical scene; only King David is directly related to the Old Testament, and he is an anachronism used to symbolize the kingdom which the Jews will go on to establish.

The Crucifixion that Chagall inserted might strike us at first as a logical reference to the New Testament. But, though Moses is shown in Christian art as a type of Christ, the crossing of the Red Sea is not a typological adumbration of the Crucifixion. Christ's passion does not follow liturgically, or with literary logic, from the main subject of the mural, but belongs, like the rest of the additional inconography, to the independent fantasy of the painter. We can better understand its presence, not by studying the Gospels or earlier representations of the Crucifixion, but by examining other versions of this scene in Chagall's *oeuvre*. Here we become aware that its meanings are unrelated to the Christian sacraments, that Chagall's crucifixion belongs, not to the vertical historical tradition of Christian art, but to the horizontal symbolic vocabulary of his *oeuvre*.

His first Crucifixion (an isolated example, for the subject was not resumed until the late 1930s) was the *Calvary* of 1912. It was conceived within a fairy-tale setting, with Jewish types and costumes. The bearded male figure near the Cross is more a father than a youthful apostle, and the whole scene suggests familial compassion rather than liturgy. "The symbolic figure of Christ had always been very familiar to me," said Chagall of this work,

and I was determined to give form to it in the guise imagined by my young heart. I wanted to show Christ as an innocent child. Nowadays I see it differently. When I painted this picture in Paris, I was trying to free myself from the icon painter's outlook.[19]

The *Calvary* is not related in spirit, as are the later Crucifixions, to the version at Assy, but it does introduce the motif of the sea and a boat with

[19] Erben, *Marc Chagall*, p. 50.

a figure in it, a purely imaginative addition by the painter, the meaning of which becomes clear in the later versions.

The White Crucifixion of 1938 (Figure 43) establishes Christ as the proto-type of the persecuted Jew. He is portrayed as an Eastern European type wearing a loin cloth made from the Jewish talis, or prayer shawl. Above Him, angels conceived as bearded patriarchs bewail His fate; about Him all is terror and destruction. Homes are burning, and the Jews are fleeing. Some of them escape in a boat crossing the waters on the left; others, like the pedlar at the right, escape overland. In the left foreground a man saves the Torah from destruction; in front of him an elderly Jew is forced to wear the sign, "Ich bin Jude." The context is that of the persecution of the European Jews just before the war, persecution which Chagall narrowly escaped by his flight to America in 1941. This interpretation is confirmed by the *Martyrdom* of 1939, in which a Jew with Christlike physiognomy and the same talis drapery is tied to a board resembling the upright of a cross. Though his arms are not outstretched, the reference to the Crucifixion is inescapable. Behind the victim is a holocaust of destruction in which houses are burning and apocalyptic Chagallesque animals float through the air. *The Yellow Crucifixion* of 1943 expands this reading of the scene by adding a sinking steamship with figures swimming helplessly in the water.

We are now in a position to explain the presence of the Crucifixion in the Assy mural. Starting with an Old Testament subject that describes how the Jews cast off oppression by escaping through the sea, Chagall's thoughts wandered to the Hitlerian persecutions. This explains the refugee-like group that surrounds Christ at Assy, as well as the little boat below them. At Marseilles, where Chagall waited to leave for America, he saw many such fugitives. "Here in the harbor close to the ship, I discovered hundreds of my Jews with bag and baggage. There is no event quite so sad as when an author and his heroes take the same ship." [20]

Foremost among the despondent figures surrounding Christ in the Assy ceramic is the Wandering Jew, or pedlar, trudging along, bent over his walking stick, a bulging sack thrown over his shoulder. A figure beloved by Chagall,

[20] *Ibid.,* p. 115.

he appears in the painter's earliest works as a reminiscence of ghetto life in his native Vitebsk. He is first discovered floating over the rooftops in *Above Vitebsk* (1914), and he wanders through Chagall's iconography with increasing frequency during the Second World War. At Assy he not only emerges from the group surrounding Christ, but reappears under the arm of the Angel, where he walks, Christlike, upon the waters. Heading towards the Promised Land, he is the avant-garde of the Red Sea Jews and the prophet, as it were, of the recent migrations to Israel.[21]

The poetic associations that led to the semi-anthropomorphic grandfather's clock to the left of the Christ in the Assy mural are more remote. Again, unlike traditional religious art, in which the symbols are related to a text or a tradition, the meanings here must be discovered within the context of Chagall's paintings. The subject first appears in *The Clock* of 1914, where it is realized without anthropomorphic additions and covers the larger part of the canvas. In the lower left-hand corner a minuscule figure stares pensively out the window. We feel that the clock represents some enigma which preoccupies him. The clock maintains a strange presence in *To My Wife* (1933–34), where it stands beside the wedded couple like a member of the family, evoking an enigmatic sense of the transitory nature of human events (much like the clock Munch placed beside himself in a late self-portrait). This mystery of time is summarized in *Time Is a River without Banks* (1930–39), where a large pendulum clock floats through the air above a river (on whose banks lovers embrace), supported by a winged fish. The mixed symbol here relates directly, of course, to the metaphor of the title.

Often the clock is rendered specifically anthropomorphic. It flies like an

[21] Although Chagall is not religious, he considers himself ethnically and spiritually a Jew and as such is deeply attached to the state of Israel. The importance of his trip to Palestine in 1931 has already been mentioned. In 1954 the Government of Israel invited him to accompany, as a guest of the state, the large Chagall retrospective held there that year. The artist replied that he fervently desired to visit Israel "in order to gather new powers and fresh inspiration." "I will not rest," he wrote, "until my feet tread upon holy soil" (quoted in Alfred Werner, "The Painter of Vitebsk," *Horizon,* January, 1955, clipping in Chagall File, Museum of Modern Art Library). Though Chagall's health prevented him from going at the time of the exhibition, he became well enough to make the trip the following year.

angel, with hands outstretched, in the *Self Portrait with Clock,* and has a female nude inscribed within it in *Winter* (1931), where the dial serves as the head of the figure. At Assy the clock stands like a Bible-reading patriarch, meditating on the Crucifixion, but in a more recent color lithograph [22] it becomes the crucified Himself (Figure 44). Here the torso of Christ, whose arms are outstretched in the position of crucifixion, is inscribed within a clock, the face of which also serves as the face of the Redeemer, while the patriarch lies on the ground to the left, Bible in hand. A further enrichment of associations is achieved in this extraordinary image by the introduction of the name Chagall, rendered so as to vaguely resemble Hebrew lettering, above the crucified figure where we normally find the inscription identifying Jesus. Here we have the final step. The Christ, who was the prototype of the suffering Jew in the crucifixions, has become identified with the painter himself.

The immense fish superimposed on the clock in this provocative lithograph serves to enlarge our understanding of the one rising from the water just below King David in the Assy mural. While this addition to the formulation of the Bible etching can be explained by purely naturalistic logic, its presence is rich in associations. Though the kinship of fish and Christ, explicit in the lithograph,[23] is probably relevant to Assy, the fish may be even more fundamentally associated with the clock (as even in the lithograph) to which it is bound in the persistent metaphor of time as "a river without banks."

Like the clock, the fish has a long history in Chagall's iconography. Sometimes it appears wholly naturalistically, as on the table of *The Drunkard* (1911–12) and in *The Soles* (1951). In *The Yellow Crucifixion* it is located in a manner analogous to that of Assy, as it projects its head above water among the survivors of a maritime disaster. In *Fish in the Street* the containing plate is enigmatically located in the middle of a town street, while in a gouache of 1952 the fish floats mysteriously towards the sun. There it circles, like a celestial body, in the immense *Creation of Man* completed in 1956. In

[22] Untitled, this original lithograph was printed by Mourlot for the de luxe edition of Jacques Lassaigne's *Chagall* (Paris: Maeght, 1957), in which it faces p. 22.

[23] The fish, the Greek word for which (*ichthus*) forms the initial letter acrostic of the Greek words meaning "Jesus Christ, Son of God, Savior," has been a familiar symbol for Christ since early Christian painting.

144

the instances thus far cited, and in fact in most cases in Chagall's *oeuvre*, the image of the fish is normal and discrete in form no matter how strange its action or setting. There are, however, some gouaches and paintings, of which *Time Is a River without Banks* is the most important, in which the fish is fused with a clock or grows wings like a bird.

The pair of embracing lovers drifting through the air in the Assy mural is even more remote from the idea of the central subject than are the clock and the fish. These figures are probably meant to suggest the joy attendant upon such a scene of deliverance, and it is precisely as a symbol of happiness that they appear elsewhere in Chagall's *oeuvre*. The prototype of the image is a painting of 1915 in the State Gallery of Moscow, sometimes also called *Above Vitebsk*, in which Chagall and his first wife, Bella, float above their native village in a partial embrace. This is one of the most familiar instances of Chagall's pictorial realization of metaphor (we have all "walked on air" or been "on top of the world").

A gouache of King David serenading the embracing couple [24] establishes a new link and reinforces our earlier reference to the David of the Assy ceramic as a harbinger of joy. Though David is absent (he would be an anachronism) in the etching of the *Crossing of the Red Sea*, his role in the etching illustrating II Samuel 6.1–5, where, harp in hand, he leads the triumphant group carrying the Ark of the Covenant into Jerusalem, is the counterpart of his function in the Assy work.

It is unfortunate that the formal achievement in Chagall's ceramic mural is not comparable to its iconographic richness. To be sure, the composition of the mural is more complex than that of the etching, more Chagallesque in its crowding of the space, but it lacks many of the refinements of the earlier work. Whereas searching and subtle contouring of forms characterize the etching, the drawing at Assy is summary and often gross. In place of the nuanced flicker of light and dark, which is a common denominator of the etching's surface and therefore an agent in the unification of the whole, we have at Assy light-dark contrasts that are blatant and tend visually to divide the composition.

[24] Illustrated in Lassiagne, *Chagall,* p. 62.

No better demonstration of these differences can be made than by a comparison of the figure of Moses as he appears in the two compositions. As with the other elements in the Assy work retained from the etching, the differences are slight but crucial. In the etching, Moses is a figure of great dignity and moral force as he stands, rod firmly in hand, commanding the course of events.[25] The silhouette is powerful, and the drawing assured. In the Assy mural the drawing has been simplified, and a series of S curves have been superimposed upon the drapery in order to assimilate the figure of Moses to the billows above him. This merging has been furthered by a restructuring of the billows, so that they come down to surround the upper part of the figure, and by making Moses a light figure against the dark sea (a reversal of the system of the etching, where Moses is a dark figure against a light sea).

While the assimilating of Moses to the billows does create a greater continuity of forms on the left side of the composition, it results in rather mechanical rhythms that do not grow from the necessities of the individual forms but constitute a facile solution applied from without. Consequently, Moses is far less convincing. Failing to hold his place, he is swept up by the external pattern, so that his gesture and pose seem no longer willed from within. The weak drawing of the figure is most evident in the manner in which he holds the rod and in the almost caricatural treatment of the face (Figure 39).[26]

Similar qualitative differences can be observed with respect to the column of Egyptians and Jews, and the Angel of the Lord. In the Bible etching the group of Jews is more open than in the Assy mural and produces, therefore, a chiaroscuro pattern continuous with the shifting lights and darks of the sea. In the mural the Jews form a denser and therefore darker group that tends to be visually isolated, boxlike, from the rest of the composition, especially as the chiaroscuro flicker of the sea has also largely vanished.

[25] "And the Lord said unto Moses, Stretch out thine hand over the sea, that the waters may come up again upon the Egyptians, upon their chariots, and upon their horsemen." Exodus 14.26.

[26] Here, as in the etching (as Schapiro observes in his introduction to Chagall, *Illustrations for the Bible*), Moses is adorned with two "radiances" which project, hornlike, from the top of his head. This iconography originated in a mistranslation in the Latin Bible.

The slight restructuring of the Angel in the Assy work has also resulted in a loss. In the etching the right leg and the skirt are carefully handled so as to assimilate the figure to the group of Jews, a continuity fostered by the common chiaroscuro of the two areas. At Assy the Angel's pose is more accidental, and the figure more detached.

Chagall himself must have felt that the Assy composition tended to pull apart; it was probably for this reason that he introduced the two broken diagonal lines that start at the sides of the mural on the level of Moses' head and lead to the Angel. These rather obvious markings are meant to reinforce the originally triangular form of the composition, weakened by the spotty quality resulting from the introduction of the new iconographic motifs. However, the vector-like lines conflict with the arabesques of the surf, intensifying instead of resolving the inherent problems of the composition. In Chagall's great early paintings, those in which his native imagination was submitted to the architectural discipline of Cubism, such structural lines appear only as edges of planes, and thus grow out of the forms of the composition.

The relatively feeble structuring of the Assy mural bears witness to a weakening that has been evident in Chagall's painting since around 1920. At that time the plastic adventure almost ceased, though the spiritual and hence iconographic development continued. But while his painting has declined, there has been a real flowering in Chagall's graphic work, among which the etchings for the Bible mark the culmination. Here the enforced discipline of the stylus and the search for nuancing necessitated by the absence of color have all worked to the advantage of his art. If the early paintings reflect a contact with Cubism, these prints show the artist under the influence of Rembrandt. They are intimate works, tender and full of love, and perhaps truer to Chagall's character than his more powerful early compositions. Yet they depend for their success in part upon their small format. Since he left Cubism behind, Chagall has not been a "big" composer. His best work has been increasingly intimate, a development contrary to the central trend in modern painting towards larger canvases and gestural painting. The deficiencies of the Assy ceramic are, in part, a function of a mistake in scale; faced with this large field and the possibilities of color, Chagall dissolved the intensity of the earlier print composition, losing the chiaroscuro flicker but not replacing it with any new structural principle adequate to the needs of a mural.

It is therefore not surprising to find the small reliefs on the side walls of the Assy baptistry higher in quality than the ceramic mural. The compression of experience into a smaller area has produced (particularly in the relief based on Psalm 124) a more structurally dense and intense composition. The searching "drawing" and richer texturing here result in part from the resistance of the material; this creates dialogue between the hand and the surface, which seems necessary for Chagall.

A word needs to be said, finally, about the inscription at the bottom of the Assy mural. It is a measure of the regret Chagall has felt in the last six or seven years for having agreed to do the work. The sympathy which he, like many other artists, entertained *vis-à-vis* the Church in the years immediately after the war was engendered by the optimistic social and artistic program of the Dominicans, and strengthened by his intimacy with the Maritains and Father Couturier. The subsequent repression of the Dominicans and the unpleasantness that surrounded the debate on sacred art precipitated by Assy have tended to alter Chagall's feelings, and his doubts and fears became very marked as a result of the "Finaly Affair" which offended the painter deeply.[27]

---

[27] Though it received little attention in America, the Finaly case became a *cause célèbre* of epic proportions in France and did much to weaken the already disintegrating *entente* between liberals and the Church. During the war, two young Jewish boys named Finaly, whose parents had died in a concentration camp, were entrusted to the care of a certain Mlle Brun, a fervent Catholic. Though they had already been circumcised, they were baptized and brought up as Catholics. After the war, their relatives, some of whom had immigrated to Israel, claimed them, but Mlle Brun refused to give them up and spirited them away to Spain, where they were kept in hiding. Her refusal to give up the baptized children was attacked vociferously throughout the nonreligious community, but she received wide unofficial support from the clergy and conservative laity. The position taken by the Catholic newspaper *La Croix* was characteristic It argued, essentially, that the Church is a perfect society which has the obligation and the authority to protect persons who have become its members by baptism. The Dominicans, *Esprit,* and Catholic intellectuals like Mauriac were in a quandary. Since there was no question here of a "forced baptism" (which according to canon law may be rescinded) some other

In March, 1956, though only firing remained for the completion of the mural, Chagall was hesitant to make it a contribution to Assy. "They want to reanimate their religion with our [the modern painter's] art," he said, raising the question as to whether he should be party to such an undertaking. By August, however, he had decided to go through with the work and was considering the sort of inscription he might place on it to render his motivation absolutely clear. After settling on the phrase, "In the Name of the Liberty of All Religions," he allowed the tiles to be baked, and the mural was set in place in the baptistry early in 1957.

---

solution had to be found. The Church finally took the position that as there was no authorization from the parents, the baptism did not "tie consciences," though it did not cease to be valid. This formula seemed to be generally satisfactory and opened the way for the children to be returned to their relatives, but not before widespread unpleasantness had been created.

II. THE ALTARPIECES BY BONNARD AND MATISSE

Though the lateral altarpieces of Notre-Dame-de-Toute-Grâce would have been executed, but for chance, by Derain and Dufy, the ultimate choice of Bonnard and Matisse was an inspired if somewhat accidental pairing. These artists represent the twin summits of twentieth century French painting. Bonnard, the master of the spot, embodies the heritage of Impressionism with its apotheosis of sensation; Matisse, the master of the colored line, orders sensation with a definition and clarity that constitute the essence of the French classical tradition. At the time they were called upon to execute their works for Assy both Bonnard and Matisse were enjoying that consummate mastery granted to only a few geniuses in the years shortly before death. Their last works are marked by an ethereality that reminds us of Mozart's *Requiem* or the visions in Shakespeare's *Tempest*.

After heroic beginnings, the art of these men had ceased, in the period between the World Wars, to be in the van of modern painting. Their glorious final years, however, not only represented a distillation and purification of their individual gifts, but recreated the artists themselves as leaders of the avant-garde. More than Picasso, it is they who are the immediate forebears of the "pure painters" of our day.[1]

---

[1] Patrick Heron observes that "by 1950 hardly one amongst the most important painters in Paris under fifty showed signs of [Picasso's] influence. The various new schools of non-figurative painting were by then in the ascendant and their leading exponents seemed . . . to be finding Matisse and Bonnard more to their liking than Picasso or Braque. Estève, Singier, Manessier et

150

In 1943, after having failed in his attempt to reach Dufy, Canon Devémy turned to Bonnard for the altar painting of Saint Francis of Sales. The choice of Dufy had been determined in part by the Canon's acquaintance with him at the Lycee. The subsequent selection of Bonnard was suggested by the cleric's friendship with Charles Terasse, Bonnard's nephew, who had been stricken with tuberculosis and was being treated at Assy; otherwise there was little to specially recommend the painter for the task. He was an agnostic who had had no particular contact with the faith, even in childhood, and who had never done anything resembling a religious picture. Moreover, his concern for the sensuous and the intimate, both in subject matter and in style, seemed hardly appropriate for sacred art.

All this notwithstanding, Devémy undertook to visit Bonnard at his little villa at Le Cannet in the hills overlooking Cannes. The painter was astonished and somewhat skeptical when the priest explained the reason for his journey, but when he learned that Rouault had already contributed a window to Assy, he began to consider the project in a more serious light. Bonnard ended the interview with a promise to think about the matter and with a request for literature on the saint, about whom he knew nothing.[2] A few months later he decided to proceed. As canvas, especially in large dimensions, was exceedingly difficult to procure in the south, owing to wartime shortages, Devémy made a trip to Paris to collect the necessary materials.

To execute a portrait of someone he had never seen was a novel undertaking for Bonnard. Not that his portraits or, for that matter, his landscapes or still-lifes were executed while confronting the subject. On the contrary, his oils were always based on small sketches or pure recollection. He considered the actual

---

al. . . . owe much to the abstract elements in Pierre Bonnard." *The Changing Forms of Art* (London: Routledge, 1955), p. 116.

Andre Lhôte (*La Peinture libérée* [Paris: Grasset, 1956], p. 204) writes that the resurrection of nuance among the young advanced post-war painters is due to Bonnard. Jean Bazaine, himself one of this group, considers the painterly problems and goals of Bonnard's late work "le plus beau risque à courir" for a young painter. Bazaine, "Bonnard et la réalité," *Formes et couleurs*, VI, No. 2 (1944), 39–48.

[2] See Jean Devémy, "Visites à Bonnard," *L'Art sacré*, September–October, 1950, No. 1–2, pp. 8–9.

models hindrances to the synthesizing process that took place when he recalled his impressions in solitude. Yet the sources of his imagery had always been located in the realities of his private world—his friends, his garden, the dining-room table, the coast below the hills of Cannet. Now he was called upon to paint something quite foreign to both his spirit and his environment. Devémy's description of the saint ("bald, bearded and squinting somewhat . . .")[3] hardly sufficed. Moreover, the standard biography,[4] which the Canon gave the painter, revealed little that had any affinity with Bonnard's intimate world. In this two-hundred-and-nine-page study of the saint, his writings, and his activities, only one sentence seems to have provided the artist with a motif for his work: "He [Francis] quickly became the master of the young in heart. The children grouped around him whenever he passed by, eager for his smile and his benediction." [5] This might have been said about Francis of Assisi or, for that matter, about most of the gentle spirits that people Bonnard's secular world.[6]

The Bonnard canvas is dominated by the presence of Saint Francis, who is located virtually in the picture plane and shown frontally from the knees up. He looks out benignly at the spectator, his arms crossed in repose, scarcely conscious of the children and the sick about him. These include two little girls and a boy in the front plane and assorted older types, among them a man with a crutch, who appear at first to surround the saint but who are actually in the space behind him. A small church closes the composition on the right, another rises among the roofs of the town in the middle ground, and a cathedral is visible in the distance. A suggestion of the fog-enshrouded alpine landscape of the Haute-Savoie constitutes the background, against which a large white dove is seen at the apex of the composition (see frontispiece).

The predominant tone of the painting is an extraordinary purple used for

[3] "Notre-Dame-de-Toute-Grâce," *Vogue* (Paris), March, 1948.

[4] Amédée de Margerie, *St. François de Sales* (Paris: Gabalda, 1927).

[5] *Ibid.,* p. 40.

[6] On page 43 I have noted the manner in which the cult of Saint Francis of Sales has gradually replaced that of Saint Francis of Assisi in the Haute-Savoie. As this change took place, however, the personality and legend of the Bishop of Geneva came more and more to resemble that of his Italian namesake.

152

the robe of the saint, the house behind him, and numerous small forms elsewhere in the composition. It is not the color usually associated with clerical garb, but a light and more transparent lilac found frequently in Bonnard's palette during his last decade of painting. There are many small areas of blue, especially in the rooftops, and an occasional patch of orange-red as in the wall of the house to the left. The figures near the saint are executed in a thin black wash scarcely used elsewhere. Except in the figures, one is struck by the extraordinary variety of color and nuances crowded into small areas, a variety even greater than is found in Renoir and Monet, once Bonnard's friends and, in effect, his masters. For example, in just a few square inches under the seated figure on the left may be seen five shades of green, three of blue, two of yellow, rust, umber and purple.

The brushstrokes span a continuum from the mere touch to the long colored line, and the shapes in the picture range from small spots to larger areas, often rectangular in shape. No forms are enclosed by line or sharply contoured. Their indeterminate edges depend upon the fading of one spot of the thin matière and the emergence of another. Between all forms there seems to be a "breathing space" of colored light, giving them the illusion of hovering in the soft space of the picture plane. Though some wonderful shapes are discovered —such as the *profil perdu* of the little girls in the foreground (Figure 45)— these silhouettes are not primary, as in Bonnard's earlier Nabis works, but rather dissolve into the tissue of color spots. This taste for impressionistic fragmentation, very marked in the last decade of Bonnard's painting, is reflected in a definition he formulated toward the end of his life, which states that a painting is "a series of spots which are joined together and ultimately form the object . . . over which the eye wanders without obstruction." [7]

The upper half of the Assy picture, depicting the rooftops and distant mountains, is one of the glories of Bonnard's *oeuvre*. The cohering principle is subtle and remote. The fabric seems less "composed" than "discovered," and it hangs together by the grace of the perfect balance and harmony of color spots which, in keeping with the "all-over" nature of the design, proliferate to the edges of the canvas. Nowhere was Bonnard more abstract than in the soft passages

[7] Tériade, "Propos de Pierre Bonnard," *Verve*, V, Nos. 17–18 (1947).

which constitute the upper fifth of the canvas—spots without literal details or even cues. We can "read" them as mountain forms only in the context of the whole work—and then, only with difficulty.

This harmony of small shapes of color, which Patrick Heron calls the "fish net" principle of Bonnard's late compositions,[8] does not obtain in the lower half of the picture, where the structuring is more old-fashioned. The difference is due, in part, to the inclusion of figures; it is probably for this reason that in the more abstract spotted pictures of the painter's last years human beings are ever fewer.[9]

Though in most of his figure scenes Bonnard dissolved the anatomies, through intimate poses and segmentations, into abstract forms assimilable to the flat pattern of his picture, he evidently considered the saint exempt from such radical pictorial handling, for he gave him a simple frontal pose that retains the full integrity of silhouette but is consequently more difficult to assimilate to the over-all design. Not that such poses are without precedent in the *oeuvre* (though I know of no others in the late work), but elsewhere they occur primarily in the uncharacteristic formal paintings like *The Loge* [10] of 1908, which are generally unsuccessful.

The symmetrical pose of Saint Francis, forming the main vertical accent of the lower half of the painting (contrasting with the horizontal divisions above), is reinforced by the heraldic handling of the two little girls at his skirts. The placement of the other figures is equally mechanical. As the saint is somewhat to the left of the vertical axis of the canvas, balance was achieved by increasing the number of figures to the right. Thus a little boy reading a book has been placed in the front plane parallel to the little girls. The same grouping (one figure looking inward on the left, two on the right) was repeated for the adults shown kneeling and sitting in a plane not far behind the saint. The two women in prayer on the third plane in depth restore the simple symmetry.

---

[8] Heron (*The Changing Forms of Art,* p. 124) imagines a fish net thrown over the canvas, and Bonnard having "to paint the picture through the square or diamond holes."

[9] See John Rewald, *Pierre Bonnard* (New York: Museum of Modern Art, 1948), p. 53.

[10] Even in this formal portrait of Gaston and Jesse Bernheim-Jeune and their wives, there is more segmentation, less frontality and hieraticism, than in the Assy work.

The special subject matter with which Bonnard was engaged here led him to an uncharacteristic hieratic structuring of the sizes of the figures. To give the saint the prominence that was his due, his size was increased disproportionately in relationship to the surrounding figures. In the context of Bonnard's informal and intimate style, the difference between the immense saint and the tiny figures at his skirts is disturbing, as is the regular staging in the sizes of the two groups of figures behind him. At first we imagine this diminution to have been necessitated by perspective, but gradually we become aware that the spatial program of the picture is ambiguous and that the mechanical staging is not its necessary correlate.[11]

Apart from establishing a stilted hieraticism, the large size given the saint raised the problem of adjusting such an isolable form to the more fragmentary pattern of the surface. The only other late canvas I know having such a dominant integral form is *The Circus Horse* (1946). Most of the works executed simultaneously with the *Saint Francis* are composed of a mosaic of small forms, as, for example, the magnificent *Interior: Dining Room* (1942–46), by which standard of perfection the frailties of the Assy picture can be measured.

The pattern Bonnard gave the folds of the saint's skirt rendered that part of his costume more assimilable. The folds were realized as vertical ridges of color of a kind employed for the horizontal roofs above. However, the large curved form representing the mantle covering the saint's shoulders and chest tends to detach itself somewhat from the surface of the composition despite the way Bonnard fractured its surface through loose brushwork.

It was the head of Saint Francis, however, that gave Bonnard the most trouble. Perhaps respect for the holy figure prompted him to employ a literalness of detail and color quite at variance with the vague color patches, sometimes virtually featureless (as in the boy at the right of *Interior: Dining Room*), that serve as human heads elsewhere in the late work. At any rate, as late as

---

[11] Viewed two-dimensionally, the figures of the sick seem to surround the saint, but taken in terms of perspective (even in the loose way Bonnard has always handled it), they appear some distance behind, the distance itself being doubtful as a result of the amorphous character of the space between the saint and the man with the crutch.

March, 1945, after two years' work on the painting, Bonnard was having difficulties assimilating this area.

"It isn't quite resolved," he told his painter friend, Jules Joëts, "because the face seems too far forward. I tried putting equivalent reds in the background but it doesn't do the trick."

"Don't you think it would be interesting to leave the figure somewhat detached from the background," Joëts asked.

"No, indeed!" Bonnard replied. "That's just what I want to avoid." [12]

The *Saint Francis of Sales* has suffered more than any other work in the Assy ensemble by its placement in the church. It made a far better impression when exhibited in 1947 at the Bonnard retrospective of the Museum of Modern Art in Paris. The tender coloring and the intimate character of the forms do not harmonize at all well with the monumental rustic interior of Assy. Unlike the bolder works of Matisse and Lurçat, Bonnard's does not project, and its presence can be appreciated only when the observer is directly before the lateral altar which it decorates. Even then the effect is spoiled by the absence of adequate lighting and by the disturbing blue, red, and rust illumination of Adeline Hébert-Stevens' window of *Our Lady of the Seven Sorrows* located at right angles to the altarpiece.

If Bonnard's *Saint Francis* seems out of place in the church, Matisse's *Saint Dominic* (see plate and Figure 47), conceived for the corresponding altar terminating the north aisle, is perfectly adapted in both scale and character to the enveloping architecture and to the other decorative works. The warm bright tones of its yellow ceramic tiles attract the observer's attention, and the presence of the boldly drawn saint communicates to the farthest reaches of the church.

The selection of Matisse for the Saint Dominic was an outgrowth of the painter's newly found interest in sacred art already manifested in his undertaking a chapel for the Dominican nuns at Vence. When, in 1948, Canon Devémy approached Matisse with the suggestion that he decorate the altar, the latter had already begun preparatory drawings for a figure of Saint Dominic

[12] Jules Joëts, "Le Dernier Entretien de Pierre Bonnard avec le peintre Jules Joëts," *Arts-Documents*, 1953, No. 29.

for the Vence Chapel; at the urging of Father Couturier—who posed for the first studies of the Saint (Figure 46)—he agreed to make a variant for Assy, using the same medium, ceramic tiles. Since at Assy the field was smaller and closed at the top by a round arch, Matisse rendered the saint in half-length and introduced mediating grapevine ornaments at left and right.

Matisse's sudden involvement with sacred art at Vence and at Assy was testimony to friendship and charity rather than religious faith.[13] During his long career, he had never evinced particular interest in Catholicism, and his few references to "God" and "religion" were vague allusions to the mystery of creation. In *Notes of a Painter* (1908), for example, Matisse wrote of preferring the human figure to still-life or landscape as a vehicle "for the so-to-say (*pour ainsi dire*) religious feeling that I have towards life." [14] Nearly forty years later, in *Jazz,* he answered a rhetorical question about belief in God by saying: "When I work . . . I feel somehow aided by someone who makes me do things that are beyond me." [15] But the casual and general character of these remarks has not prevented their being exploited by critics interested in suggesting the possibility of Matisse's conversion.[16]

[13] The events leading to Matisse's essay in sacred art were rather casual. During his recovery from an operation in 1941 he was attended by a young nurse with whom he became quite friendly. She later became a Dominican novice and went to Vence to serve in a conventual rest home for tubercular girls called the "Foyer Lacordaire." As Matisse's villa was just across the road, the nurse, now called Sister Jacques, often went to visit him. One day she brought a watercolor design she had made for a window in the convent's new oratory. Matisse encouraged her and very soon began designing windows himself. In the end, he offered to do the whole chapel and personally underwrote a considerable part of the cost.

[14] Henri Matisse, "Notes d'un peintre," *La Grande Revue,* 12th year, No. 52, November–December, 1908, pp. 731–45.

[15] Matisse, *Jazz* (Paris: Editions Verve, 1947).

[16] Cf., for example, Michel Florisoone ("Matisse et la main de Dieu," *Études,* 79th year, Tome 248, February, 1946, pp. 246–50), who builds upon the earlier citation; and *La Vie Catholique illustrée,* which took the later citation out of context, headlining an article on Matisse: "Every time I work I believe in God." (Cf. Barr, *Matisse: His Art and His Public,* p. 287.) The most disturbing misinterpretation of Matisse's intent received the widest circulation. This was a Reuters dispatch datelined Vance [*sic*], June 25, 1951, published in the United States by the New York *Times,* in which the painter was quoted as having said: "I started this work four years ago, and as a result I know I now believe in God."

157

THE ALTARPIECES

Until the 1940s Matisse had completely avoided religious subject matter, and, as late as a year before he undertook the chapel at Vence, he still considered such themes foreign to his creative spirit. Asked by Brother Rayssiguier (who subsequently became important in the planning of the chapel) to try a religious subject, "a Virgin, for example," Matisse replied: "No, I do not feel such subjects. . . . When I paint something profane, God directs me, and it goes beyond me. If I tried to make a Virgin, I would be forcing. God would leave me to myself." [17] His final decision to do the Vence chapel involved no change in fundamental attitude. "I did not feel the need to convert in order to do the chapel," he told André Lejard. "My interior attitude has not altered; it has remained the same as it was when I was confronted by a face, a chair, or a bowl of fruit." [18]

The *Saint Dominic* of Assy exemplifies that linear purity and perfection which characterized the works of Matisse's last years. Preceded by somewhat fussier drawings, the image was gradually purged of nonessentials and synthesized until each line became endowed with maximum evocative power. Nowhere is this more remarkable than in the head of the saint. As in the Vence version, no features are delineated,[19] but unlike the later work, that of Assy shows the head turning sideways. It is extraordinary how this single outer contour line seems to suggest not only the motion of the head but the entire expression of the visage. The motif of the turning head imparts to the saint a mobility he lacks in the more hieratic, frontal version at Vence.

At Assy, Dominic's body is frontal, the symmetry broken only by the emergence of his left arm from under the cassock. His left hand holds a holy book, the form of which balances the protruding sleeve. But if we are at first struck by the symmetry, we gradually realize that the drama of the work lies in the many subtle deviations from this principle. The whole figure, for example, though constructed on an axis formed by a vertical fissure between the

[17] Régamey, *L'Art sacré au XXe siècle,* pp. 232–33.

[18] André Lejard, "Propos de Henri Matisse," *Guilde du livre,* June, 1952 (Matisse File, Museum of Modern Art Library).

[19] In *Notes of a Painter,* Matisse observed, in reference to the figure paintings by which he expressed his "so-to-say religious feeling": "I do not insist upon the details of the face."

HENRI MATISSE, *Saint Dominic*
CERAMIC TILE, ALTAR DECORATION

ceramic panels, is, like Bonnard's saint, slightly to the side of the axis of the field. All the forms and lines that at first seem symmetrical are subtly individuated. The hood rises higher on the saint's left than on his right and the contours of the shoulders are quite different. There is nothing predictable in the way the lines progress. The contours alter direction subtly, their thickness changing suddenly in response to the varying pressures of the brush. The direction of each line seems discovered en route.

On the symbolic level, the grapevine ornament at the side hovers ambiguously between the "Luxe, calme et volupté"[20] of Matisse's private world and allusion to the "true vine" (John 15.1). But its "message" is primarily formal, as it always is in Matisse. The small, irregular forms of the leaves and the spot-marks representing grapes provide a wonderful foil for the more ascetic contours of the figure. The stems, while beautifully interrelated with the forms of the figure, constitute in themselves an interesting system. In the lower half of the image they run roughly parallel, bending out towards the right and then shifting direction, but from the neck of Saint Dominic to the top of the image they are symmetrical with respect to the central axis (i.e., mirror images). At the point (above the sleeve) at which the parallelism of the rinceaux halts, however, a new parallelism is established between the vine on the (viewer's) right and the line formed by the inner contour of the cloak and the side of the collar.

The rinceaux break out at the top in directions opposite to the contour of the arch-shaped frame thereby counteracting the oppressive weight of the rusticated voussoirs of the arch (see plate) and emphasizing the lateral expansion of the space of the image. Since the ceramic is of but one color (save for the black lines of the drawing) and contains no trace of chiaroscuro, the image remains wholly in the picture plane.

[20] This title (of a painting of 1904–5), along with those like *Joie de vivre* and *Dance,* constitute an ideal index to Matisse's art. The phrase is borrowed from the refrain of Baudelaire's "Invitation au voyage," which reads: "La tout n'est qu'ordre et beauté, / Luxe, calme, et volupté."

12. THE RICHIER CRUCIFIX

Little did Germaine Richier realize that a visit to her tubercular niece at the sanatorium of Sancellemoz in 1948 would lead to one of the most significant works of her career and one destined to become a *cause célèbre* in the bitter debate on sacred art. It was on that trip that she met Canon Devémy, who was first to interest her in doing something (no subject in particular was mentioned) for the church of Assy. A short time later Father Courturier prevailed on her to collaborate in the project, suggesting that she create a crucifix, a liturgical object he considered appropriate for her "dry" style. At first Madame Richier rejected the idea, preferring to make some sculptural decoration in the form of a pure abstract sign, but finally she agreed to do the crucifix. From that moment Father Couturier studiously refrained from trying to influence the outcome of the work; indeed, he did not even discuss the liturgical character and significance of the cult object with the artist.[1]

For Madame Richier the task was totally novel. Herself an atheist, she had never had occasion to make a religious figure, even a mythological one, save for an early abstraction which she thought of partly as a head of Christ. "But this," she has noted, "was really just a study of form." A trip south to Assy helped her to develop a better sense of the character and atmosphere of the

[1] Both Fathers Couturier and Régamey have always insisted in their writings that the interested priest must "educate" the artist, discussing with him not only the canon laws concerning art but the spiritual implications of the subject being represented. But these statements appear to have been intended for ecclesiastical consumption. The fact is that with the partial exception of Léger and Bonnard, this "instruction" never took place in connection with Assy. Given the creative processes of most of the artists involved, it is doubtful that such discussion would have been profitable—or even welcome.

church and resulted in several quick sketches since destroyed. Though the process of her art remained the same and though she felt no special inspiration as a result of the liturgical subject matter, she sensed more and more as work progressed that "unconscious things of a unique kind were being translated."

The first sketches made at Assy were utilized for a plaster maquette with a figure of Christ much larger than it was to be in the final work; this the artist set aside as too static. Down at the church once again, she began a new series of sketches. By now the Lurçat tapestry, against which the crucifix could be seen, was temporarily installed, and Madame Richier was able to adjust the proportions and dimensions of the piece to its future setting.

In Paris again, she began to elaborate a large plaster cross. The surface was handled so as to resemble craggy and weathered wood—the textural common denominator of much of her mature sculpture.[2] Its tortured and sacrificial appearance evoked appropriate associations for a crucifix.

As she worked over the plaster (Figure 52A), the body of Christ slowly began to take shape, emerging from the structure of the Cross. A large curve was introduced by bowing out the legs and the upper torso, which thus became distinctly separated from the upright of the Cross. This separation does not obtain horizontally, where the slight suggestions of a cross-bar are buried by being fused with the arms of the figure. Vague indications of a head, a chest cavity, and some drapery about the hips were gradually worked into the plaster but, as even in the final state, these were suppressed "so as not to interfere with the sign quality of the work."

Some significant changes occurred between this preparatory plaster maquette and the final work (Figures 52B, 53). The right leg of Christ, considerably shorter than the left in the former, was equalized in length, and forms identifiable as feet were added to the terminations of the legs. As a result, the vertical emphasis was proportionately increased, and whereas a marked horizontality obtained in the preparatory state, the final version reads in an ascending manner. Moreover, the suggestion of a horizontal bar extending

[2] The raw, seemingly ugly, textural character of Richier's work relates her to the movement of "L'Art brut," which has emerged since the war, its major exponent in painting being Jean Dubuffet.

beyond Christ's arms was eliminated so that the horizontal section of the definitive work consists simply of the arms, which now terminate clearly in hands.

Beyond adding hands and legs to the figure, Madame Richier also clarified the articulation of the torso. This is particularly noticeable in the handling of the muscles of the shoulders, elbows, and wrists. The apparent laying bare of anatomy led one critic to compare Madame Richier with Ligier Richier.[3] In the visage two small holes suggesting eyes have become barely visible, and below the ridge which we read as the nose, a slight horizontal incision has been made to represent the mouth.[4]

After the single bronze cast of the final plaster was made, Madame Richier worked over its surface with abrasives, creating the rich contrasts between the polished highlights of the ridges and the dark encrusted valleys in the surfaces. This treatment rendered the surface even more like petrified bark, and upon seeing the Crucifix Father Couturier was immediately reminded of Isaiah 53: "For he shall grow up . . . as a root out of a dry ground; he hath no form nor comeliness. . . . He is despised and rejected of men; a man of sorrows." Madame Richier had not had this passage in mind, but she did not object to

---

[3] De Mandiargues, "Germaine Richier," *Le Disque vert,* I, No. 4 (July–August, 1953). Though both would appear to be concerned with the corruption of the flesh, the resemblance noted here is more apparent than real. Ligier Richier conveys the late medieval horror of death through gruesome and exceedingly realistic representations of human anatomy in various states of disintegration. What appears to be putrefaction (I prefer to call it "weathering") in the sculpture of Germaine Richier belongs, not to the figure represented (here the Christ), but to the material employed, i.e., it is a texture common to a large part of her *oeuvre* and exists a priori as a "vocabulary" element before its application in specific works. If considered an attribute of Christ's body (as it is widely misread), such texture would certainly constitute sacrilege.

[4] In the scandal surrounding this work (see Chapter 3), certain writers, basing their opinion on photographs alone, described the work as "faceless," e.g., Walter Bernardi, "Der Streit um Assy," *Rheinischer Merkur,* May 3, 1951 (File of Father Régamey). Were this true, the work would run afoul of ecclesiastic regulations insuring the humanity of Christ in imagery. First promulgated by the Council of Trent in its twenty-fifth session, these regulations were later incorporated into the Corpus of Canon Law (No. 1279). Mariani, *La Legislazione ecclesiastica in materia d'arte sacra,* p. 99. Madame Richier, however, was, in any case, unaware of the canonical requirement.

162

its being inscribed on a placard near the work when, shortly afterward, it was set on the central altar at the church.

Germaine Richier was hardly prepared for the agonized clamor and cries of sacrilege that erupted shortly after the Crucifix was delivered to the church. "A scandalous and anti-Christian thing," wrote Monseigneur Touzé,[5] director of the Chantiers du Cardinal, his comment typifying the almost universal re-action of conservative clerics. Soon the Crucifix became, above all other con-tributions to Assy, the *cause célèbre* and the rallying point of the traditionalists in the extended debate that ensued.

Of the various criticisms focusing specifically on the Crucifix, the most im-portant related to its special role as cult object in the liturgy. The Catholic sculptor Henri Charlier, alluding to the qualities that separate a crucifix from other elements of church decoration, attacked Madame Richier's work as "liturgically insufficient," though he did not indicate the failing,[6] and even Father Régamey admitted the possibility of difference of opinion on "the rightness of so pathetic a work for its liturgical function." [7] Stanislas Fumet was more specific, asking how the priest could unveil in three movements (as is required in the Easter Service) Christ's head, right arm, and finally, whole body if the anatomical readability of the sculpture was insufficient.[8]

More important, however, than the way in which the Crucifix might contra-dict the letter of the liturgy was the way in which it related to its spirit. Did the work display that transcendence of physical suffering which is the heart of the liturgical message? On this subjective question opinions differed considerably; even a critic familiar with the language of modern art attacked the Crucifix as a "bit of hacked and writhing skin," in which he was unable to discover "the

---

[5] Touzé, "L'Art sacré," 18th year, No. 8, 1951, p. 3. *Le Christ dans le bainlieu.*

[6] Charlier, "À propos de Christ de l'église d'Assy," *Écrits de Paris,* September, 1951, pp. 50–55.

[7] Régamey, "La Querelle de l'art sacré," *La Vie intellectuelle,* November, 1951, pp. 3–48.

[8] Stanislas Fumet, "Un Christ d'atelier peut n'être pas un Christ d'église," *Recherches et débats,* July, 1951, No. 15–16. It would seem that Fumet's impression of the work was based either on hearsay or on a very poor photograph, for no one, no matter how unfamiliar with modern art, would have difficulty in discerning at least the broader anatomical elements in Madame Richier's Crucifix.

victory of Christ over suffering and death." [9] The Jesuit Father Henri de Montrond, by the same token, saw the Crucifix as sinning paradoxically "by excess of realism." Criticizing what he considered an over-emphasis on the physical aspects of the crucifixion, he argued that the sculpture reflected "less the sacrifice of Christ than the expression of Madame Richier's own confusion in the face of vast contemporary suffering." "Her language," he continued, "realistically translates . . . more of this personal sentiment than the profound thought of the Church." [10]

Yet this violence had its defenders. Denise Kohler considered the *horreur sacrée* of the sculpture precisely the antidote to today's widespread spiritless exercise of the liturgy. "Recent churches," she observed, "do not cry loudly enough the price paid for the 'good news.' . . . [Madame Richier's piece] is of a hallucinatory theological and scriptural truth. . . . It enters our skin like a red hot iron." [11]

[9] "Testis" [Gabriel Marcel], "Le Pseudo-Christ de Germaine Richier banni de l'église d'Assy," *L'Homme nouveau,* July 29, 1951.

[10] De Montrond, "Art sacré et théologie," *Etude,* December, 1951.

[11] Denise Kohler, "Le Christ d'Assy est un Christ d'église," *Recherches et débats,* January, 1952, No. 18.

CONCLUSION

The revival of religious art which took place at Assy could not have been generated from within the ranks of Catholicism alone; rather it depended upon a new, unorthodox, and tenuous alliance between the community of artists and a liberal minority within the Church. Before the Second World War the attempt to reanimate sacred art, carried out completely within the confines of the Catholic world, had succeeded only in substituting poor modernistic art for the older academic and pseudo-historical styles. The church of Assy was made possible solely by a radical change in policy through which the community of genuine artists, few of them Catholic and many of them actively opposed to religion, was invited to participate in the church.

The surprising acceptance of some of these artists was due to a momentary convergence of normally conflicting interests, producing a coalition that took place only in France and that depended on a number of unusual circumstances created by the war. In the five years from the end of the war until the dedication of the church the patriotic front of the Resistance, which comprehended both priests and Communists, continued to exercise a cohesive influence. As a result of the Worker-Priest movement a new rapport developed between the liberal priesthood and some Socialists (and even Communists), a rapport between the French Left and the Church that was greatest among the intellectuals and artists on both sides. The Resistance ideal of a new world, which the Liberation was to have rendered possible, had not yet gone up in the smoke of cynicism.

The modern masters who worked at Assy in no way embraced the tenets of Catholicism. Nor did they surrender their almost universal distrust of institutional religion. They were, and remain, largely unfamiliar with the liturgy

165

CONCLUSION

which sacred art celebrates. The subjects chosen by the Dominicans, particularly as they were revised to suit the participating artists, did not constitute, as is customary, an affirmation of the dogma, hierarchy, or calendar of the Church. Moreover, in some instances (e.g., Lurçat's tapestry and Chagall's ceramic mural) even this limited iconography was handled so that its traditional meanings were altered or translated into purely personal philosophies.

The work of Rouault, the single major Catholic artist of our century, emerges as foreign in spirit to the liturgy and, paradoxically, more antisacramental than the efforts of the Communist Léger. As a person and as a painter we see Rouault isolated from the community of believers towards whom the Communists Léger and Lurçat and the religious Jew Lipchitz seem more directly oriented. In Rouault's windows at Assy, and to varying extents in the contributions of the others, the religious subject matter becomes a way of expanding the hegemony and variety of modern art. But this modern imagery in no way enlarges or develops the sacramental iconography of Christianity. The decorations at Assy thus constitute neither a resumption of the centuries-old tradition of sacred art nor a new beginning of artistic experience that can be assimilated into the spirit of the liturgy.

Participation at Assy led to no new stylistic or compositional discoveries in the works of the artists involved, and in some cases (e.g., Bonnard's altarpiece) the religious focus of the task fostered uncharacteristic and limiting hieratic formulations. None of the artists testified to any special inspiration as the result of the religious nature of the commission; in fact, some questioned the central place traditionally accorded faith as a generator of religious art, even in the Middle Ages.

The Dominican promoters of the church of Assy appear as prophets without honor in their own country, for the Catholic Church at large did not support the venture. The works at Assy were not commissioned through normal ecclesiastical channels but were, to a large extent, gifts of the artists involved: testimonials to friendships (with men like Father Couturier and Jacques Maritain), to alliances (Lurçat fought alongside priests in the Resistance), and to supra-Catholic social and spiritual ideals. When the church was finished, it was viewed with alarm by the Vatican, which soon opened an attack upon Assy

166

as a part of its general repression of the New Gallicanism. Begun in 1950, this struggle has abated in the last few years, but only with the triumph of the Ultramontanists and the dissipation of the Sacred Art Movement and the Worker-Priests mission.

In the disheartening wake of these bitter disputes the prestige of Catholicism among artists and intellectuals, which was at its height in the five years following the end of the war, has largely disappeared, and the Church's opportunity to take advantage of the spiritual vacuum that existed in France appears to have passed. Many of the artists who participated at Assy would no longer be inclined to do so. Far from being the beginning of a "Renaissance" of sacred art, the church of Assy now seems destined to go down in history as an anomaly—in company with the equally unique chapel of Matisse and the church of Le Corbusier.

Modern churches will be built, and occasionally a great modern painter will decorate one of them, but reunions of masters, such as the church of Assy witnessed, will probably never take place again. An undertaking of comparably great scale and meaning must wait upon the time when established religions recreate themselves as spiritual leaders of the artistic and intellectual world or are replaced by a new idealistic synthesis having the power to inspire men of vision.

BIBLIOGRAPHY

Abbé Belloin. Lettre à Son Excellence Mgr. Touzé, Directeur des "Chantiers du Cardinal," dated Sanarose Martel, February 1, 1953.

Agnel, Arnaud d'. L'Art religieux moderne. Grenoble, B. Arthaud, 1936.

Aubert, R. Le Pontificat de Pie IX. Paris, Bloud and Gay, 1952.

Auvert, Guy-Jean. Défense et illustration de l'art sacré. Paris, Nouvelles Editions Latines, 1956.

Bardet, Gaston. "La Maison de Dieu," Temoignages de la Pierre-Qui-Vire, January, 1953, No. 36, pp. 50–56.

———— "Una Polemica si allarga," Arte cristiana, XXXVIII, No. 11–12 (November–December, 1951), 129–30.

Barr, Alfred. Matisse: His Art and His Public. New York, Museum of Modern Art, 1951.

Bartoli, Luciano. L'Arte nella casa di Dio. Turin, Società Editrice Internazionale, 1950.

Bazaine, Jean. "Bonnard et la réalité," Formes et couleurs, VI, No. 2 (March, 1944), 39–48.

———— "Marie-Alain Couturier, o.p.," Esprit, XXII, No. 5 (May, 1954), 774–81.

———— Notes sur la peinture. Paris, Éditions du Seuil, 1953.

———— "Sens de l'art moderne" (interview), Zodiaque, II, No. 18–19 (January, 1954), 61–66.

Bernardi, Walter. "Der Streit um Assy," Rheinischer Merkur, May 3, 1951 (File of Father Régamey).

Bloy, Léon. "Notes de Léon Bloy sur Rouault," Cahiers d'art, III, 3 (1928).

Bourniquel, Camille. "La Querelle de l'art sacré," Esprit, XIX, No. 10 (October, 1951), 563–72.

Bourniquel, Camille, and Jean Guichard-Meili, Les Créateurs et le sacré. Paris, Éditions du Cerf, 1956.

Bréhier, Louis. L'Art chrétien. 2d ed. Paris, Laurens, 1928.

169

BIBLIOGRAPHY

Brenson, Theodore. "Abstract Art and Christianity," *Liturgical Arts,* XXII, No. 3 (May, 1954), 76–78.

Breton, Guy. "L'Église la plus moderne du monde sonne le glas du style Saint Sulpice," *Noir et blanc,* 6th year, No. 286, August 16, 1950, p. 563.

Brillant, Maurice. L'Art chrétien en France au XXme siècle. Paris, Bloudet Gay, 1927.

Bulletin paroissial liturgique. Paris, Les Éditions du Cerf, No. 15, 1939.

Canons and Decrees of the Council of Trent. Translated by H. J. Schroeder. St. Louis and London, 1941.

Cassou, Jean. "Paris: Controversy and Quintessence," *Art News,* L, No. 2 (April, 1951), 18–19, 57–58.

Chagall, Marc. "Ceramics," a note dated Vence, September, 1952, printed in the catalogue of the Chagall Exhibition at the Curt Valentin Gallery, New York, November, 1952.

———— Illustrations for the Bible. Introduction by Meyer Schapiro. Additional text by Jean Wahl. New York, Harcourt, Brace, 1956.

———— Lecture delivered at the University of Chicago. English translation in *The Works of the Mind*. Edited by Robert Haywood. Chicago, University of Chicago Press, 1947.

Charlier, Henri. "À propos du Christ de l'église d'Assy," *Écrits de Paris,* September, 1951, pp. 50–55.

———— "L'Art dans la communauté chrétienne," in *Problèmes de l'art sacré.* Edited by Debidour. Paris, Le Nouveau Portique, n.d.

Chastel, André. "Les Problèmes de l'art religieux," Pt. I, *Le Monde,* December 13, 1951, No. 2140, p. 7; Pt. II, *Le Monde,* December 14, 1951, No. 2141, p. 7.

Cingria, Alexandre. La Décadence de l'art sacré. Lausanne, Cahiers Vaudois, 1917.

Claudel, Paul. "Lettre à Alexandre Cingria," in *Positions et propositions,* Vol. II. Paris, Gallimard, 1934.

Cocteau, Jean. Lettre à Jacques Maritain. Paris, Stock, 1926.

Cogniat, Raymond. "Rouault: l'inspiration religieuse et la recherche des signes," *Les Arts plastiques,* 5th series, No. 4, January–February, 1952, pp. 252–58.

Corte, Marcel de. "La Querelle de l'art sacré," *La Libre belgique,* February 5, 1952 (File of Father Régamey).

Costantini, Celso. "Dell'arte sacra deformatrice," *Osservatore Romano,* June 10, 1951, p. 1.

———— "Réponse à diverses critiques," *Osservatore Romano,* August 20, 1951, p. 1.

———— "San Pio X e l'arte," *Fede ed arte,* 2nd year, No. 6, June, 1954, pp. 169–77.

———— "Signore ho amato il decoro della tua casa," *Fede ed arte* (entire issue), 2nd year, No. 2, February, 1954, pp. 33–63.

Costantini, Giovanni. "Accordo e collaborazione fra artisti e clero," *Fede ed arte,* 1st year, No. 9, September, 1953, pp. 258–63.

———— "Norme pratiche per l'ordinazione e l'esecuzione delle opere d'arte sacra," *Fede ed arte,* 1st year, No. 5, May, 1953, pp. 149–51.

Costantini, Celso, and Giovanni Costantini. Fede ed arte, Vol. II. Rome, Pontificia Commissione Centrale per l'Arte Sacre, 1946.

Coulton, G. G. Art and the Reformation. Cambridge, The University Press, 1953.

Couturier, Marie-Alain, O.P. Art et catholicisme. Montreal, Éditions de l'Arbre, 1945.

———— "L'Art religieux moderne," *Le Figaro,* October 24, 1951, p. 3.

———— "The Assy Church," *Life,* XXVIII, No. 25 (June 19, 1950), 72–76.

———— "Byzance et nos efforts," *L'Art sacré,* May–June, 1953, No. 9–10, pp. 26–27.

———— "Deux églises Savoyards," *L'Art sacré,* 4th year, No. 29, May, 1938, pp. 117–21.

———— "L'Église d'Assy," *Art et decoration,* 1950, No. 16, pp. 17–22.

———— "L'Église d'Assy," *Arts,* April 16, 1948, p. 1.

———— "Historique de l'église d'Assy," *L'Art sacré,* September–October, 1950, No. 1–2, pp. 2–7.

———— "La Leçon d'Assy," *L'Art sacré,* September–October, 1950, No. 1–2, pp. 16–20.

———— "Léger et le moyen âge," in *Fernand Léger: La Forme humaine dans l'espace.* Montreal, Éditions de l'Arbre, 1945.

———— "Note on Assy," *Liturgical Arts,* XIX, No. 2 (February, 1951), 30–31.

———— "Religious Art and the Modern Artist," *Magazine of Art,* XLIV, No. 7 (November, 1951), 268–72.

———— "Sur le plateau d'Assy," *La Vie catholique illustrée,* August 13, 1950, No. 265 (File of Father Régamey).

———— "Trois églises" (unpublished project for a preface), January, 1954 (File of Father Régamey).

———— Unpublished letter to M. Frank Elgar in reply to his articles on Assy and Audincourt published in *Carrefour* (File of Father Régamey).

Cram, Ralph. The Catholic Church and Art. New York, Macmillan, 1930.

Crooy, F. Chanoine. Dogme et art. Brussels, Goemaire, 1947.

Debidour, Victor-Henri. "Autour de l'église d'Assy," in *Problèmes de l'art sacré.* Edited by Debidour. Paris, Le Nouveau Portique, n.d.

———— "Une Enquête sur quelques aspects actuels des problèmes de l'art sacré,"

BIBLIOGRAPHY

in *Problèmes de l'art sacré*. Edited by Debidour. Paris, Le Nouveau Portique, n.d.

Denis, Maurice. Histoire de l'art religieux. Paris, Ernest Flammarion, 1939.

Descargues, Pierre. Fernand Léger. Paris, Editions Cercle d'art, 1955.

Devémy, Jean. "L'Église d'Assy et l'art sacré," *Courier de l'ouest,* January 6, 1951, p. 1.

―――― "Die Kirche von Assy," *Werk,* April, 1949 (File of Father Régamey).

―――― "Visites à Bonnard," *L'Art sacré,* September–October, 1950, No. 1–2, pp. 8–9.

Doncoeur, Paul. "Confusions et clartés dans le débat sur l'art sacré," *Etudes,* 85th year, Tome 273, April, 1952, pp. 30–39.

―――― "Au service de l'art sacré," *Etudes,* 80th year, Tome 252, January, 1947, pp. 110–15.

Dorival, Bernard. "Le Divorce de l'art et du public," *L'Art sacré,* January–February, 1951, No. 5–6, pp. 4–8.

―――― "L'Église d'Assy ou la résurrection de l'art sacré," *Médecine de France,* 1950, No. 18, pp. 29–32.

―――― "Épurons les églises," *La Table ronde,* June, 1951, No. 42, pp. 160–62.

Douaire, Richard. "Pilgrimage to Assy, an Appraisal," *Liturgical Arts,* XIX, No. 2 (February, 1951), 28–30.

Duthuit, Georges. "Documents," *Transition, Forty-nine,* 1949, No. 5, pp. 125–26.

Elgar, Frank. "L'Église d'Assy, une magnifique tentative manquée," *Carrefour,* 6th year, No. 313, September 12, 1950, p. 9.

Erben, Walter. Marc Chagall. London, Thames and Hudson, 1957.

Farge, M. "Saint esprit contre Saint Sulpice," *Cahiers des Alpes,* 1st year, No. 2, November, 1951, pp. 80–85.

Ferrand, Gabriel. "The Wonderful Wak-Wak Tree," *Encyclopedia of Islam,* Fasciculus R, pp. 1106–7.

Florenne, Yves. "Prière pour un agonisant: fin de l'art sacré?" *Mercure de France,* CCCXVII, No. 1073 (January–April, 1953), 54–62.

Florisoone, Michel. "Matisse et la main de Dieu," *Etudes,* 79th year, Tome 248, February, 1946, pp. 246–50.

Frank, Carlo Borromeo. Kernfragen kirchlicher Kunst. Vienna, Herder, 1953.

Froger, Pierre. "L'Art bafoué," *Courrier de l'ouest,* January 2, 1951 (File of Father Régamey).

Fumet, Stanislas. "Un Christ d'atelier peut n'être pas un Christ d'église," *Recherches et débats,* July, 1951, No. 15–16.

Gennep, Dr. A. van, "Essai sur le culte populaire des saints franciscains en Savoie," *Revue d'histoire franciscaine,* IV, No. 2 (April–June, 1927), 113–210.

172

Grenier, Jean. "Idées de Georges Rouault," *L'Oeil,* April, 1957, No. 28, pp. 30–41.

Guerrisi, Michele. "L'Arte religiosa e la crisi del gusto contemporaneo," *Fede ed arte,* 1st year, No. 3, March, 1953, pp. 77–84.

——— "L'Estetica del cubismo," *Fede ed arte,* 1st year, No. 7, July, 1953, pp. 194–97.

Guide (to the church of Assy), *L'Art sacré,* September–October, 1950, No. 1–2, pp. 11–15.

Hennig, John. "Liturgy and Modern Art," *Liturgical Arts,* XIII, No. 1 (November, 1944), 2–4.

Henze, Anton, and Theodor Filthaut. Contemporary Church Art. Translated by Cecily Hastings, ed. by Maurice Lavanoux. New York, Sheed and Ward, 1956.

Heron, Patrick. The Changing Forms of Art. London, Routledge, 1955.

Hirsch, Pierre. Jean Lurçat et la tapisserie. Paris, Victor Michon, 1946.

Hope, Henry. The Sculpture of Jacques Lipchitz. New York, Museum of Modern Art, 1954.

Houvet, Etienne. Cathédrale de Chartres, Vol. VII. Chelles, A. Faucheux, 1926.

Hurel, Abbé J. A. L'Art religieux contemporain. Paris, Didier, 1868.

Joëts, Jules. "Le Dernier Entretien de Pierre Bonnard avec le peintre Jules Joëts," *Arts-documents,* February, 1953, No. 29, pp. 8–9.

Kohler, Denise. "Le Christ d'Assy est un Christ d'église," *Recherches et débats,* January, 1952, No. 18.

Kreitmaier, Joseph. "Die Beuroner Kunstschule," *Stimmen aus Maria Laach,* LXXXVI (1913), 48–66.

Kuh, Katherine. Fernand Léger. Chicago, Art Institute of Chicago, 1953.

Labourt, Le Chanoine. "Réponse à une enquête sur l'art sacré: presentée par Maurice Brillant," *La Croix,* May 10, 1952, pp. 2–3.

Lacôte, René. "Jean Lurçat et l'avenir de la tapisserie française," *Arts de France,* January, 1951, No. 34, pp. 62–63.

LaFarge, John. "Private Opinion and Church Authority," *Liturgical Arts,* XVI, No. 4 (August, 1948), 124–25.

Laprade, Jacques de. "Notes sur Rouault," *Le Point,* 5th year, No. 26–27, August–October, 1943, pp. 59–75.

Larrea, Juan. "An Open Letter to Jacques Lipchitz," *College Art Journal,* XIII, No. 13 (Summer, 1954), 251–88.

Lassaigne, Jacques. Chagall. Paris, Maeght, 1957.

Lavanoux, Maurice. "The Authentic Tradition in Art," *Liturgical Arts,* XXII, No. 4 (August, 1954), 122–25.

BIBLIOGRAPHY

Lavanoux, Maurice. Editorial, *Liturgical Arts,* XXVI, No. 2 (February, 1958), 41–42.

———— "Preliminary Report: First International Congress of Catholic Artists," *Liturgical Arts,* XIX, No. 1 (November, 1950), 4–6.

Lebesque, Morvan. "Le Scandale du Christ d'Assy," *Carrefour,* 6th year, No. 356, July 11, 1951, p. 3.

Ledeur, Chanoine. "Conseils fraternels," *L'Art sacré,* January–February, 1951, No. 5–6, pp. 15–17.

Léger, Fernand. "À propos du corps humain consideré comme un objet," in *Fernand Léger: La Forme humaine dans l'espace*. Montreal, Editions de l'Arbre, 1945.

———— "L'Architecture moderne et la couleur," *Formes et vie,* 1951, No. 1, pp. 24–28.

———— "Byzantine Mosaics and Modern Art," *Magazine of Art,* XXXVII, No. 4 (April, 1944), 144–45.

———— "Discorso egli architetti," *Casabella continuità,* September–October, 1955, No. 207, pp. 69–70.

———— Letter from Léger, *L'Art sacré,* March–April, 1954, No. 7–8, p. 6.

———— "Reflexions sur l'intégration de la peinture et de la sculpture dans l'architecture," *I Quattro Soli,* I, No. 1 (January, 1954), 8.

———— "Sens de l'art moderne" (interview), *Zodiaque,* II, No. 18–19 (January, 1954), 36–40.

Lejard, André. "Propos de Henri Matisse," *Guilde du livre,* June, 1952 (Matisse File, Museum of Modern Art Library).

Lemaître, Henri (ed.). "L'Art sacré, le clergé et les fidèles," Centre d'Informations Catholiques, Paris, May 19, 1952 (mimeographed).

Lhôte, André. La Peinture libérée. Paris, Grasset, 1956.

Lhotellier, Auguste. "Nos Frères dominicains," *Esprit,* XXII, No. 3 (March, 1954), 407–9.

Lipchitz, Jacques. "Symposium (statement) on Art and Religion," *Art Digest,* XXVIII, No. 6 (December 15, 1953), 8–11, 31–33.

———— The Drawings of Jacques Lipchitz. New York, Curt Valentin, 1944.

Lurçat, Jean. "Un Artiste devant le métier," *Art et décoration,* 1946, No. 2, pp. 120–25.

———— Le Bestiaire de la tapisserie du moyen âge. Geneva, Cailler, 1947.

———— Tapisserie française. Paris, Bordas ed., 1947.

Machard, Albert. "L'Église d'Assy et l'art chrétien," *Ouest-France,* 7th year, No. 1921, January 5, 1951, p. 4.

174

Mâle, Émile. L'Art religieux après le concile de Trente. Paris, Colin, 1932.

Malraux, André. "De l'art et des masses," *Liberté de l'esprit,* 3rd year, No. 22, June, 1951, pp. 177–80.

——— "Rouault," *Formes,* December, 1929, No. 1, pp. 5–6.

——— The Voices of Silence. Translated by Stuart Gilbert. New York, Doubleday, 1953.

Mandiargues, André Pieyre de. Germaine Richier. Brussels, Editions Synthèses, n.d.

——— "Germaine Richier," *Le Disque vert,* I, No. 4 (July–August, 1953).

Marcel, Gabriel. "Lettre à La Table ronde sur le Christ de l'église d'Assy," *La Table ronde,* July, 1951, No. 43, pp. 181–82.

Marchand, André. In *Cahiers de l'art sacré,* 1946, No. 7, p. 35.

Margerie, Amédée de. St. François de Sales. Paris, Gabalda, 1927.

Mariani, Goffredo. La Legislazione ecclesiastica in materia d'arte sacra. Rome, Ferrari, 1945.

Maritain, Jacques. Art and Poetry. New York, Philosophical Library, 1943.

——— Art and Scholasticism with Other Essays ("The Frontiers of Poetry," "An Essay on Art," "Some Reflections on Religious Art"). Translated by J. F. Scanlan. New York, Scribner, 1930.

——— "Chagall," *Selection,* Cahier 6, June, 1929, pp. 27–39.

——— Creative Intuition in Art and Poetry. New York, Meridian Books, 1955.

——— Foreword to the Catalogue of the Rouault Retrospective Exhibition, Museum of Modern Art, New York, 1953.

——— "On Artistic Judgment," *Liturgical Arts,* XI, No. 2 (February, 1943), 46–47.

——— Réponse à Jean Cocteau. Paris, Stock, 1926.

Maritain, Raïssa. Adventures in Grace. New York, Longmans, Green, 1945.

——— Marc Chagall. New York, Maison Française, 1943.

——— We Have Been Friends Together. New York, Longmans, Green, 1945.

Marois, Pierre. "La Foi et l'art religieux," *La Revue des hommes et des mondes,* August, 1951, No. 61.

Mathey, François. "Situation du vitrail en France," *Quadrum,* December, 1957, No. 4, pp. 84–98.

Matisse, Henri. Jazz. Paris, Editions Verve, 1947.

——— "Notes d'un peintre," *La Grande Revue,* 12th year, No. 52, November–December, 1908.

Mauriac, François. "Des couleurs et des goûts," *Le Figaro,* December 4, 1951.

Mellquist, Jerome. "Chapel at Assy: A 20th Century Canterbury," *Art Digest,* XXVI, No. 6 (December 15, 1951), 10, 23.

BIBLIOGRAPHY

Mezzana, Corrado. "Rome 1950," *Arte cristiana,* XXXVIII, No. 7–10 (July–October, 1951), 110–12.

Montrond, Henri de. "Art sacré et théologie," *Etudes,* 84th year, Tome 271, December, 1951, pp. 314–21.

Morel, Maurice. "Phisionomie de Rouault," *Etudes,* 80th year, Tome 253, May, 1947, pp. 188–91.

——— "Rouault parmi nous," *Cahiers de l'art sacré,* 1946, No. 3, pp. 4–7.

Mounier, Emmanuel. "Aux avant-postes de la pensée chrétienne," *Esprit,* XV, No. 9 (September, 1947), 436–44.

Newton, Eric. "Modernism and Religious Art," *Liturgical Arts,* XVIII, No. 4 (August, 1950), 88–90.

Notre-Dame-de-Toute-Grâce, Assy. Lyon, Imp. M. Lescuyer, 1951.

"Notre-Dame-de-Toute-Grâce" (An interview with Léger), *Vogue* (Paris), March, 1948 (Léger File, Museum of Modern Art).

Ochsé, Madaleine. La Nouvelle Querelle des images. Paris, Editions du Centurion, 1952.

——— Un Art sacré pour notre temps. Paris, Librairie Arthème Fayard, 1959.

Onimus, Jean. "L'Art cruel," *Etudes,* 86th year, Tome 277, June, 1953, pp. 344–55.

Paluzzi, Carlo. "Il Papa agli artisti," *Fede ed arte,* 1st year, No. 4, April, 1953, pp. 115–16.

Pantalini, Oreste. Arte sacra e liturgia. Milan, Enrico Hoepli, 1932.

Parmoissin, R. Mystère de l'art sacré. Paris, Nouvelles Éditions Debresse, 1957.

"Le Père Couturier," *L'Art sacré,* March–April and May–June, 1954. (Two double issues devoted to a review of the life and work of Father Couturier, including his last articles, excerpts from his letters, and numerous testimonials.)

Pichard, Joseph. L'Art sacré moderne. Paris and Grenoble, B. Arthaud, 1953.

——— "L'Oeuvre de Rouault," *L'Art d'église,* January, 1953, No. 1, pp. 3–7.

Pius XII, Pope. "Address to the First International Congress of Catholic Artists," *Liturgical Arts,* XIX, No. 1 (November, 1950), 3–4.

——— "The Function of Holy Art" (Papal address), *Catholic Mind,* 50th year, No. 1079, November, 1952, pp. 697–99.

——— Mediator Dei. Encyclical Letter on the Sacred Liturgy, November 20, 1947. Revised ed. New York, The America Press, 1954.

——— Musicae sacrae disciplina. Encyclical Letter of December 25, 1955, French text in *La Documentation Catholique,* January 22, 1956, No. 1217, pp. 74–75.

Racz, André. "Tradition: Fertile Soil for Growth," *Liturgical Arts,* XVII, No. 4 (August, 1949), 108–12.

Ramelli, A. Cassi. Edifici per il culto. Milan, Edizione Vallardi, 1953.

Read, Herbert. "Art and Religion," *Listener,* XVI, No. 395 (August 5, 1936), 256–58.

———— "Georges Rouault," in *A Coat of Many Colors.* London, Routledge, 1945.

Régamey, Pie-Raymond, O.P. Art sacré au XXe siècle? Paris, Editions du Cerf, 1952.

———— "L'Art sacré, sera-t-il chrétien?" *Recherches et débats,* New Series, I, No. 1 (May, 1952).

———— "Cinq tendances dominantes," *Cahiers de l'art sacré,* 1946, No. 3, pp. 17–29.

———— "Les Conditions de l'art sacré dans le monde moderne," *La Vie intellectuelle,* 16th year, No. 12, December, 1948, pp. 8–34.

———— "Débat sur l'art non figuratif," *La Vie intellectuelle,* 19th year, No. 7, July, 1951, pp. 40–62.

———— "L'Education artistique du clergé," *Cahiers de l'art sacré,* 2nd series, No. 9, 1946, pp. 4–30.

———— "Les Etapes de l'académisme," *L'Art sacré,* New Series, October, 1947, No. 10, pp. 245–87.

———— "Exégèse de quelques lieux communs en matière d'art sacré," in *Problèmes de l'art sacré.* Edited by Debidour. Paris, Le Nouveau Portique, n.d.

———— "Gardez le mésure . . . ," *L'Art sacré,* January–February, 1953, No. 5–6, pp. 28–31.

———— "Lettre ouverte à M. Debidour sur l'église d'Assy," in Appendix to *Problèmes de l'art sacré.* Edited by Debidour. Paris, Le Nouveau Portique, n.d.

———— "Les Lois de l'église sur l'art sacré," *Cahiers de l'art sacré,* 1945, No. 1, p. 6.

———— "Note sur l'orientation," *Cahiers de l'art sacré,* 1945, No. 1, p. 30.

———— "Les Possibilités chrétiennes des artistes incroyants," *La Vie intellectuelle,* 19th year, No. 3, March, 1951, pp. 4–23.

———— Les Principes d'un véritable renouveau des arts sacrés. Liége, La Pensée Catholique, 1948.

———— "La Querelle de l'art sacré," *La Vie intellectuelle,* 19th year, No. 11, November, 1951, pp. 3–48.

———— "La Querelle des vitraux," *L'Art sacré,* 5th year, No. 38, February, 1939, pp. 49–53.

BIBLIOGRAPHY

Régamey, Pie-Raymond, o.p., "Réponse à une enquête sur l'art sacré: presentée par Maurice Brillant," *La Croix,* May 18, 1952, p. 2.

———— "Rome, 1950," *L'Art sacré,* January–February, 1951, No. 5–6, pp. 22–26.

Régamey, Pie-Raymond, and Cardinal Suhard. "Les Lois de l'église sur l'art sacré," *Cahiers de l'art sacré,* 1946, No. 1, p. 6.

"Religion and the Intellectuals: A Symposium," *Partisan Review,* XVII, No. 2 (February, 1950), 103.

Rewald, John. Pierre Bonnard. New York, Museum of Modern Art, 1948.

Rey, Robert. Preface to *Dessins de Couturier.* Paris, Les Trois Epis, 1947.

Richardson, John. "Le Nouvel 'Atelier' de Braque (et les vitraux de Varengeville)," *L'Oeil,* June 15, 1955, No. 6, pp. 20–26, 39.

Roger-Marx, Claude. "La Chapelle-musée d'Assy," *Le Figaro littéraire,* 5th year, No. 227, August 26, 1950, p. 8.

Rouault, Georges. "Anciens et modernes," *Le Point,* 6th year, No. 34–35, March, 1947, pp. 48–54.

———— "Climat pictural," *La Renaissance,* XX (October–December, 1937), 2–4.

———— "Réponse à une enquête sur l'art sacré: presentée par Maurice Brillant," *La Croix,* May 11, 1952, p. 2.

Roulin, Dom E. Nos églises. Paris, P. Lothielleux Ed., 1938.

Rousseau, André. "Encore l'art sacré," *Le Figaro,* August 4, 1951, p. 8.

Roy, Claude. Jean Lurçat. Geneva, Pierre Cailler, 1956.

Russoli, Franco. "Fernand Léger e l'architettura," *Casabella continuità,* September–October, 1955, No. 207, p. 68.

Sacred Congregation of the Holy Office. "On Sacred Art" (Instruction to Bishops), June 30, 1952, English translation in *Catholic Mind,* 50th year, No. 1079, November, 1952, pp. 699–702.

Schapiro, Meyer. "Courbet and Popular Imagery," *Journal of the Warburg and Courtauld Institutes,* IV, No. 3–4 (1940–41), 164–91.

———— "On the Aesthetic Attitude in Romanesque Art," in *Art and Thought: Essays in Honor of Dr. Ananda K. Coomaraswamy.* London, Luzac and Co., 1947.

———— "Review of Arnaud d'Agnel, *L'Art religieux moderne,*" *Review of Religion,* III, No. 4 (1939), 468–73.

Schwob, René. Chagall et l'âme juive. Paris, Correa, 1931.

Scortesco, Paul. Saint Picasso peignez pour nous. Paris, Nouvelles Editions Latines, 1953.

———— Satan voici ta victoire. Paris, Nouvelles Editions Latines, 1953.

Segy, Ladislas. "The Meaning of Jacques Lipchitz' Sculpture" (typescript).

Severini, Gino. Du Cubisme au classicisme. Paris, Povolozsky, 1921.

———— "Toujours l'art sacré: l'église a-t-elle trahi le Christ?" *Arts,* April 10, 1952, No. 354, p. 7.

Sidoine. "Assy fait scandale à Angers," *Arts,* January 26, 1951, No. 295, pp. 1, 3.

Sjöberg, Yves. Mort et résurrection de l'art sacré. Paris, Grasset, 1957.

Soby, James Thrall. Georges Rouault. New York, Museum of Modern Art, 1947.

Stahly, F. "The Church of Assy," *Graphis,* V, No. 26 (1949), 128–33, 203–5.

Steinmann, Jean. Léon Bloy. Paris, Editions du Cerf, 1955.

Suhard, Joseph Cardinal. Essor ou déclin de l'église (pastoral letter). Paris, Lahure, 1947.

Surchamp, Dom Angelico. "Assy-Vence-Audincourt," *Temoignages de la Pierre-Qui-Vire,* January, 1953, No. 36.

Sweeney, James Johnson. "An Interview with Marc Chagall," *Partisan Review,* XII, No. 1 (Winter, 1944), 88–93.

———— Marc Chagall. New York, Museum of Modern Art, 1946.

Tea, Eva. "Le Immagine sacré," *Arte cristiana,* XXXIX, No. 2 (February, 1952), 32–35.

Teriade. "Propos de Pierre Bonnard," *Verve,* V, Nos. 17–18 (1947), pages unnumbered.

"Testis" [Gabriel Marcel]. "Le Pseudo-Christ de Germaine Richier banni de l'église d'Assy," *L'Homme nouveau,* July 29, 1951.

Theôte, Daniel. "Intimate Moments with Rouault," *Tricolor,* May, 1944, No. 2, pp. 65–98.

Tillich, Paul, and Theodore Greene. "Authentic Religious Art," *Arts Digest,* XXVIII, No. 19 (August, 1954), 13.

Touzé, Msgr. Paul Louis. "L'Art sacré," *Le Christ dans le bainlieu,* 18th year, No. 8, 1951, p. 3.

Venturi, Lionello. Georges Rouault. 2d ed. Paris, Skira, 1948.

Vollard, Ambroise. Recollections of a Picture Dealer. Boston, Little, Brown, 1936.

Waldemar-George. "Georges Rouault, peintre sacré et maudit," *La Renaissance,* XX (October–December, 1937), 5–30.

Wall, Bernard. Report on the Vatican. London, Widenfeld and Nichols, 1956.

Warnach, Walther. "Rom und die moderne Kunst," *Wort und Wahrheit,* VII, No. 12 (December, 1952), 927–32.

Watkin, Edward I. Catholic Art and Culture. New York, Sheed & Ward, 1944.

Werner, Alfred. "The Painter of Vitebsk," *Horizon,* January, 1955 (Chagall File, Museum of Modern Art Library).

BIBLIOGRAPHY

Wind, Edgar. "Traditional Religion and Modern Art," *Art News,* LII, No. 3 (May, 1953), 18–23, 60–63.

Zervos, Christian. "Fernand Léger," *Cahiers d'art,* 8th year, No. 3–4, 1933, pages unnumbered.

Zographos, Praxitele. "Les Rapports du peintre avec Dieu," *Tuileries,* May, 1951, No. 8.

INDEX

INDEX

INDEX